TALES OF THE WOLF

TALES OF THE WOLF

FIFTY-ONE STORIES OF WOLF ENCOUNTERS IN THE WILD

COMPILED BY DENISE CASEY AND TIM W. CLARK
WITH ILLUSTRATIONS BY BETH KROMMES

HOMESTEAD PUBLISHING
Moose, Wyoming

Library of Congress Cataloging-in-Publication Data

Tales of the wolf : fifty-one stories of wolf encounters in the wild / compiled by Denise Casey and Tim W. Clark ; with illustrations by Beth Krommes.
      p.   cm.
      Includes bibliographical references (p.   ).
      ISBN 0-943972-40-X (acid-free paper)
      1. Wolves. 2. Wolves—North America. 3. Wolf hunting 4. Wolves—North America—Folklore. 5. Indians of North America—Folklore. 6. Tales—North America. I. Casey, Denise. II. Clark, Tim W.
      QL737.C22T36 1995
      599.74'442—dc20   95-38298
                                                           CIP

1 3 5 7 9 10 8 6 4 2

Published by
HOMESTEAD PUBLISHING
Box 193
Moose, Wyoming 83012

TALES FROM NATIVE AMERICA

"The Sun, the Wolf, and the Buffalo," by Ella E. Clark. From *Indian Legends from the Northern Rockies* by Ella E. Clark. Copyright © 1966 by the University of Oklahoma Press. Reprinted with permission of the University of Oklahoma Press.

"The End of Laugher," by James Willard Schultz. From *Why Gone Those Times? Blackfoot Tales*, by James Willard Schultz (Apikuni). Edited by Eugene Lee Silliman. Copyright © 1974 by the University of Oklahoma Press. Reprinted with permission of the University of Oklahoma Press.

"Wolf Dance," by Randolph B. Marcy. First published in *Thirty Years of Army Life on the Border* (New York: Harper & Brothers, 1866).

"The Wolf Helper," by George Bird Grinnell. From *By Cheyenne Campfires*, by George Bird Grinnell. Copyright © 1926 by Yale University Press. Reprinted with permission of Yale University Press.

"Forsaken Boy," by Henry Rowe Schoolcraft. First published in *Algic Researches, Comprising Inquiries Respecting the Mental Characteristics of the North American Indians,* First Series, Indian Tales and Legends (New York: Harper & Brothers, 1839).

"The Wolf-Warrior," by George A. Dorsey. First published in *The Pawnee: Mythology* (Washington: Carnegie Institution of Washington, 1906).

"Black Wolf and His Fathers," by George Bird Grinnell. From *By Cheyenne Campfires,* by George Bird Grinnell. Copyright © 1926 by Yale University Press. Reprinted with permission of Yale University Press.

"The Song of the Old Wolf," by Melvin R. Gilmore. From *Prairie Smoke*, by Melvin R. Gilmore. Copyright © 1929 by Columbia University Press. Reprinted with permission of the publisher.

"The Wolf Ritual," by Alice Henson Ernst. From *The Wolf Ritual of the Northwest Coast*, by Alice Henson Ernst. Copyright © 1952 by the University of Oregon Press. Reprinted with permission of the University of Oregon Press.

EARLY EXPLORERS AND NATURALISTS

"A Swedish Naturalist in America," by Peter Kalm. First English publication in 1770. *Peter Kalm's Travels in North America, the English Version of 1770*, edited by Adolph B. Benson (New York: Wilson-Erickson, Inc., 1937).

"Samuel Hearne, Arctic Explorer," by Samuel Hearne. From *A Journey from Prince of Wales's Fort in Hudson's Bay to the Northern Ocean, 1769, 1770, 1771, 1772*, by Samuel Hearne, edited by Richard Glover (Toronto: Macmillan Company of Canada Ltd., 1958). First published 1795.

"Flower Hunter Meets Black Wolf," by William Bartram. *The Travels of William Bartram; Naturalist's Edition*, edited by Francis Harper (New Haven: Yale University Press, 1958). First published in 1791 as *Travels through North and South Carolina, Georgia, East and West Florida, the Cherokee Country, the Extensive Territories of the Muscogulges, or Creek Confederacy, and the Country of the Chactaws*.

"Our Hearts Failed Us," by David Thompson. From *David Thompson's Narrative, 1784-1812*, edited by Richard Glover (Toronto: The Champlain Society, 1962). Reprinted with permission of The Champlain Society, Toronto, Canada. First published 1916 as *David Thompson's Narrative of His Explorations in Western America, 1784-1812*, edited by Joseph B. Tyrell.

"Buffalo and Wolves," Meriwether Lewis and William Clark. First published in *Original Journals of the Lewis and Clark Expedition, 1804-06*, edited by Reuben Gold Thwaites (New York: Dodd, Mead & Company, 1904-1905). Reprinted by Antiquarian Press, New York, 1959.

"Pitting of Wolves," by John James Audubon. First published in *Ornithological Biography, or an Account of the Habits of the Birds of the United States of America, Accompanied by Descriptions of the Objects Represented in the Work Entitled* The Birds of America, *and Interspersed with Delineations of American Scenery and Manners*, vol. III (Edinburgh: Adam & Charles Black, 1835).

"On the Barren Grounds," by John Richardson. First published in *Fauna Boreali-Americana; or the Zoology of the Northern Parts of British America* (London: John Murray, 1829).

"Myths and Medicines," by Maximilian, Prinz von Wied. First published in *Travels in the Interior of North America*. First English translation published in 1843. Reprinted in *Early Western Travels, 1748-1846*, v. 22-24, edited by Reuben Gold Thwaites (Cleveland: Arthur H. Clark Co., 1906).

"The Rite of Life," by George Catlin. From *Letters and Notes on the Manners, Customs, and Condition of the North American Indians*, 2 v., 2nd ed. (New York: Wiley and Putnam, 1842).

FRONTIER ENCOUNTERS, OLD WORLD ATTITUDES

"None But Monsters of the Desert," by David Humphreys. From *The Life and Heroic Exploits of Israel Putnam, Major-General in the Revolutionary War* (New York: Ezra Strong, 1835).

"Trading Along the Columbia," by Alexander Ross. From *Fur Traders of the Far West*, by Alexander Ross, edited by Kenneth A. Spaulding. Copyright © 1956 by the University of Oklahoma Press. Reprinted with permission of the University of Oklahoma Press. First published in 1855 (London) as *Fur Hunters of the Far West; a Narrative of Adventures in the Oregon and Rocky Mountains*.

"Having Two Hearts," by Warren Angus Ferris. From *Life in the Rocky Mountains; a Diary of Wanderings on the Sources of the Rivers Missouri, Columbia, and Colorado, 1830-1835*, edited by Leroy R. Hafen (Denver: The Old West Publishing Company, 1940). Second edition 1983. Reprinted with permission of Old West Publishing. First published serially in *Western Literary Messenger* in 1843-44.

"A Hat Trick," by Josiah Gregg. From *Commerce of the Prairies*, by Josiah Gregg, edited by Max L. Moorhead (Norman: University of Oklahoma Press, 1954). First published in 1844.

"Mad Wolf in Camp," by Charles Larpenteur. From *Forty Years a Fur Trader on the Upper Missouri*, by Charles Larpenteur, edited by Elliott Coues (New York: Francis P. Harper, 1898). "Mad Wolf in Camp," by Washington Irving. From *The Adventures of Captain Bonneville, U.S.A., in the Rocky Mountains and the Far West*, by Washington Irving, edited by Edgeley W. Todd (Norman: University of Oklahoma Press, 1961). "Mad Wolf in Camp," by Warren Angus Ferris. From *Life in the Rocky Mountains; a Diary of Wanderings on the Sources of the Rivers Missouri, Columbia, and Colorado, 1830-1835*, edited by Leroy R. Hafen (Denver: The Old West Publishing Company, 1983). Reprinted with permission of Old West Publishing.

"Scenes in the Rocky Mountains," by Rufus B. Sage. From *Rufus B. Sage, His Letters and Papers, 1836-1847, with an annotated reprint of his "Scenes in the Rocky Mountains and in Oregon, California, New Mexico, Texas, and the Grand Prairies,"* edited by LeRoy R. Hafen and Ann W. Hafen, 2 vols. (Glendale, Calif.: Arthur H. Clark Company, 1956).

"One Night Among Wolves," by Darius B. Cook. First published in *Six Months Among Indians, Wolves and Other Wild Animals, in the Forests of Allegan County, Mich., in the Winter of 1839 and 1840* (Niles, Michigan: Niles Mirror Office, 1889).

"Skater Chased by Wolves," by C. W. Webber. First published in *The Hunter-Naturalist; Romance of Sporting; or, Wild Scenes and Wild Hunters* (Philadelphia: J. W. Bradley, 1851).

"A Bushel of Fun Shooting Wolves," by Sutherland McCoy. First published in "Mr. McCoy's Story, His Buffalo Hunt, and Battle with Mountain Wolves," from Origen Thomson, *Crossing the Plains, Narrative of the Scenes, Incidents and Adventures attending the Overland Journey of the Decatur and Rush County Emigrants to the "far-off" Oregon, in 1852* (Greensburg, Indiana: Orville Thomson, Printer, 1896).

"Wolves of the Plains," by Richard Irving Dodge. From *The Plains of North America and their Inhabitants*, by Richard Irving Dodge, edited by Wayne R. Kime (Newark: University of Delaware Press, 1989).

"An Encounter in India," C. G. C. T., *The Spectator*, Sept. 3, 1927. Reprinted with permission of *The Spectator* (London).

"Why Is the Wolf Ferocious?" translated by M. Gaster. First published in *Rumanian Bird and Beast Stories* (London: Sidgwick & Jackson, Ltd., 1915).

SERIOUS KILLING

"The War on the Wolf," by Stanley P. Young. First published in *American Forests*, November and December 1942. Reprinted with permission of *American Forests*.

"A Very Profitable Business," by James R. Mead. From *Hunting and Trading on the Great Plains, 1859-1875*, by James R. Mead and edited by Schuyler Jones. Copyright © 1986 by Schuyler Jones. Reprinted with permission of the University of Oklahoma Press.

"Bidden to a Feast," by L. S. Kelly. First published in *Forest and Stream* 48(8):144-145 (Feb. 20, 1897). Reprinted courtesy of *Field and Stream*.

"Wolf Coursing," by Parker Gillmore. First published in *Gun, Rod, and Saddle: A Record of Personal Experiences* (London: W. H. Allen & Co. Ltd., 1893).

"Badlands Billy," by Ernest Thompson Seton. First published in *Animal Heroes* (New York: Charles Scribner's Sons, 1905).

"The Home Life of the Big Wolves," by Vernon Bailey. First published in *Natural History* 49:120-122 (September 1940). Copyright © 1940 by the American Museum of Natural History. Reprinted with permission of *Natural History*.

"The Wolf Tracker," by Zane Grey. First published in *Ladies' Home Journal*, v. 41, November

1924. Copyright © 1924, The Meredith Corporation. All Rights Reserved. Reprinted from *Ladies' Home Journal* magazine with permission of Loren Grey.

"The Last Stand of the Lobos," by Donald Kenneth Stevens. First published in *Sunset Magazine*, v. 54, January and February 1925. Reprinted with permission of Sunset Publishing Corporation.

"Ghost Wolf of the Little Belts," by Elva Wineman. First published in *Montana Wild Life*, May 1930. Reprinted courtesy of *Montana Outdoors*.

"Old Three Legs," by A. M. Thompson. First published in *Field and Stream* 35(12):30-31, 75-76 (April 1931). Reprinted courtesy of *Field and Stream*.

A CONTRARY POINT OF VIEW

"A Grave Mistake," by Emily Henrietta Hickey. Originally entitled "A Wolf Story" and first published in *The Leisure Hour* 41:594 (1892).

"In Van Tassel's Corral," by Franklin Welles Calkins. First published in *Outing Magazine* 39:174-177 (1901).

"The Price of Heredity," by John Franklin Lewis. First published in *Outing Magazine* 52:590-591 (August 1908).

"The Wilds Without Firearms," by Enos A. Mills. First published in *Wild Life on the Rockies* (Boston and New York: Houghton Mifflin Company, 1909).

"The Polite Wolf," by Gilbert Coleridge. First published in *The Contemporary Review* (1914).

"Winning a Wolf's Heart," by Lawrence Trimble, The Literary Digest 92:50-54, January 29, 1927.

"The Wolf Pack," by Vilhjalmur Stefansson. First published in *The American Mercury*. II:327-330 (1927).

"Yellowstone Wolves," by Marguerite L. Arnold. First published in *Nature Magazine* 30:111-112 (August 1937). Copyright © 1937 by the American Museum of Natural History. Reprinted with permission of *Natural History*.

"Three Years in the Wolves' Wilderness," by John F. Stanwell-Fletcher. First published in *Natural History* 49:136-147 (March 1942). Copyright © 1942 by the American Museum of Natural History. Reprinted with permission of *Natural History*.

"Departure for the Night Hunt," by Adolph Murie. From *The Wolves of Mount McKinley* (Washington: Government Printing Office, 1944).

EPILOGUE

Excerpt by Thomas J. Farnham. From *Travels in the Great Western Prairies, the Anahuac and Rocky Mountains, and in the Oregon Territory*, reprinted in *Early Western Travels, 1748-1846*, v. 28, edited by Reuben Gold Thwaites (Cleveland: Arthur H. Clark Co., 1906).

Excerpt by Father Pierre Jean de Smet. From *Letters and Sketches: With a Narrative of a Year's Residence among the Indian Tribes of the Rocky Mountains* (1841-42), reprinted in *Early Western Travels, 1748-1846*, v. 27, edited by Reuben Gold Thwaites (Cleveland: Arthur H. Clark Co., 1906).

Excerpt from "The Scribbler." From "In Frontier Days," *Forest and Stream* (January 1901).

Excerpt from James R. Mead. From *Hunting and Trading on the Great Plains, 1859-1875*, by James R. Mead, edited by Schuyler Jones. Copyright © 1986 by Schuyler Jones. Reprinted by permission of the University of Oklahoma Press.

Excerpt from Washington Irving. From *A Tour on the Prairies*, by Washington Irving, edited by John Francis McDermott (Norman: University of Oklahoma Press, 1956).

Excerpt from N.A.T. From *Forest and Stream* (February 2, 1888).

Excerpt from Adolph Murie. From *A Naturalist in Alaska*, by Adolph Murie. Copyright © 1961 by the Devin-Adair Co. Reprinted with permission of the publisher.

Dedicated
to our longtime friends and supporters
Cathy Patrick and Hopie and Bob Stevens

ACKNOWLEDGMENTS

Many people took an interest in this project and suggested possible sources of stories, sent us stories, or otherwise helped in putting this book together. In this regard, we would like to thank Norm Bishop, Matt Black, Winfred Blevins, Franz Camenzind, Lisa Diekmann, Stephen Kellert, Barbara and Heather Merbs, Cathy Patrick, and Carl Schreier. We especially appreciate Norm Bishop's careful reading of an earlier draft, and his many helpful comments. We are grateful to John Wargo for temporary use of his office at Yale University. The staff at several branches of the Yale University Library System were most helpful in locating and retrieving materials. Many thanks to Joe Cinquino and his staff of Management Information Services at Yale University for extensive photocopying from old books. And a heartfelt thanks to Beth Krommes for her wonderful illustrations.

CONTENTS

INTRODUCTION

THE great gray wolf that haunts the imagination of North Americans does not travel lightly. Wherever he goes, whatever he does, he is burdened with a heavy load that we have laid on him—all our images of him, our dreams, our fears, our stories. They have accumulated over the centuries, carried from many lands in the Old World, dredged from the ancient past of North America's own people, fashioned anew in the New World's peculiar geography, history, and society.

People have done a good job of recording and documenting the burden. Enough words have been written about the wolf to fill a library—children's fables, literary and psychological analyses, hunting stories, manuals about how to kill wolves, folklore and myths from around the world, newspaper reports, reams of public comment about wolf management, biological treatises, and anthropological analyses. The images, stories, and meanings represented by these writings are too many to count. But beyond the fairy tales and fables and the six-hour-battle-royal-between-four-grizzlies-and-four-wolves fictions, there is a wealth of recorded encounters between real people and real wolves. That's what this book is about. As Stephen Kellert concluded from his studies of attitudes toward nature, some people "have only recently begun to re-discover that the symbolic and historic are insufficient substitutes for the fundamentally meaningful experience of the real."

The wolf remains an emotionally charged management issue in parts of the continent (the Yukon, Minnesota, Yellowstone, and Alaska, for instance). The debate is whether we as a society value the wolf as a species to be protected and restored to portions of its former range, although underlying this, of course, is the ancient philosophical question of humans' relationship and responsibility to the natural world. The stories recorded here offer some useful historical background, show trends in our thinking and attitudes about wolves, and illustrate changes in context that have led to changes in thinking. Thus grounding the current debate about wolves may help lead it away from the vehement ranting of recent years and toward more informed, democratic discourse.

The purpose of this book is not to clarify misperceptions about wolves, argue their dangers or benefits to various regions, or advocate wolf restoration in the false belief that we can thus recreate real wilderness or even a "balance of nature." Wolves and wolf stories have too strong a hold on the human psyche to dismiss or reduce to their scientific or political dimensions. As novelist Cormac McCarthy tells us, "Things separate from their stories have no meaning." There is something about wolf stories that is tremendously potent, some irresistible thrill we get from them. Many people have acknowledged this grip on our minds:

> There must be something in a wolf which appeals powerfully to human imagination; otherwise there would be no proper wolf stories. The wolf, being a natural beast, is timid and peaceable; but the story, being "merely psychological," must account for our nervous reactions.
> William J. Long, "The Peaceable, Timid Wolf,"
> *The Independent* (May 31, 1919).

> No place is so apt for the origin of such widely exaggerated reports [of wolves] as the Arctic and sub-Arctic regions, since in these remote sections there is little possibility of the fallacy of the stories ever being established. Their elusive source may be likened unto the proverbial rainbow's end. The truth of the matter is that we do not seriously endeavor to have them discredited. Who will deny that such stories thrill our fertile imagination and, beneficially, send our thoughts wandering through distant fields of adventure?
> J. Stokley Ligon, "When Wolves Forsake Their Ways,"
> *Nature Magazine* (March 1926).

> No wild animal of Europe has won a fame at all comparable with that of the wolf. In myth, legend and history it figures above other beasts with an insistence which at first sight seems mysterious. What the grizzly bear is to our own far West, the tiger to India, the lion to parts of Africa, all that and much more was the wolf to our ancestors over the sea. Not only is it the chief hero among all brutes in the folk-lore of all countries of Europe, but it continues to this day to be an object of superstition among the peasantry, and its very name is a metaphor of dread.
> Lynn Tew Sprague, "The Wolf in Myth, Legend and History,"
> *Outing Magazine* (1902).

Russia does not disappoint you as far as the wolves go. All through the winter wolves form a part of every peasant's calculations, and stories of wolves are still the tales that most easily draw the old men from the chimney corner and the children from play. They never grow stale, and it is only foreigners who disbelieve them.

> Francesca M. Wilson, "Wolves,"
> *The Living Age* (February 16, 1924).

This book of 51 stories about encounters with wolves illustrates some of the range of perceptions and feelings about the wolf. The stories come from across the continent—from Florida to Connecticut to the Great Lakes to the Great Plains to the Northwest Coast. (For contrast, one story from Europe and two about wolves from Asia also are included.) The earliest dated account is from Swedish naturalist Peter Kalm's visit to colonial America in 1748. The latest is from biologist Adolph Murie's pioneering research in Alaska in the early 1940s. Many different images of the wolf appear in the book, real and metaphorical—the wolf as god, devil, ghost, and trickster, as helper and hunter, as father and mother and pup, as creator and destroyer, as talisman and as animal, as "a fierce green fire dying." No wolves but rabid ones kill people in this collection (as is believed to be true of North American history), but people kill plenty of wolves in plenty of ways.

Some of the storytellers are well-known, including Revolutionary War hero Israel Putnam, naturalist John James Audubon, and novelist Zane Grey. Others are ordinary people, including a wagon-train traveler, a few mountain men, the wife of a Yellowstone Park ranger, and a Montana librarian. In the case of some of the Indian tales, collectors recorded their stories but not their names. Most of the encounters are reported firsthand, a few are secondhand, a couple are fictional, and some are legendary. They come from personal journals, outdoor and sporting magazines, ladies' magazines, newspapers, books of travel and life on the ever-westering border, scientific and anthropological reports, previously published collections of Native American stories, biographies, and other sources.

The stories are arranged in five categories that show different basic attitudes that have characterized the last 250 years of American environmental history. Within each section, the stories are generally chronological.

TALES FROM NATIVE AMERICA: *Of Wolves and Men*, by Barry Lopez, does a superb job of describing the Native American world in which wolves were esteemed. In this world, wolves hunted the same game species that people did and in much the same way. Indians watched wolves, knew them, and respected their hunting abilities, their elusiveness, and their familial devotion. In Henry Beston's words: "They are not brethren, they are not underlings; they are other nations." One fundamental characteristic of the hundreds of indigenous cultures, from pre-Columbian times to the present, is their deeply religious connection to the land and its inhabitants. This situation naturally gave rise to a certain range of ways of comprehending the wolf, as well as certain attitudes, values, and meanings attached to it.

Within this broad perspective, the nine tales in this section of the book are richly varied in kind. There are teaching stories, creation stories, helping stories, mystery stories, trickster stories. They come from Crow, Blackfeet, Cheyenne, Ojibway, Nootka, Tonkawa, Lakota, and Pawnee peoples. In all, there is a general attitude of attentiveness and respect, of something to be learned from the wolves. Discovering what this something is may not be easy, though, for the original audience or for modern readers. In *Ojibway Heritage* (1976), Basil Johnston offered some ideas for studying and understanding all Indian stories:

> The stories recorded are not to be interpreted literally; but freely, yet rationally according to the Ojibway views of life. Readers and listeners are expected to draw their own inferences, conclusions, and meanings according to their intellectual capacities.
>
> Because each Ojibway story may embody several themes and meanings, time and deliberation are required for adequate appreciation. There is no instantaneous understanding. Ojibway stories are as broad and deep in meaning and mystery as are the tales, legends, and myths of Greek, Roman, Egyptian and other peoples and just as difficult to understand as are the parables of the Bible.

EARLY EXPLORERS AND NATURALISTS: Beginning, of course, in 1492 and continuing even into the 20th century in the Arctic, the European explorers (including the fur-company men) and early naturalists who came to the New World had particular interests and interactions with the land and animals—and no livestock to lose to wolves. In the spirit of discovery (albeit with economic aims), they attempted to find, observe, and report accurately whatever the New World had to show them. As historian Reuben Gold Thwaites pointed out, "In the early nineteenth century, scientific collection was the chief object of ambition among thoughtful explorers—to secure for the world a complete catalogue of its plants and animals was worth much toil and hardship, heroic endeavor, and mighty daring." Naturalist William Bartram expressed his delight and wonder at the country's bounty, its newness, and its diversity: "Continually impelled by a restless spirit of curiosity, [I was] in pursuit of new productions of nature, my chief happiness consisted in tracing and admiring the infinite power, majesty, and perfection of the great Almighty Creator and in the contemplation, that through divine aid and permission, I might be instrumental in discovering, and introducing into my native country, some original productions of nature, which might become useful to society."

In nine stories that cover the period from 1748 to 1835, several early explorers and naturalists report their experiences with wolves. Unlike many New World plants and animals, wolves were not new to them, so they often only briefly mentioned distribution, kinds (coyotes were often called wolves and distinguished only by their smaller size), differences from European wolves, and utility of the fur. But amongst the dry, scientific reports, there are stories of wonder, adventure, cruelty, pathos, and ritual.

FRONTIER ENCOUNTERS, OLD WORLD ATTITUDES: European settlers came to North America in the early 1600s and brought with them their crops, livestock, and fences, and also their hatred of wolves. William Wood wrote in 1634 of the wolves of Massachusetts, "They be the greatest inconveniency the Countrey hath, both for matter of dammage to private men in particular, and the whole Countrey in generall," and he lamented, "yet is there little hope of their utter destruction, the Countrey being so spacious, and they so numerous." The 17th century left us few if any stories about encounters with wolves, but it did leave an institutionalized system of bounties, along with several ways of destroying wolves and pervasive attitudes, with religious overtones, of fear, hatred, and disgust.

The twelve stories in this section, from the 1750s to 1927, are about how people's attitudes and cultural norms were transported—unconscious and unexamined—to new situations, no matter how much they differed from the situations where the perspectives evolved. But these encounters do not all focus on passionate emotions and knee-jerk reactions. Some of them illustrate the basic lack of knowledge of wolf behavior and ecology that remained true until the first scientific research was done in the 1930s and 40s.

The peculiarity of the English legacy is shown in this 1874 comparison with French attitudes:

> When the wolf appears in the day-time amongst the flocks of the Morvan villages [France], a vigorous young shepherdess will even go and kick him with her wooden shoes, and the lads, instead of running away, pelt him heartily with stones. The wolf in England, where he is seen in menageries, like a savage panther behind strong bars of iron, enjoys a much more imposing reputation than in France, where he is more familiarly known. Indeed the word *wolf* and the word *loup* do not convey the same impression to my mind, because 'wolf,' to me, is associated with the grand mystic conception of the animal, whereas *loup* is associated with the simple reality.
>
> Philip Gilbert Hamerton,
> *Chapters on Animals* (1874).

The very early extermination of wolves from England probably influenced the attitudes of the English and English-speaking Americans and permitted this "grand mystic conception" to flourish unfettered by reality.

SERIOUS KILLING: As the Euro-American people and culture took over more and more of North America, placing less emphasis on discovery and more on mastery, the wolf fell victim to the widespread extermination that included Native Americans, buffalo (for various recreational and utilitarian purposes, not the least of which was to starve the Plains Indians), passenger pigeons, and all predators, among other species.

This section begins with an extraordinary two-part history of "The War on the Wolf" by wolf expert Stanley P. Young in 1942, which chronicled wolf extermination from its antecedents in medieval Europe to the last renegade lobos of the American West in the 1920s and 30s. The nine stories that follow, dating from 1859 to 1931, demonstrate the intensity of this slaughter. In the mid-19th century, the value of wolf pelts led to an industry of poisoning and skinning wolves. Wolf coursing was also a popular sport akin to fox hunting. But it was largely the growing livestock empire in the West (with strong support from the government) that developed a habit, an industry, a justification, and almost an *ethic* of killing wolves.

The basic argument was that, as Vernon Bailey put it, "wolves are meat-eaters and so is man; and there was not enough meat to go around," and that both livestock growing and game hunting would be immensely more profitable if no animals were "lost" to wolves. Consequently, poison, guards, traps, fences, snares, guns, and the prestige of a "wolfing" profession all were employed in addition to the bounties that long had served to eliminate wolves. Aldo Leopold wrote, "In those days we had never heard of passing up the chance to kill wolves." And according to Young, "A sort of range law was adopted whereby no ranch man would knowingly pass up a dead carcass without first inserting a goodly dose of strychnine, in hopes of eventually killing a wolf or two."

Needless to say, we won the war.

A CONTRARY POINT OF VIEW: The emergence of a new and different attitude is shown in ten stories that date from 1892 to 1944—or possibly it was the re-emergence of a more mature, more resonant perspective of wolves, similar to that of Native Americans. Wolves came to be seen as sentient, intelligent, sociable creatures with the respectable profession of hunting. They possibly even deserved ethical consideration. Americans have become increasingly fascinated with a species that is, in many ways, so like ourselves (not to mention our companion dogs), but yet so mysteriously, so elusively *other*. And after wolves had been removed from much of the United States, they were deeply missed by some.

This new set of attitudes grew, again, out of changes in context. One factor in this change has been the gradual enlargement of the conservation idea during the last 120 years. (Of course, there are some who would still deny protection to wolves.) At the same time, we have developed standards for the humane treatment of animals, although their extension to the trapping of fur bearers and predators still has not been entire. Another factor has been the shift from rural to urban living, which has removed people from direct interaction with nature, including wolves. Indeed, the disappearance of the "frontier" has perhaps dampened the urge to conquer nature. The collection and distribution of scientific knowledge about wolves has resulted in a more realistic understanding of the species. Besides, there is a growing appreciation of other cultural viewpoints, such as those of Native Americans. And finally, although the actual loss of wolves and other species has been accumulating a long time, it seems that the *sense of loss* has only in recent decades motivated us to appreciate, protect, and restore species wherever possible.

Many authors, in fact, have suggested that we humans require natural experiences and forces beyond ourselves. Scientists, philosophers, psychologists, and others now are inquiring into the validity of the "biophilia hypothesis," which "proclaims a human dependence on nature that extends far beyond the simple issues of material and physical sustenance to encompass as well the human craving for aesthetic, intellectual, cognitive, and even spiritual meaning and satisfaction" (Stephen Kellert and E. O. Wilson, *The Biophilia Hypothesis*, 1994). In Thoreau's words, "We need to witness our own limits transgressed and some life pasturing freely where we never wander."

❖❖❖

We have not tried to correct or reinterpret or justify or explain the wolves or the humans that inhabit these tales. The old stories stand as they originally were set down, complete with the authors' and narrators' observations, perceptions, and responses. Many statements and assertions are made in these accounts that modern science has shown to be untrue—for instance, that wolves exhaust their prey by loping tirelessly after them and disable them by hamstringing, that they are no more than big lovable dogs, or that wolf packs are made up of dozens of animals. The *assertions of fact* blend, unremarked, into the *assertions of opinion*—that wolves are "the most degenerate and unmoral mammal species on earth," or that they are "noble and heroic" or "altogether offensive, having a savage look, a frightful howl, an insupportable smell, a perverse disposition, and brutal manners. . . . [t]he most hateful while living, and the most useless when dead."

Many historical incidents, vivid descriptions, and eloquent evocations in these stories could be taken out of context and misused to feed the rhetoric in the ongoing debates about wolves in parts of North America. We hope this doesn't happen. Just as we can't judge the wolf of today by these old stories, neither can we judge the wolf or the stories of old by the knowledge, attitudes, or values that are integral to today's world. As the context has changed through history, so have views of the wolf changed, and the appropriateness and meaningfulness of those views.

"I listened even as gold-hunters listen to stories of treasure trove, for these were the things of my world." That was how Ernest Thompson Seton listened to stories about wolves. And a rich cultural hoard it is, this very large accumulation of stories about wolves, our own singular American literature, borne by the wolf. We should cherish it, even though we can't grasp all its elusive, conflicting, or painful ideas and even though the ongoing wolf-management debate makes it seem more like Pandora's box than a treasure chest. The wolf's stories, his unshakeable burden, together make up one long and endlessly fascinating story. In the most fundamental sense, it is a story about ourselves as much as it is about wolves.

Such is the tradition of his fame that when your horse breaks into a wild gallop at wintry midnight, and your companion points to the next field and whispers, 'The wolves!' and you see them dimly in the pale snowlight, there comes a thrill, not so much of fear as of an old poetry that has descended to you through all the generations of our race.

Philip Gilbert Hamerton,
Chapters on Animals (1874).

TALES OF THE WOLF

TALES FROM NATIVE AMERICA

BECAUSE its range extended over most of North America, the wolf was known to nearly all native American peoples. Here are nine stories that reveal a little of the wide range of meanings attached to the wolf.

The wolf is a helper and intermediary to the people in the ancient Crow tale of "The Sun, the Wolf, and the Buffalo." In the Cheyenne tale called "The Wolf Helper," a wolf leads some survivors of the Sand Creek Massacre in 1864 to food and safety. Their initial fear of the animal quickly turns to gratitude, acceptance, and companionship: "They knew that he was their friend, and that he was true; they knew that he would do something for them." And in "The Forsaken Boy," an Ojibway story, wolves show pity, kindness, and fidelity to a child abandoned by his relatives.

In "The Wolf-Warrior," a Pawnee story, the wolf is the giver of powerful gifts that enable a man to help his people. Similarly, "The Wolf Ritual" tells the origin story of the Nootkan people, who receive powerful but dangerous gifts from wolves. Wolves also give life to the Tonkawas in "Wolf Dance."

"Black Wolf and His Fathers" is a wonderfully rich Cheyenne story of mystery, while "The Song of the Old Wolf," a Lakota tale, is a mournful lament for the infirmity and loneliness of old age. The aged storyteller in "The End of Laugher" muses that "about the only pleasure old men have, you know, is to live over in memory the stirring times of their youth," and he recounts the adventures he and a friend had as young men with their pet wolf.

Throughout these Native American wolf stories, there is an appreciation of the shared origins and destiny of people and of the creatures of the natural world. And there is a desire to maintain this natural order, not only through ritual and thanks-giving, but also through respectful attitudes and behaviors.

THE SUN, THE WOLF, AND THE BUFFALO
Crow

 IN her introduction to the book from which this story is taken, Ella E. Clark quotes Chief Plenty-Coups about the importance of buffalo to the Crow people:

When the buffalo went away, we became a changed people.... Idleness that was never with us in the buffalo days has stolen much from both our minds and bodies. The buffalo was everything to us. When it went away, the hearts of my people fell to the ground, and they could not lift them up again.

The Sun and the Buffalo were two key beings in the world of the Crows, and standing between them in this story, and between them and the people as an intermediary and helper, was the Wolf.

Clark's source for this tale was Lieutenant James A. Bradley, who was stationed among the Crows from 1871 to 1877 and who recorded many of their "traditions and facts." This story was told to him by Little Face, a scout, who was about sixty years old. It is from Indian Legends from the Northern Rockies *(Norman: University of Oklahoma Press, 1966).*

❖❖❖

Many years ago the Crow nation was very large, and our people were the favorites of the Sun. One time the Sun came down among them and took a Crow woman as his wife. They had a handsome lodge, where the woman lived, greatly respected by the tribe. Occasionally the Sun came down and lived with her for a while. Because of his love for his wife, the Sun blessed her people with an abundance of food, corn, and buffalo, and also with success over their enemies in war.

But there was a fool-dog among the Crows, a man with an evil spirit. He roamed about the village, doing harm to anyone he could harm. No one punished him, because he was a fool-dog and could not help it. Once when the Sun was away from his lodge on earth, the fool-dog visited it and abused his wife. She bore her shame in silence, but prepared herself for death. When the Sun came to see her, she told him what the fool-dog had done and then put herself to death before her husband's eyes.

The Sun was so angry that he determined to destroy the entire Crow nation. He caused their corn to fail, prevented buffalo from coming to their country, and gave their enemies power over them. The Crows were forced to become wanderers over the earth, to seek a new home where they might have food and rest.

A long time they wandered, suffering greatly from hunger. When they were in danger of total destruction from starvation, White Wolf, a servant of the Sun, took pity on them and made up his mind to save them.

"Make a pile of rice stalks and other fuel," White Wolf told them. "Make little pellets of meat and corn meal and throw them upon the pile, one by one, until the pile bursts into flames. Ten buffalo will rise from the midst of the flames. You must kill all of them. If one should escape, he would be sure to go to the Sun and tell what you have done. Then there would be no hope for you."

The people were distressed by these orders. Although they could find enough meat for the sacrifice, they thought there was not so much as a kernel of corn among them. But at last they learned that an old woman had preserved a small amount of corn for seed. She gladly contributed it to save her people from starvation.

They made ten pellets of meat and corn meal; they made a pile of rice stalks and other fuel. The best hunters stood by with their bows drawn while the pellets were thrown upon the pile, one by one. There was no flame after the first pellet, none after the second, none after the third or even the ninth. The Crows were almost in despair. But when the tenth pellet was thrown into the pile, a bright flame burst forth and ten fat buffalo galloped out of the midst of the flames.

The hunters let fly a shower of arrows, and the ten buffalo fell dead. The women prepared a big feast amid rejoicing throughout the camp. At the suggestion of White Wolf, the people repeated the charm. The next flames produced twenty buffalo, the next thirty, and so on until the number reached ninety. The hunters killed all of them and all the people had an abundance of food.

In those days there were no firearms and no horses. It was difficult for the men on foot, using bows and arrows, to kill so many animals. The number troubled all the people; they feared that one might escape and would cause the Sun to show his anger against them again. When the number of buffalo galloping out of the flames reached one hundred, one animal did escape. He ran directly to the Sun and told the whole story.

The Sun was very angry—with White Wolf more than with the Crows, who had showed themselves to be brave in a time of trouble.

"Go to the Crow people," the Sun said to White Wolf, "and tell them that I shall no longer work to destroy them. You yourself will forevermore be a vagabond, an outcast among the animals of the world."

Wolf has been a vagabond to this day. And Sun has never again taken a wife among the Crow women.

THE END OF LAUGHER
Blackfeet

 JAMES Willard Schultz, author of this story, traveled west to Montana from his native New York in 1876. He lived with the Blackfeet Indians for more than two decades, at first following the buffalo across the plains, and later ranching, guiding hunters, and writing stories, articles, and books about his adopted people. He continued to visit and write about them—"with love and insight"— until his death in 1947.

In this story, from Why Gone Those Times? Blackfoot Tales *(edited by Eugene Lee Silliman, Norman: University of Oklahoma Press, 1974), Apikuni— Schultz's Blackfeet name—and his friends listen to the second installment of a tale about a tame wolf. The storyteller is Red Eagle, now an old man, who recalls the adventures of his youth.*

❖❖❖

Apsi and Jackson had not been present the evening Old Red Eagle related the story of Laugher, the tame wolf, how his chum Nitaina had captured it when a little pup, and taught it many things, they at last taking it with them on a raid against the Sioux, on which occasion it twice saved them from the enemy. But while we were skinning some wolves at one of our baits down on Cow Creek I retold the story and they were as anxious as was I to hear more of the life of the truly remarkable animal. To that end Apsi told his mother one evening to prepare a little feast for us, and himself invited Red Eagle to come over and eat and smoke.

"Ha! That is why you invited me here; you want to hear more about the wolf!" the old man exclaimed, after the feast was over and Apsi had lit a big pipe for him.

"Well, you shall hear. I like to tell about the happenings in those long dead days. About the only pleasure old men have, you know, is to live over in memory the stirring times of their youth.

"Let me think. Where did I leave off the other night? Oh, yes. Well, when we came home with the big band of horses we had taken from the Sioux, and told what a great help Laugher had been to us, Nitaina's mother fell upon the animal and hugged and kissed him, and so would have my mother have done had she dared. The news spread all through the great

7

camp how Laugher had saved us from the enemy. The war party that had refused to let us go with it because of the wolf, returned home on foot defeated, and with three of their number missing. The leader felt worse than ever when he learned of our success, and offered to start right out again with us. A great many warriors, old and young, wanted us, with Laugher, to go with them on a raid. We refused to do so, and prepared to go, just we two and Laugher, into the country of the Cheyennes. That tribe had a fine breed of horses; most all of them pintos. We wanted some of them. My father had once been to war against the Cheyennes, and gave us directions how to go. Leaving the Missouri at the mouth of the Marias, we were to strike off southeast across the plains to the lower Yellowstone, and from there on to the headwaters of the Little Missouri, or some other stream not far beyond it. Somewhere in that vicinity, he said, we would find the enemy.

"At that time the people were preparing to put up the medicine lodge so we waited to take part in the ceremonies before setting out on our far expedition. On the first day of the lodge we made sacrifices to the sun, partook of the sacred dried tongues, and prayed the great god to have pity and give us long life and happiness, and success in all things, this coming raid in particular. Our mothers and fathers also prayed for us. On the fourth day of the lodge Nitaina and I stood before the people and counted our coups, not many at that time; we were but youths, and had been only twice against the enemy.

"When Nitaina counted this coups Laugher stood beside him. When he finished he called out its name and the wolf raised up and put its forepaws on his shoulders: 'No, no, not that way,' he said, 'turn around so all can see you.' He turned it around, holding it up by its forelegs.

"'Friends,' he went on, 'Laugher is going to count his coups. He does not speak our language so I shall be his interpreter. Now, then, listen.' And raising his voice he shouted: 'Laugher. That is me. That is my name. I went on a raid with Nitaina and Red Eagle. On a bare rock butte of the Little Rockies I discovered the trail of the enemy and gave warning, and saved the lives of my two men. Later, I helped them round up and drive off a band of Sioux horses. Still later, while I alone was awake, I saw the enemy running to kill my sleeping men and take the horses, and again I gave warning, and assisted them to escape. There. I have said.'

"Oh, how that great crowd of people shouted, and when he finished, and the waiting drummers whanged their big drums: 'Laugher! Laugher! A chief is Laugher, the wolf,' they cried, and the women longed to pet the animal and dared not. He seemed to sense what was going on. Nitaina released him and he ran around and around, wagging his tail and jumping up time and again to lick his master's face. The three of us soon left the lodge and went home to get ready to start out that evening.

"We left camp at sundown, well outfitted for the long trail. Each of us had six extra pairs of moccasins, and Laugher packed them and our lariats. We had plenty of powder and ball; some extra flints; and our guns were good guns for those days, at the distance of one hundred steps we could usually kill a buffalo or elk or deer the first shot, if it was standing still. No one at that time risked the loss of a charge by shooting at running game. Beside our guns we each carried a bow and arrows in bow case and quiver slung on our backs, these for silent killing of meat, and for use in all ways should anything go wrong with the other weapons.

"In three days time we arrived at the mouth of the Marias, there crossed the Missouri on a raft of driftwood, climbed out of the valley to the plain, and went southeasterly across it to Arrow Creek. The narrow valley of this stream, you remember, is mostly cut cliffed; from its head in the Highwood Mountains to its mouth are only a few places where one can cross it. We struck the rim of the deep cut before daylight one morning, and waited for the sun to drive the darkness away. We took the little pack off from Laugher's back and laid down for a rest. We were very thirsty; the sound of running water down at the foot of the cliffs made us even more thirsty and restless; we could not sleep. Laugher was even more thirsty than we were; he kept going to the edge of the cliff and looking down and whining. If there had been a way for him, he would have gone down to the creek. He was in such distress that he presently began to howl, oh, so sadly. This he did a number of times before light began to rise in the eastern sky.

"As the light grew we noticed three wolves coming toward us, one a very large one, and so old that his hair was almost white. Laugher went trotting out to meet them, and they stopped and watched his approach. The morning wind was from the west: from them to us. They could not smell us. Laugher went close to them, wagging his tail, wiggling his body, showing, puppy-like by all his actions that he was somewhat afraid of them. The smaller of the three advanced to meet him, and he playfully bounded off to one side, circled and ran to the far side of the three, and stopped. At that they all suddenly threw up their heads and nosed the air, went close to him and put their noses to his side, took a smell and then bounded away out on the plain as only frightened wolves can run. Not once did they stop so long as they were in sight. Laugher stood still and watched them go, and then came whining to us and looking very foolish: 'Now, what do you make of that—what think you frightened them?' I asked.

"'Easily answered: Laugher carries the odor of man in his long, thick hair. Our odor; the odor of his pack, and smoke of campfire. It is no wonder that they ran from him,' Nitaina answered.

"He was right enough and we were glad that it was so. There was little chance of Laugher's brothers becoming friendly to him, and enticing him away from us.

"The canyon and breaks of Arrow Creek was the home of band after band of bighorn; to this day they are there very plentiful. As we descended one of their tails, three big males saw and smelled us, and ran off to the right along a narrow ledge. Laugher ran after then—we were carrying his pack down—and pressed them so closely that the hindmost of the three sprang from the ledge up on a little shelf just large enough for footing. It was a big leap it had made; Laugher did not even try to follow; but he stopped right under and raising up on his hind legs pawed the cliff wall and whined, looking up at the bighorn and then at us. I handed Nitaina my gun and got out my bow, and walking right under the shelf fired an arrow clear to the feathering into the animal's body. With one big leap it shot straight out over my head, struck another shelf far below, and went bouncing and rolling clear to the bottom of the canyon. The fall did not injure the fine, fat meat. We stopped right there for two days, drying thin sheets of it in the hot sun, and then went on. We saved that meat for a possible time of need, and kept killing fresh meat from day to day, as wanted.

"From Arrow Creek to Yellow River [Judith River], from it to It-Crushed-Them-Creek [Arnell's Creek—named for some women digging red paint who were killed by the collapse of the high cutbank], and from there to Black Butte, at the east end of the Judith Mountains, we saw no people, nor any sign of them; but beyond that, down in the valley of On-The-Far-Side Bear River [Musselshell River], we found some—and right there came very near ending our trail. It was still night when we looked down into the valley from the edge of the plain. Night Light, low in the western sky, was broken in two and the small part of her in sight did not enable us to see things at any distance. Great black patches below were of course groves of cottonwoods, and lighter places were open, grassy bottoms. We thought to stop right where we were until daylight; a patch of young quaking aspens offering good concealment; but thirst, intense thirst, drove us on; the far, low call of the river drew us to it. We descended the hill and struck out across the bottom for the lower point of a big grove.

"As we neared it there arose from the upper end of it a sudden thunder of noise and we stopped to listen. It was coming toward us; the ground trembled from the pounding of hundreds of heavy hoofs; dead branches cracked and snapped; leafy branches and brush swayed and swished; a stampeded herd of buffalo was headed our way.

"'Run! Run! Get behind a tree,' Nitaina cried.

"He had no need to do so; I was already running to shelter as fast as I could go. I passed through the outer brush of the grove; the first trees were very small; there was not time for me to go on to larger growth; I stopped at one not larger than the width of my hand, too small to climb, and pressed against it, Nitaina taking the one next to me on my right; and at that instant came the buffalo, an almost solid mass of them, hundreds of them, smashing past us. One lunged against my tree, struck my right shoulder, and though I was gripping the trunk with both arms and held on, the shock knocked me out to the other side where I was hit again, and so hard that time that I almost lost my hold. The hot, steamy breath of the big animals made me gasp for air. Flying pieces of hoof-spurned wood and earth stung my face. Again and again, now on one side and then on the other an animal brushed against me, and every instant I expected to be knocked from my hold and trampled to death.

"And then the last of the big herd passed. It went thundering on down the valley. The air cleared and, wiping the dust out of our nostrils, we again breathed freely. Said Nitaina: 'Laugher is gone. Perhaps he is killed—'

"'Your mouth, close it. Something comes,' I told him.

"'Yes. Lie down!' he answered, and we threw ourselves flat on the ground. There had been a faint snapping of sticks in the distance; more sticks snapped; nearer and nearer; and then with soft tread came men; many men; one behind another, passing on our left, and very close. In the dim glow of Night Light and her children we could no more than make out their moving forms.

One spoke, another answered, and several laughed. Their talk was strange in our ears. They could not see us, lying near them on the ground, itself as dark as night. They went steadily on with hurrying step and were gone. Once more we breathed freely and our throbbing hearts slowed down. In the distance a wolf howled: 'Ha! There is Laugher. I feared that he had been trampled to death. He did not leave me until a part of the herd had passed,' said Nitaina.

"Said I: 'Our medicine is good; the gods have listened to our prayers; all this that we have safely passed through is a sign that we are to be successful on this long trail.'

"'Do not boast. Keep on praying—'

"Laugher interrupted him by leaping up and licking his face. He had lost his little pack; our moccasins, lariats, and a part of the dried bighorn meat were gone.

"'We can make new ropes and kill more meat, but without those moccasins right here we turn back,' said I.

"Nitaina did not answer. We went to the river and drank and drank of the cool water, then crawled into the thick willows lining the shore and laid down and slept until almost midday, when we drank again, and washed ourselves, and ate a little of the dried meat that we carried. I then went up on the rim of the plain and stood watch, and Nitaina hunted for the lost pack. After a long search he found it in thick sagebrush near the point of the grove, and signalled me to return to him. I had seen nothing of the war party that had passed us in the night. The whole country was quiet. At sundown we struck out for the Bull Mountains, a group of low buttes east of the On-The-Far-Side Bear River.

"On and on we went night after night, past the small mountains and across the big plains. Nothing happened; of buffalo and antelope there was no end, but of riders, or people afoot not even a sign. And at last, in the early part of a night, we descended a steep, but short hill, crossed a wide bottom, and drank from the waters of Elk River, or as you whites call it, the Yellowstone. There we camped for the rest of the night, and at daylight, putting our guns and clothing and other things on a couple of dry logs lashed together, we swam and pushed our way to the other shore.

"There were no trails, no signs of people in the big flat there, except some fire places of the past winter, rain beaten and grass grown. We climbed to the rim of the plain for a look at the country and saw that we had struck the river far too high up. My father had said for us to cross it midway between its mouth and the mouth of the Crow's Bear River—as you say, Powder River—and right below us was the Crow's Bear River. We crossed the wide point and went down into its valley, and there struck a fresh trail; a big, dusty, fresh trail of many travois and dragging lodge poles, and countless horses. A big camp of people had recently passed there, travelling up the valley. When evening came we followed the trail, hoping that the makers of it were those we sought—the Cheyennes, breeders of the spotted horses.

"In the early morning, just before daylight, Laugher began to whine, and sniff the air, and then leaving us was gone sometime. We didn't know what to think of his actions; we were alarmed; we stopped right there and waited for him and for daylight. When he returned he was quiet enough and laid down beside us in the tall sagebrush. Morning broke and we found ourselves at the edge of a recently deserted camp ground; in more than one of the many lodge fire places the ashes were still warm. We moved quickly through the trampled brush and fresh broken strong smelling sage toward a shelter in a grove, picking up here and there a cast off, worn out moccasin. The porcupine quill embroidery of the tops was of strange design; neither Sioux nor Crow; we were undoubtedly following a Cheyenne trail.

"Two nights later as we were following the big trail, Laugher all at once halted in front of us and howled. We could hear nothing and wondered what disturbed him. Farther on he howled again; our ears were quick to catch the noises of the night but still we could hear nothing except the hooting of an owl over by the river. Somewhat later he howled again, and then we knew that his ears were much more keen than ours; what he had long since heard we now heard: the distant howling of a multitude of dogs; where they were was of course the big camp we were trailing.

"Right there we took to the hills, first filling a couple of buffalo bladders with water, and some time before morning cached ourselves in some thick brush overlooking the bottom in which were the lodges. When the light came we saw about two hundred of them over against a belt of cottonwoods by the river. And horses, they were as plentiful as the grass, and they were pintos mostly. Band after band grazed in the bottom, and on the hills on the far side of the river, and in among the lodges were tethered the choice stock: the valuable stallions and swift buffalo runners: 'Those are the ones we want—the ones we must have,' said Nitaina.

"'Right you are,' I answered. 'We have come far; only the best of them will pay us for the long trail that we are making.'

"We lay quietly there in the brush all day, sleeping by turns and watching the Cheyennes. Many of the hunters rode out early for the chase but none came near us. In the later part of the day a lot of young men held a war dance. They were fine dancers; their drums were loud and deep toned; their singing was fine. But it made Laugher uneasy; Nitaina was obliged more than once to slap his ears to keep him from howling.

"Toward evening we made our plan to raid the camp. We would wait until the last lodge fire died out and then sneak in among the tethered horses and lead out one or two at a time until each had ten of them. That was the number we decided upon, ten big, swift pintos each. A small grove of cottonwoods at the lower end of the bottom was to be the place where we were to lead, and tie the horses as fast as we obtained them, and there, too, Laugher was to be hobbled until our work was finished: we well knew that it would never do to allow him to get in among the camp dogs.

"Some time after dark we went down to the lower grove. Then, waiting until every lodge was dark, Nitaina tied Laugher's four feet together with a moccasin string and we left him lying there on the ground and whining, and slowly advanced toward the camp: 'Before taking any animals let's go all through it and pick out the very best of them,' I proposed, and Nitaina answered that that was the right thing to do.

"Night Light was not quite strong; she enabled us to see our way some distance ahead. We did not sneak into the camp; we walked naturally in past the outer lodges just as though we belonged there, and so did not arouse the suspicions of the dogs and get them after us. But, once inside, we went more slowly, looking at this horse, and that one, deciding which of the many to take. And all the time we kept a sharp lookout all around for the enemy; someone might come out at any time and discover us. All was quiet enough, however. In several lodges people snored. In another someone talked in his sleep; we prayed that all would sleep until we got away with what we wanted.

"We had gone about half way up the length of the camp when some dogs at the lower end began to bark as though they were attacking something. More and more dogs joined them. They all seemed to be coming straight up along the lodges. Their howls and yelps and growlings grew until the noise was deafening, and wakened people began to call out to one another. And then, away ahead of the rush, came Laugher and jumped up against his master. He had gnawed off his hobbling string! Oh, how frightened we were. We ran; at first through a howling mass of dogs that tripped us several times. They passed on, hundreds of them, Laugher leading them out from the lodges and away off across the bottom toward the hills. We ran the other way; into the grove and down it, the shouts of the whole camp of aroused men and women and children ringing in our ears. None followed us, doubted that any of them had discovered us, but still we ran, out from the big grove and down the bottom to the small one from which we had started. There we stopped and watched and listened; there was still some commotion in the camp; one after another the lodges began to glow with the light of freshly kindled fires; but out at the foot of the hills the dogs had given up the chase; there was never one that could overtake a wolf. With occasional yelps they were going back to camp, and presently, panting loudly, Laugher came to us, wagging his tail, jumping around us and whining, proud of what he had done. We were very angry at him; our hearts heavy with our failure of the night; but we agree that it was useless to whip him, to scold him: he could not know that he had done us wrong. We gathered up our things and went away back down the river, and remained in hiding for three nights.

"People passed down and up the bottom in front of us every day, so we knew that camp had not been moved. On the fourth night we again approached it and stopped in the small grove below. There I remained with Laugher while Nitaina went on, and after a time returned with two horses, I then took my turn and brought back two; and so we worked until we had ten each, the number we had in the first place decided to take, and with that many we were content. We had had no trouble whatever in getting them out of the sleeping camp that was a good sign for the future. We each mounted an animal, and with Laugher helping, herded the rest up out of the valley and over the plain on a swift run for home. If any of the Cheyennes followed, we never saw them. On the whole way back we saw no enemies, and had no trouble of any kind; and how our people did cheer us when we rode into camp with our band of beautiful pintos.

"And now I come to the end of my story. In the latter part of the following winter Laugher began to absent himself from camp; at first for a day; then for several days; and at last for many days at a time. We knew why he went: his kind were calling him; he was looking for a wife among them, and we could not help it. It was useless to tie him—he would snap ropes in two as fast as they were put on, and to keep him hobbled was too cruel. And then came a day when he came home no more. Later on we saw him one last time. We were hunting, and away out on the plain noticed two wolves sitting on a low butte watching us. As we neared them one came trotting down to meet us, and lo! it was Laugher, oh, so glad to see his master. Nitaina got down off his horse and petted him, then remounted and called him to follow. He sat down and watched us starting on, and whined, and trotted back to the butte and the wife he had found. He jumped around her, wagging his tail, and then started toward us, looking back—by all his actions coaxing her to follow, but she would not move. Again and again he did that, and at last gave up and howled. He loved Nitaina, but he loved his young wife most.

"We had thought in the spring to capture several wolf pups and tame them, and saw that it would be only a waste of time and trouble. The call of kind to kind is stronger than any other love."

WOLF DANCE
Tonkawa

 THE Tonkawas were a small group of central Texas Indians who were known, historically, as great buffalo hunters and skilled horse riders. In 1854, the War Department sent Colonel Randolph B. Marcy to locate and survey reservations for several tribes, among them the Tonkawas. Marcy was well aware of their situation:

The borderers of Texas have often made war upon them without the slightest provocation, and have, time and time again, robbed them of their fields, and forced them to abandon their agricultural improvements, and remove farther and farther away as the white settlers encroached upon them. They have been robbed, murdered, and starved, until they have been reduced to mere skeletons of nominal tribes, which, when we went among them, were so much disheartened and discouraged that they were perfectly willing to submit to any change that held out to them the least guarantee of security.

The Tonkawas did not hunt wolves: they believed that if they killed a wolf, they would be stricken with blindness, fevers, or madness. When they encountered a wolf, they asked it to provide them with deer when they hunted, and when returning hunters hung game meat in trees in camp, they conducted special rites to protect it from being carried off by wolves.

This second-hand account of the Wolf Dance commemorating the Tonkawa creation comes from Marcy's book Thirty Years of Army Life on the Border *(New York: Harper & Brothers, 1866).*

❖❖❖

It appears that, during the existence of the Republic of Texas, [my friend and associate, Major Neighbors] was appointed agent for the Tonkawas, and went out into the Plains and took up his abode with them. After about a year he succeeded in gaining their confidence, and ingratiated himself into especial good standing and favor with the principal chief, who manifested every disposition to oblige him whenever an opportunity offered.

These Indians, in common with all the aborigines of this continent, were eminently superstitious, believing in the agency of invisible spirits in controlling the every-day affairs of life, and in the efficacy of "medicine-bags" and

charms in healing diseases, etc. They also, like the other tribes, had their
national dances for different important occasions, and among these ceremonies
was one which seemed to me very curious, and entirely different from any other
I had heard of. It was called the *"Wolf Dance,"* and was intended to commemo-
rate the history of their origin and creation. Their traditions have handed down
to them the idea that the original progenitor of the Tonkawas was brought
into this world through the agency of the wolves.

The dance is always conducted with the utmost solemnity and secrecy,
and with all the pomp and ceremony their limited means allows; and it was
only by the most urgent entreaty, and the exercise of all his influence with the
chief, that he was permitted to become a spectator upon the important occasion, and then upon the express condition that it should be kept secret from
the other Indians.

Before the performance commenced he was clandestinely introduced into
a large dance-lodge, where he was secreted by the chief in such a position
that he could observe what was going on without himself being seen.

Soon after this, about fifty warriors, all dressed in wolf skins from head
to feet, so as to represent the animal very perfectly, made their entrance upon
all-fours in single file, and passed around the lodge, howling, growling, and
making other demonstrations peculiar to that carnivorous quadruped.

After this had continued for some time, they began to put down their
noses and sniff the earth in every direction, until at length one of them suddenly stopped, uttered a shrill cry, and commenced scratching the ground at
a particular spot. The others immediately gathered around, and all set to
work scratching up the earth with their hands, imitating the motions of the
wolf in so doing; and, in a few minutes, greatly to the astonishment of the
major, they exhumed from the spot a genuine live Tonkawa, who had previously been interred for the performance.

As soon as they had unearthed this strange biped, they ran around, scenting his person and examining him throughout with the greatest apparent
delight and curiosity. The advent of this curious and novel creature was an
occasion of no ordinary moment to them, and a council of venerable and sage
old wolves was at once assembled to determine what disposition should be
made of him.

The Tonkawa addressed them as follows: "You have taken me from the
spirit land where I was contented and happy, and brought me into this world

where I am a stranger, and I know not what I shall do for subsistence and clothing. It is better you should place me back where you found me, otherwise I shall freeze or starve."

After mature deliberation the council declined returning him to the earth, and advised him to gain a livelihood as the wolves did; to go out into the wilderness, and rob, kill, and steal wherever opportunity presented. They then placed a bow and arrows in his hands, and told him with these he must furnish himself with food and clothing; that he could wander about from place to place like the wolves, but that he must never build a house or cultivate the soil; that if he did he would surely die.

This injunction, the chief informed the major, had always been strictly adhered to by the Tonkawas.

THE WOLF HELPER
Cheyenne

 THIS is a Cheyenne "story of mystery," its meaning and power arising from its setting in the horrifying historical episode of the Sand Creek massacre. Some have called this massacre the beginning of the war for the Plains that did not end until twenty-five years later with another massacre, Wounded Knee. On the morning of November 29, 1864, Colonel John Chivington made a surprise attack on a village of Cheyennes and Arapahoes who believed themselves to be under the protection of nearby Fort Lyon. After a swift and brutal attack with rifles and howitzers, which was met with only a brief defense by the Indians, the drunken soldiers slaughtered the wounded and mutilated the bodies. Some 200 Indians, mostly women and children, were murdered. This story is about a few survivors who escaped the devastation.

The tale was collected by George Bird Grinnell and published in his book By Cheyenne Campfires *(New Haven: Yale University Press, 1926).*

❖❖❖

After the Sand Creek massacre was over, the the troops had gone, there were left alive two women. In 1902 these women were still living. One was named Two She-Wolf Woman, and the other, Standing in Different Places Woman. They were sisters, and each had a little daughter—one ten years old and one of six years. Their husband was badly wounded and likely to die, and he told them they must leave him and go on home to the camp, so that they might save themselves and their children. They started. They had no food, and no implements except their knives and a little short-handled axe. They had their robes.

They traveled on and on, until they reached the Smoky Hill River. Here they found many rose berries, and they pounded them up with the little axe and ate them. After they had pounded the rose berries they made flat cakes of them to give to the children, and started on. They did not know where the camp was, and did not know where to go. They just followed the river down.

One night after they had been traveling for six or seven days, they went into a little hole in the bluff for shelter, for it was very cold. They were sitting up, one robe under them, with the other in front of them, and with the children lying between them. In the middle of the night something came into the hole and lay down by them, and when this thing had come near to them, standing between them and the opening of the hole, they saw that it was a big wolf, and were afraid of it; but it lay down quietly.

Next morning they started on, and the wolf went with them, walking not far to one side of them. Their feet were sore, for their moccasins were worn out, and they often stopped to rest, and when they did so the wolf lay down near by. At one of these halts the elder woman spoke to the wolf, just as she would talk to a person. She said to him: "O Wolf, try to do something for us. We and our children are nearly starved." When she spoke to him, the wolf seemed to listen and rose up on his haunches and looked at her, and when she stopped speaking he rose to his feet and started off toward the north. It was the early part of the winter, but there was no snow on the ground.

The women still sat there resting, for they were weak and tired and footsore. They saw the wolf pass out of sight over the hill, and after a time they saw him coming back. He came toward them, and when he was close to them they could see that his mouth and jaws were covered with blood. He stepped in front of them and turned his head and looked back in the direction from whence he had come. The women were so weak and stiff they could hardly get up, but they rose to their feet. When they stood up the wolf trotted off to the top of the hill and stopped, looking back, and they followed him very slowly. When they reached the top of the hill and looked off, they saw, down in the little draw beyond, the carcass of a buffalo, and in a circle all about it sat many wolves. The wolf looked back at the women again, and then loped down toward the carcass. Now the women started to walk fast toward the carcass, for here was food. All the wolves still sat about; they were not feeding on the carcass.

When the women reached it they drew their knives and opened it. They made no fire, but at once ate the liver and tripe, and the fat about the intestines, without cooking, and gave food to the children. Then they cut off pieces of the meat, as much as they could carry, and made up packs and started on their way. As soon as they had left the carcass, all the wolves fell upon it and began to eat it quickly, growling and snarling at each other, and soon they had eaten it all. The big wolf ate with the other wolves. The women went on over the hill and stopped; they had eaten so much that they could not go far. In the evening, when the sun was low, one of the women said to the other, "Here is our friend again"; and the wolf came trotting up to them.

Soon after he had joined them they started on to look for a hollow where they might sleep. The wolf traveled with them. When it grew dark they stopped, and the wolf lay near them. Every day they tried to find a place to camp where there were willows. They used to cut these and make a shelter of them, and cover this with grass, and make a bed of grass, and then put down their robes and cover themselves with grass. So they were well sheltered.

One morning as they were going along they looked over the hill and saw in the bottom below them some ponies feeding. They started down to see whose they were, the wolf traveling along, but off to one side. Before they had come near to the horses two persons came up over a hill, and when these persons saw the women coming they sprang on their horses and ran away fast. The women walked on to the place where the men had been. Here there was a fire, and meat that the men had left—a tongue and other food roasting. The women took the meat and ate, and they cut the tongue in two and gave the smaller end of it to the wolf, which had come up and was lying by the fire.

After they had finished eating they went on, and soon came to a big spring with a hollow near by—a good place to camp. They were glad to find the place, for the sky looked as if it were going to snow. They made a good camp, a house of willows and grass, and covered it with bark from the trees. By this time they had become so accustomed to having the wolf with them that every night they used to make a bed near the door of the house, piling up grass for him to sleep on.

That night the women heard a noise down in the hollow—something calling like a big owl. Two She-Wolf Woman was watching; for they were afraid during the night, and used to take turns keeping watch. They could hear this thing breaking sticks as it walked about. The watcher awoke her sister, saying, "Wake up! something is coming." The wolf now stood up, and soon he began to howl with a long-drawn-out cry, which was very dismal. Soon from all directions many wolves began to come to the place. After a little while this thing that was making the noise began to come closer, and when it did so all the wolves rushed toward it and began fighting it, and the women seized their children and ran away into the night. They got far out on the level prairie and stopped there, for their feet were sore, and they were very tired. In the morning just as day was breaking they saw the big wolf coming toward them. When he reached them he lay down.

The elder woman now spoke to him again, and said, "Wolf, take pity on us; help us to find the trail of our people." When she had ceased speaking, the wolf trotted away, leaving the women, and they followed on very slowly. Before long they saw him coming back toward them fast—loping. When he got to them they saw that he had in his mouth a big piece of dried meat. He dropped the meat in front of them. They seized the meat and divided it, and gave some of it to their children and ate of it themselves. The wolf did not lie down, but stood waiting, and when they had eaten, he led them to an old camp where there were sticks standing in the ground, and on each stick hung a parfleche sack of meat. Their relations had left these things for them, knowing that they were lost and thinking that they might pass that way.

Now the women had plenty of food; they went to the water and built a shelter with a place in it for the wolf. That night it snowed. When they arose the snow was above their ankles. Again the woman spoke to the wolf, and asked him to go and find their camp, and he went away. The women stayed there. The wolf was not gone a long time; he came back the same day. They were watching for him, for now they knew that he was their friend, and that he was true; they knew that he would do something for them. The two women went to the top of the little hill near by, and before night they saw the wolf coming. He came up to them and stopped, and then began to look back. The women felt sure that he had found something, and went back to their camp and got their children, and went to the wolf, who started back as he had come, traveling ahead of them. On the point of a high hill he stopped, and when the women overtook him they looked down, and there they saw a big Cheyenne camp on the river below. This was the head of the Republican River.

They went on down to the camp, and to the lodge of Gray Beard. The wolf remained on the hill. After the women had eaten, the older woman took meat, and told the people that a wolf had led them to the camp, and she was going back to give him something to eat. She went back and gave the wolf the food, and after he had eaten she said to him, "Now, you have brought us to the camp, you can go back to your old ways." Late that evening the woman went up on the hill again to see if the wolf was there, but he was gone. She saw his tracks going back the same way that he had come. This happened in the winter of 1864 and 1865. The women and one of the children are still alive.

THE FORSAKEN BOY
Ojibway

THE idea of wolves adopting human children has always intrigued people, from Romulus and Remus in ancient Rome to the much-debated account of Amala and Kamala in twentieth century India. Little is said directly about the wolves in this tale, but the implicit message is unforgettable.

This story was recorded and published quite early by pioneer ethnologist Henry Rowe Schoolcraft. The Ojibways were somewhat better known than other Indians partly because of Schoolcraft's studies and partly because of the large area they occupied and the early presence of whites among them. Beginning in 1822 as an Indian agent and later as Superintendent of Indian Affairs, Schoolcraft spent many years in the Old Northwest Territory (around Lake Superior and in Michigan). He studied Ojibway language and mythology and was among the first scholars to base his studies on first-hand interviews. "Sheem; or, The Forsaken Boy" is from Algic Researches, Comprising Inquiries Respecting the Mental Characteristics of the North American Indians, *First Series, Indian Tales and Legends (New York: Harper & Brothers, 1839).*

❖❖❖

A solitary lodge stood on the banks of a remote lake. It was near the hour of sunset. Silence reigned within and without. Not a sound was heard but the low breathing of the dying inmate and head of this poor family. His wife and three children surrounded his bed. Two of the latter were almost grown up; the other was a mere child. All their simple skill in medicine had been exhausted to no effect. They moved about the lodge in whispers, and were waiting the departure of the spirit. As one of the last acts of kindness, the skin door of the lodge had been thrown back to admit the fresh air. The poor man felt a momentary return of strength, and, raising himself a little, addressed his family.

"I leave you in a world of care, in which it has required all my strength and skill to supply you food, and protect you from the storms and cold of a severe climate. For you, my partner in life, I have less sorrow in parting, because I am persuaded you will not remain long behind me, and will therefore find the period of your sufferings shortened. But you, my children! my poor and forsaken children, who have just commenced the career of life, who will protect you from its evils? Listen to my words! Unkindness, ingratitude, and every wickedness is in the scene before you. It is for this cause that, years ago, I withdrew from my kindred and my tribe, to spend my days in this lonely spot. I have contented myself with the company of your mother and yourselves during seasons of very frequent scarcity and want, while your kindred, feasting in a scene where food is plenty, have caused the forests to echo with the shouts of successful war. I gave up these things for the enjoyment of peace. I wished to shield you from the bad examples you would inevitably have followed. I have seen you, thus far, grow up in innocence. If we have sometimes suffered bodily want, we have escaped pain of mind. We have been kept from scenes of rioting and bloodshed.

"My career is now at its close. I will shut my eyes in peace, if you, my children, will promise me to cherish each other. Let not your mother suffer during the few days that are left to her; and I charge you, on no account, to forsake your youngest brother. Of him I give you both my dying charge to take a tender care." He sank exhausted on his pallet. The family waited a moment, as if expecting to hear something farther; but, when they came to his side, the spirit had taken its flight.

The mother and daughter gave vent to their feelings in lamentations. The elder son witnessed the scene in silence. He soon exerted himself to supply, with the bow and net, his father's place. Time, however, wore away heavily. Five moons had filled and waned, and the sixth was near its full, when the mother also died. In her last moments she pressed the fulfilment of their promise to their father, which the children readily renewed, because they were yet free from selfish motives.

The winter passed; and the spring, with its enlivening effects in a northern hemisphere, cheered the drooping spirits of the bereft little family. The girl, being the eldest, dictated to her brothers, and seemed to feel a tender and sisterly affection for the youngest, who was rather sickly and delicate. The other boy soon showed symptoms of restlessness and ambition, and addressed the sister as follows: "My sister, are we always to live as if there were no other human beings in the world? Must I deprive myself of the pleasure of associating with my own kind? I have determined this question for myself. I shall seek the villages of men, and you cannot prevent me."

The sister replied: "I do not say no, my brother, to what you desire. We are not prohibited the society of our fellow-mortals; but we are told to cherish each other, and to do nothing independent of each other. Neither pleasure nor pain ought, therefore, to separate us, especially from our younger brother, who, being but a child, and weakly withal, is entitled to a double share of our affection. If we follow our separate gratifications, it will surely make us neglect him, whom we are bound by vows, both to our father and mother, to support." The young man received this address in silence. He appeared daily to grow more restiff and moody, and one day, taking his bow and arrows, left the lodge and never returned.

Affection nerved the sister's arm. She was not so ignorant of the forest arts as to let her brother want. For a long time she administered to his necessities, and supplied a mother's cares. At length, however, she began to be weary of solitude and of her charge. No one came to be a witness of her assiduity, or to let fall a single word in her native language. Years, which added to her strength and capability of directing the affairs of the household, brought with them the irrepressible desire of society, and made solitude irksome. At this point, selfishness gained the ascendency of her heart; for, in meditating a change in her mode of life, she lost sight of her younger brother, and left him to be provided for by contingencies.

One day, after collecting all the provisions she had been able to save for emergencies, after bringing a quantity of wood to the door, she said to her little brother: "My brother, you must not stray from the lodge. I am going to seek our elder brother. I shall be back soon." Then, taking her bundle, she set off in search of habitations. She soon found them, and was so much taken up with the pleasures and amusements of social life, that the thought of her brother was almost entirely obliterated. She accepted proposals of marriage; and, after that, thought still less of her hapless and abandoned relative.

Meantime her elder brother had also married, and lived on the shores of the same lake whose ample circuit contained the abandoned lodge of his father and his forsaken brother. The latter was soon brought to the pinching turn of his fate. As soon as he had eaten all the food left by his sister, he was obliged to pick berries and dig up roots. These were finally covered by the snow. Winter came on with all its rigours. He was obliged to quit the lodge in search of other food. Sometimes he passed the night in the clefts of old trees or caverns, and ate the refuse meals of the wolves. The latter, at last, became his only resource; and he became so fearless of these animals that he would sit close by them while they devoured their prey. The wolves, on the other hand, became so familiar with his face and form, that they were undisturbed by his approach; and, appearing to sympathize with him in his outcast condition, would always leave something for his repast. In this way he lived till spring. As soon as the lake was free from ice, he followed his newfound friends to the shore. It happened, the same day, that his elder brother was fishing in his canoe, a considerable distance out in the lake, when he thought he heard the cries of a child on the shore, and wondered how any could exist on so bleak and barren a part of the coast. He listened again attentively, and distinctly heard the cry repeated. He made for shore as quick as possible, and, as he approached land, discovered and recognised his little brother, and heard him singing, in a plaintive voice,

> Neesia—neesia,
> Shyegwuh goosuh!
> Ni my een gwun iewh!
> Ni my een gwun iewh!
> > Heo hwooh.

> Ke ge wai bin im
> She gwuh dush
> Ni my een gwun iewh!
> Ni my een gwun iewh!
> > Heo hwooh.

> Tyau, tyau! sunnagud,
> Nin dininee wun aubun
> She gwuh dush
> Ni my een gwun iewh!
> > Heo hwooh.

> Listen, brother—elder brother!
> Now my fate is near its close;
> Soon my state shall be another,
> Soon shall cease my day of woes.

Left by friends I loved the dearest,
All who knew and loved me most;
Woes the darkest and severest,
Bide me on this barren coast.

Pity! ah, that manly feeling,
Fled from hearts where once it grew,
Now in wolfish forms revealing,
Glows more warmly than in you.

Stony hearts! that saw me languish,
Deaf to all a father said,
Deaf to all a mother's anguish,
All a brother's feelings fled.

Ah, ye wolves, in all your ranging,
I have found you kind and true;
More than man—and now I'm changing,
And will soon be one of you.

At the termination of his song, which was drawn out with a peculiar
cadence, he howled like a wolf. The elder brother was still more astonished,
when, getting nearer shore, he perceived his poor brother partly transformed
into that animal. He immediately leaped on shore, and strove to catch him in
his arms, soothingly saying, "My brother, my brother, come to me." But the
boy eluded his grasp, crying as he fled, "Neesia, neesia," &c., and howling in
the intervals.

The elder brother, conscience stricken, and feeling his brotherly affection strongly return, with redoubled force exclaimed, in great anguish, "My
brother! my brother! my brother!"

But, the nearer he approached, the more rapidly the transformation went
on; the boy alternately singing and howling, and calling out the name, first of
his brother, and then of his sister, till the change was completely accomplished,
when he exclaimed, "I am a wolf!" and bounded out of sight.

THE WOLF-WARRIOR
Pawnee

 THE wolf was an important creature in the world of the Pawnee people of the central Great Plains, who were known as the Wolf People. This story was told by Thief, of the Kitkehahki Pawnee, to George A. Dorsey, who collected tales under the auspices of the Carnegie Institution and published them as The Pawnee: Mythology *(Washington: Carnegie Institution of Washington, 1906). The Pawnee recognized two main kinds of tales, those that were true and those that were invented, especially by the old men, for the purpose of "impressing some moral precept, illustrating some phase of ethical life, or of conveying a warning, etc." "The Wolf-Warrior" is a true story of the power one man obtained from a wolf and is one of the stories "which treat of the wonderful doings of the supernatural beings of the earth."*

Dorsey noted that while the Pawnee were still in Nebraska, before they were removed to Oklahoma in 1874, the trickster or transformer stories were called not Coyote stories but Wolf stories. Such tales "suggest to the Pawnee the mischievous performances of the Wolf sent by the Wolf-Star, who, in attempting to steal people from Lightning, introduces mortality on earth, and through Lightning's failure to sacrifice Wolf the earth becomes subject to warfare and death."

❖❖❖

A company of warriors were out on the war-path. One man was separated from the party and could not find it again. He climbed a high hill and as he neared the top of the hill he heard a song. The song was like this:

> Here and there over this earth,
> Here and there I have traveled.

The man looked around for the singer, and there on top of the hill sat an old Wolf on his haunches with his body erect. He was looking towards the heavens and singing. He sang the song several times, and the man heard the song and recognized it as the Wolf-Warrior song. The wolf was old, his hair had fallen, and there were few hairs upon his head, paws, and the end of his tail. The Wolf saw the man and said: "Come, my son, I want you to see me. This is my medicine that you see before me; although I am old I eat a little of this root and it makes me strong so that I can walk a long distance without growing weary. You can take the root, powder it fine, mix the root with white clay so that it will become dust, and when you are on the war-path and are very tired, take the pounded root and snuff it up your nose, and the tired feeling will go from you and you can travel fast. When you go home kill a wolf and make you a robe; then kill two more wolves and have moccasins made; have the front paws upon your moccasins, the hind paws back on your heels. Always wear the moccasins and wolf robe when you are on the war-path and want to travel fast. Do as I have told you and you shall become a great warrior and you shall have long life."

The man answered the Wolf, saying: "My father, you are a wonderful being. Tirawa watches over you and has given you long life. Give me long life, my father; make me a great warrior and I will keep the things you have told me. I will always have my tobacco bag filled with sumach leaves mixed with tobacco, so that I can smoke to you." The Wolf then said: "My son, lie down by me to-night. I am dying of old age; by the time the sun comes up and looks upon me I shall be dead. When I am dead, cut my nose and then cut a strip up the scalp about the length of the forefinger to the wrist. This you must dry and wear upon your scalp-lock, for this nose shall be my spirit, and if you keep it you shall live to be old and you shall not die until your skin is wrinkled and you have only a few hairs left upon your head. Then give these things to your children and tell them about me, so that they will take care of my things." The man sat down and the Wolf began to howl again and raised his head towards the heavens. As he kept on howling, the man listened and he heard a song. He heard it so plainly that he could sing the song:

> Often when the sun is high,
> Then I despise myself.

This song was to belong to the man, for he was to get old like the Wolf. The Wolf kept on howling, and that night the man lay down by the Wolf. As darkness came on, the Wolf crawled nearer to the man and sat down by him, and so the Wolf and the man slept side by side. The Wolf's power was transferred to the man through the medium of a dream. Towards morning, when the first morning star, "Wolf-Star," came up, the Wolf sat up and gave one big howl, then lay down again. At dawn the man awoke and saw that the

Wolf was still sleeping. He sat up faced the east, and waited for the sun to come up from the horizon. As its first ray shot across the land, the Wolf lifted up its head and looked at the sun, gave a howl, and as the sound died away the Wolf died. The man went up to where the Wolf lay and spoke to him, with deep feeling, and wept. He remained upon the hill several days, and one night the Wolf came to him in a dream and said: "My son, take the nose off from my body and keep it, as I told you. Do not stay upon the hill any more, for the Sun, my father, who gives me my power, has given me permission to follow you all the time. When I last cried, it was a cry to the Sun, for now the Sun has helped me to pass out of this world to our home, to a place unknown by man." When the man awoke, he looked about him and saw the Wolf lying there. He took his knife out and laid it on the ground. He took some sumach leaves and tobacco and placed them inside the nostrils of the Wolf. After this, he took his knife and cut the nose with a piece of the scalp on. He left the Wolf on the hill; for the Wolf in the dream had told him that he should leave his body on the hill. The man took the things that he was to take with him, the root and the nose of the Wolf. The man did not go to join the war party, but went on home.

When he reached home, people asked about the others who were with him. He told them that he was lost from the others and had not seen them any more, and so he had come back home. The people called him a coward and said, "You should have remained with them." The man did not say anything. Days went by. The man was always absent from the village. While he was gone one day, the war party came over the hills as if to attack the village. They were on fine ponies that they had captured from the enemy, and each was singing his victory song. As they approached the village men went out to meet the victorious party, while the women and children climbed the mud-lodges to see the victorious war party come in. Some of them had white clay all over their bodies, and others were painted black with prairie grass that they had burned, to let the people know by the smoke that a victorious war party was coming. When the men came home the people told them that they did not go out to meet the man who had come home alone. The warriors then told the people that they thought the man had strayed off and perhaps been killed by the enemy, for he had never been seen by them again. Wolf-Man returned to the village when he saw the war party approaching, and listened to all they said, but remained silent.

The summer passed. In the fall when the people were gathering their corn, another warrior of distinction sat in his lodge and invited a few of his friends to join him, telling that he intended to go out among the Comanche. Wolf-Man heard about the war party, and he stole away from home and joined the party. There were good warriors in this party, so Wolf-Man was not so prominent. When they reached the enemy's country he made up his mind that he would scout on ahead. Every morning when the war party began to journey, Wolf-Man would remain behind. In the evening he would be the last to come to camp, and he would tell of all he saw farther south, where the other scouts had failed to go. Most of the warriors did not believe him.

One day he stayed behind, but when he did travel he went far beyond the others. He turned back, and on his way the other scouts saw him. They were surprised, for these scouts had started out before anyone. Wolf-Man went to where the main company had made the camp. The two scouts reported carefully all they had seen and they also told that they had seen Wolf-Man coming from a long distance in advance of them and that he had a report to make. Wolf-Man then told how he walked and passed the other scouts and how he had gone a long way from the scouts. There were no signs of any enemy, so Wolf-Man recommended that they go southeast to the land of the Osage. The two leaders were glad to hear the man speak. The next morning, before daylight, he was told to scout on ahead. The man went out, and before daylight he was back, for he had seen Cheyenne and Arapaho breaking camp.

The company hid until noon; then they came out from their hiding place and followed the trail. The trail was plain. They could see the enemy making camp. They could also see where they were taking their ponies. After night scouts were sent to capture the ponies. Wolf-Man was one of the six scouts selected. He went with the men, but finally went away from them to the place where the leader was, with the other young men. As he drove the ponies up, the leader came and met him. "All these ponies I give you," said Wolf-Man. The leader thanked him and said, "This day you shall be known among our great warriors as the Man-Who-Has-No-Leader." Wolf-Man went back to camp and found more ponies, brought them to the leader, and again he gave them all to him. The young men surrounded the herd of ponies. Each man had his lariat rope trying to rope a pony. Everybody was told to catch his pony and to drive the herd. Most of the men caught ponies and got on them. While the men were riding and driving the ponies they saw

Wolf-Man walking, sometimes running, and he did not seem to get tired. The leader, when he divided the ponies, let Wolf-Man take his choice of all. Wolf-Man took one pony. The leader divided the ponies so that even the young men who for the first time had gone on the war-path received a pony, and every one of the warriors had a pony. As they neared the village the leader started a prairie fire and made the young men take the burnt grass and paint their faces black.

The people in the village saw the smoke. Soon they saw the warriors coming over the hills on ponies and singing their victory songs, and they knew that it was the war party which had gone out. When the warriors were in their lodges, they told of Wolf-Man's wonderful endurance in walking. After that when a leader wanted to go on the war-path he invited Wolf-Man. Wolf-Man was always ready to go. He was the leader of scouts. The war party always came back successful, for they had Wolf-Man with them.

Among the warriors was a famous leader who determined to go on the war-path. He sent for only the best men in the tribe, and Wolf-Man was among them. This party of warriors started out for the Mexican country, for in that country they could capture mules and fine ponies. Before starting, Wolf-Man had a wolf robe made. He also had moccasins made from wolf hide. The nose and scalp of the wolf he wore on his scalp-lock all the time, and he wore the wolf robe and his wolf moccasins. When the company had gone far south into the enemy's country, the leader found two men who seemed never to grow tired, and yet they traveled farther every day than the others. They soon were recognized as leaders of all the scouts. They were sent out in different directions one day, and when they were far away from the others they met. There were no enemies in sight. They could see no sign, and so they started back to the place where the leaders were with the other men. As they journeyed, both seemed to be equal in endurance. Wolf-Man 's companion said: "How do you travel so fast? You must possess some power." "Well," said Wolf-Man, "I will let you know. See my moccasins? They are made of wolf hide. I wear them on my journey; when I near the camp, I take them off. I also use this dust in my buckskin sack. Take some and snuff it up into your nostrils." The other man took the dust and snuffed it. The tired feeling wore off and he felt like walking a long distance. They went on for many miles, and then Wolf-Man said to the other man: "Have you no guardian nor helper? I have told you my secret, now tell me yours." The man reached for his scalp-lock and took from it a small root. This he broke and gave to Wolf-Man, and said, "Chew; swallow." Wolf-Man took the root, chewed it, and swallowed the juice. He felt as though it were morning and he had not been traveling all day. As he swallowed the juice from the root he felt relieved from hunger, for the root tasted like fat. Wolf-Man said, "This is wonderful; who or what animal gave you this root?" The man answered and said: "This root I got from a Horse; the Horse did not speak to me, but I had a dream, and the Horse told me in my dream that I must go with him and he would show me the Horses' root. I followed the Horse and he showed me the root; I dug it up and tasted it; I knew how it tasted; I woke up. The next day I went out and found the root, and dug it up and tasted it and it was the same, and so I kept it." Wolf-Man did not say any more, for he had found one man equal to himself in traveling. Wolf-Man also knew that the man did not tell all of his story.

When they reached camp they told the leaders where they had been, and it was hard for the leaders to believe them; for it was a journey of several days to the place where they said they had been. These two men were the ones who found a Mexican village and took from a corral many ponies and mules, giving them to the leader. The leader thanked them.

After this trip Wolf-Man made friends with the other man who could walk fast. They became old and were often invited by young warriors to tell their war stories to them. Wolf-Man outlived the other man and came to Oklahoma in 1872. He was then a very old man, but still a good walker. He had a son whom he took pains to teach his secrets and songs. One night after the old man had given all of his things to his son, he lay down in his earth-lodge and waited through the night for the first ray of the morning sun to come, for he knew that when it came he had to die. The ray came through the lodge and rested on the old man. He gave one cry and died, as the wolf had died, of old age.

BLACK WOLF AND HIS FATHERS
Cheyenne

 THIS Cheyenne "story of mystery" was recorded by George Bird Grinnell in By Cheyenne Campfires *(New Haven: Yale University Press, 1926). Based on his thirty years' close contact with the Cheyenne, he also wrote his most highly regarded work,* The Cheyenne Indians, *and* The Fighting Cheyennes. *Although Grinnell was an Eastern businessman and publisher, he is best remembered for his ethnological and historical studies of the West. He was an ardent conservationist and advocate for Native Americans.*

The symbolic richness and depth of this story rival any traditional European legends about wolves.

❖❖❖

Black Wolf was a fine-looking young man and many girls liked him, but his father did not wish any of them as daughter-in-law. He used to say, "I do not want my son to get married."

Every day Black Wolf used to go up on the hill and sit there on a white buffalo robe, looking over the valley.

There was talk in the camp that they were going to move. Black Wolf's father said: "If the camp moves, I shall stay here. The people give me too much trouble."

He did not like it because so many young girls wanted to marry his son.

Two girls, who thought they would be smart, determined to play a trick on Black Wolf, and agreed that when the camp moved they would stay behind. They said, "We will see what we can do to this young man who thinks he is too nice for any girl."

The robe on which Black Wolf used to sit was never moved. It lay always in the same place on the hill. One night after the camp had gone the girls, who had remained hidden during the day, went up on the hill and took the robe from its place, and where it had lain they dug a deep hole. They worked all night, digging the hole and carrying the dirt far away, so that it could not be seen. When they had finished they spread the buffalo robe smoothly over the hole, just as it had been before.

Next morning Black Wolf went up to sit on the hill and when he sat down on the robe he fell into this deep hole. He could not get out.

When night came and he did not return to the lodge, his mother said to her husband: "Where is my son, that he has not yet come in? He must feel lonely since the camp has left. My son wanted to follow the camp, and if you had had good sense you would have done as he wished. Let us pack up now and follow the camp."

They packed up and started, and when they reached the main camp the mother said, "Is my son in camp?"

The father said to his friends, "My son got lonely and followed up the camp." Both supposed he was there.

The two girls were watching the lodge, and after the father had moved his camp, the girls came to the hole on the hill and looked down into it and saw the young man sitting there. He could not get out. The girls spoke to him and said, "You were very hard to get, but we have got you now."

Black Wolf answered them, saying, "If you will take me out of this hole I will marry you both."

"Very well," said the girls; "but first hand us up the white buffalo robe. If we should take you out first, there would be no way of getting the robe."

After he had handed the robe up to them they said, "Now we have you where we want you." Close by were many buffalo bones, and they gathered these and threw them down at Black Wolf and hit him on the head and shoulders so that he was bleeding from many places. They did not take him out of the hole. They went away and left him there suffering. His parents in the camp kept asking people if anyone had seen their son, but no one could tell them about him, and at last they concluded that he was lost and began to mourn for him.

One night a big white wolf that was trotting along the hillside smelled the man and following up the scent found the hole. When he had looked into the hole the wolf said, "I have found a human being. I will take him for my son."

Another wolf, a mad one, came up, looked into the hole, and said: "I have found a human being. Now I shall have something to eat."

The white wolf wanted the young man for his son, and the rabid wolf wanted to eat him. They disputed for a long time as to what should be done with him, and finally they agreed that each one should dig down to the man, and that the one that first got to him should have him.

They began to dig, and the man, who had overheard the dispute, took one of the buffalo bones that had been thrown into the hole and began to dig on the side where the white wolf was digging and so helped him, and the white wolf got first into the hole.

When both wolves had dug into the hole they again began to dispute, for the rabid wolf still wanted to eat Black Wolf. Then they began to discuss how they should get out of the hole and up on to the ground again. The rabid wolf said to the white wolf, "I will first creep out of the hole and then the man may follow, and you can come last."

"No," said the white wolf, "that will not do." He turned to the young man and said, "If you come following him out of the hole he will turn around and bite you and begin to eat you." At last the rabid wolf gave up to the white wolf and let him have the man. The rabid wolf said, "You go ahead and our son can follow you and I will follow him."

"No," said the white wolf, "this human being may be a great help to us. We must protect him so that he can help us. You go out first, I will follow, and our son can follow me."

The mad wolf went first and the white wolf followed. When he got to the entrance the white wolf just put his head out of the hole and the rabid wolf, who had already turned around, started forward to bite him and then when he saw who it was stopped and said, "I have made a mistake." The man came out last and all three stood there together.

The white wolf said to him, "Now, we will take you to our home."

"Yes," said the mad wolf, "you will go to our home. There you will see many fathers."

They started and pretty soon the mad wolf began to edge closer and closer to the man and to act as if he wanted to eat him. As they went the white wolf said to his son, "We live inside a big round hill."

The mad wolf said: "Our son has traveled a long way. He must be getting hungry. Why do you not go off and see if you can find something for him to eat."

The white wolf would not go away from the man. He said to the mad wolf: "No, you are a better hunter than I, and always have better luck than I. You go and get something for our son. He is getting very hungry."

"Yes," said the mad wolf, "I will go. You see that hill ahead of us,"— pointing—"you try to meet me there."

The mad wolf went off and as he went over the hill the white wolf said to the man: "There are four of us just like him, and they are very cross and ugly, and there are four of us just like me who have taken you for my son."

Just then the mad wolf came back, and said to the white wolf, "Have you been telling our son bad things about me—abusing me?"

"No," said the white wolf, "I have just been telling him what a good hunter you are, and how you never get tired."

The mad wolf went off again, and as they were going along the white wolf said to the man, "He will carry the news to where we are going and there you will see many wolves and they will all be your fathers."

When the mad wolf came back to them, appearing over the point where he had said he would meet them, he carried in his mouth a buffalo kidney for the man to eat. Black Wolf took the kidney and the white wolf said, "I told you that your father was a great hunter and that he would bring you something to eat."

The mad wolf said, "I think you have been telling this man all about me."

Where they met they slept that night. The mad wolf said, "I will sleep next to our son."

"No," said the white wolf, "I will sleep next to my own son." The mad wolf always seemed to be wanting to get near the young man to harm him.

Next morning they started again, and the mad wolf said to the white wolf, "Now, do you go off and get something to eat for our son."

"No," said the white wolf, "you go. I have told you once that I have taken this person for my son, and I shall not leave him."

The mad wolf started, and before he left the white wolf told him the direction they were going and where they should meet. When they met the mad wolf had in his mouth a piece of liver for the man. That night they stayed at the place of their meeting.

Next morning they started, and the white wolf said to the young man, "To-night, at the next camp we make, before we get home, you shall have a robe."

As they traveled that day the white wolf said to the mad wolf, "Now, try again and make another hunt, and get something to eat."

The mad wolf started off and then turned back and said, "No, I have gone twice; you go now."

"No," said the white wolf, "I have told you that this is my son and I will not leave him. Besides he is going to have a robe at our next camp." So the mad wolf went off to look for food. When he met them he had in his mouth a tongue, cooked, and the young man ate it. After the young man had eaten the tongue, the white wolf said to the mad wolf, "Our son now must have a robe so that he can sleep warmer."

The white wolf lay down and rolled on the ground and when he rose to his feet, he left a wolf hide lying on the ground. He said to the young man, "Now, take the front and the hind feet in your hands, just as you would pick up a robe to place on your shoulders, lift the hide straight up, and give it one shake."

The young man did as he had been told and when he had given the hide this one shake, he was holding in his hands a nice big robe, made of four large wolf hides sewed together.

The white wolf told him to put the robe on. They stopped here all night.

Next morning as they started, the white wolf showed the young man a great butte, away far off. "There is where we are going," he said, "but we shall not reach it to-day."

The mad wolf said, "Now, do you go out and hunt, and we will meet halfway to the butte."

The white wolf answered him as before, and then the mad wolf went off to hunt. After he had gone the white wolf said: "When we get to that place where we are going, the mad wolf will ask you to pick out your father from among the other wolves. You cannot do this, for there are four of us just alike, and if you do not do it they kill you and eat you. I will refuse to let you do it. When I refuse, perhaps they will say that you must do it. If they do so, when you look at me as we stand in the line I will try to wink my right eye and you must take hold of me and pull me out of the line and say, 'This is my father.' The first time you try to pick me out I will wink my right eye, but then we will all mingle and walk about and howl. Then we will form in line again. The second time you have to choose me I will move my right ear and you must say, 'This is my father.' The third time we will again mix up and howl and when they fall in line that time I will move the third toe of my right foot. The fourth time after we mix up and howl, we will all sit down on our tails with the tails sticking out between our fore-feet and as we sit there I will move the tip of my tail. Then choose me."

That night the mad wolf met them with a piece of roasted meat. They were then very near to the butte. The white wolf again pointed to it and said, "There is where I am taking you."

When they started next morning, the mad wolf left them and went on fast to the butte to carry the news. When he got there he said, "We are bringing with us a human being who will be a help to us wolves."

As the white wolf and the young man approached the butte, there seemed to be a wave of wolves and coyotes rushing toward them over the prairie. When they reached the butte they found there four mad wolves just alike and four white wolves just alike. The ground inside the butte was beaten down hard.

The man-eating wolf said to the white wolf, "If this son of yours can pick you out every time for four times, then we will all take him for our son."

The white wolf said, "Yes, we will have our son look for his father."

They told the young man to cover up his head and all the wolves moved about among themselves and howled. Then they walked in a circle and the four white wolves fell into the center of the circle and stood in a row. Now the son was told to uncover his head and to look for his father. The four white wolves stood there in a row in the center of the circle. The young man looked at the four and watched their heads and presently he saw one of the wolves wink his right eye. The young man said, "This is my father," and the man-eating wolf gave a grunt. He did not like it.

Again they told the young man to cover his head, and the wolves all walked around and howled as before and when the young man uncovered his head and they said, "Now look for your father." He looked again and one of the white wolves moved his right ear. The young man said, "This is my father," and again the man-eating wolf gave a grunt. He did not like it.

The same thing happened again, and when the young man looked for his father he chose the white wolf that moved the third toe on his right foot. Again the man-eating wolf gave a grunt of anger.

The same thing happened again, but before the young man chose, the man-eating wolf said, "This is your last choice." The young man chose the white wolf that moved the tip of this tail that was under him. After he got through, the man-eating wolf thought more of the son than the white wolf did.

The white wolf said: "Now, our son has been here a long time and so have we, and we are all hungry. We must send off for a bow and arrows. We will send Walking Rabbit (a jack rabbit)."

"No," said Walking Rabbit, "do not send me, they might hurt me; send Standing Rabbit."

Standing Rabbit went and found a camp of people and went close to it and presently people began to shoot arrows at him and he went so close to some people that they even threw their bows at him. He dodged the arrows and the bows, and managed to pick up all these things, and to carry back with him to the butte the arrows shot at him and bows thrown at him. When he returned he had a lot of arrows.

The young man was glad to get these things. He began to try his bow to see how strong it was, and when he snapped it he frightened the wolves and they began to run away.

"Look out," said the white wolf, "do not frighten your fathers; they are easily scared."

"Very well," said the young man, "but let them get some buffalo here so that I can try my bow on them."

The wolves went to drive the buffalo up and soon did so.

The young man had twenty arrows, and he killed twenty buffalo. Then they needed a knife to cut up the meat and decided to send the Swift Fox for it, for he could go fast and would make a quick trip.

Before long the Swift Fox got back, bringing a knife with him. They did not know how he got it but supposed that it was thrown at him.

The young man was glad to get the knife and went out and cut places in the buffalo, so that the wolves could eat. He took the tongues for himself.

Now the wolves said: "Our son needs something to cook with. He must have fire."

To the Coyote they said, "Now, you are sly; you go and get fire."

Presently the Coyote got back with a whole sack of punk and some flint stones and he went to the young man and gave these things to him saying, "Now, here is something to make fire with, if you know how to use it."

The young man made the fire in the lodge where he was, and the smell of the fire frightened the wolves almost to death. The white wolf said to him: "My son, you are frightening all your fathers. After this you must build your fire outside."

So Black Wolf built his fire outside that night and was sitting by it roasting his meat when a wolf came up that had been into a buffalo pound where people were, and had been shot. The arrow was still sticking in him. The white wolf told his son to pull the arrow out. Another wolf came with an arrow sticking in him and again the white wolf said, "Go and pull the arrow out of your father, for you understand how to do this."

One day the young man said to his father, "I will go to that place where my fathers got wounded." He did so. After the buffalo had been surrounded and killed, the wolves went down to the buffalo and began to eat, and the young man went with them. He acted wild and seemed to be afraid of the smell of people. Some of the people saw him and said, "That looks like the young man who was lost." These people took the news back to camp saying that among the wolves that came to eat was one who walked upright and acted like a human being. Black Wolf's father said: "That must be my son. I want you to try hard to catch him so that I can have him back."

The next morning the wolves decided to go back to feed on the buffalo and the man went with them. The news had gone through the camp that the lost young man had been seen with the wolves, and all the people went out and got around the pound and when the man tried to run away he found that they had surrounded him, and they caught him. He acted very wild and tried to bite them. He had big tusks like a wolf. For a long time he struggled, but the people talked to him and told him that his father wanted to see him, and at last he became quiet. After they had taken him to camp, he still tried to get away and his father talked to him and asked him where he had been and why he was living with the wolves, and at last he became quiet, but the people still held him.

All the wolves went home crying and said that they had lost their son; that the people had got him. When they told this at the butte, the wolves all said that they would go to war for him to-morrow.

A wolf came near to the camp and howled, telling the young man that the wolves had gone back to notify the others, and that they would come for him next day and would surround the camp and make a charge on it.

The young man said to the people: "That one that howled has said something very bad. There are a great many of those people that took me for their son. None of you should wander out from camp in the morning. There are many of those people, and they will eat you up. On the place where I used to sit on the hill on my white buffalo robe I was treated very badly and I felt angry about it. No one ever came to look for me."

The next morning the wolves were thick about the camp. The young man said: "Father, I was treated very badly by two girls. I have promised them to the wolves to eat and when I have given them to the wolves, I will tell the wolves to go away."

He asked if he might go out to speak with the wolves but his father said, "No, speak from where you are." Then the young man howled like a wolf and the wolves all began to go away.

Black Wolf went out of the lodge with his father to walk about and as he was walking he saw the two girls who had thrown him into the hole, at work scraping on a buffalo hide. They saw him and, as he passed, nudged each other.

"Father," he said, "if you will give me those two girls for my fathers to eat, I may remain with you all the time."

He said, "Father, let us go back to the lodge."

When they had entered he said, "Father, give me two arrows." When they had been given to him he went out and killed the two girls. He asked his father to have dried meat piled up in the center of the camp, and the father had an old man cry it through the village to have dried meat so piled up. After it had been piled up, he told the people to carry it outside the circle and to make four piles of it to the four directions. After that, he cut up each of the girls in two pieces and put one piece on each pile. After that was done he told his father that he was going to call the wolves and that none of the people should go out of the lodges, but they might look out of the holes. Then he went to the center of the camp and howled four times, and wolves appeared all about the camp. In his howlings he said, "My fathers, I give you human beings to eat."

When the wolves began to eat he went among them. He called out to the people, "Now, you will see me with my four fathers," meaning the four white wolves.

His four fathers stood close to him all the time. After he came back to the camp from the wolves he said to his father: "Father, I will now stay with you, but not all the time. Whenever my other fathers call me I will go back to them and kill them something to eat. After I have killed some buffalo for them, I will come home. I will live part of the time with each of you."

THE SONG OF THE OLD WOLF
Lakota

 THE old man in this story was not alone in being inspired by the scenery from a hilltop overlooking the Missouri River. In the early 1830s, George Catlin stopped at "Floyd's Grave," a beautiful hill above the river where Lewis and Clark had thought it most fitting to bury the remains of Sergeant Charles Floyd, the only fatality of their expedition. Catlin wrote:

> *I several times ascended it and sat upon his grave, overgrown with grass and the most delicate wild flowers, where I sat and contemplated the solitude and stillness of this tenanted mound; and beheld from its top, the windings infinite of the Missouri, and its thousand hills and domes of green, vanishing into blue in distance, when nought but the soft-breathing winds were heard, to break the stillness and quietude of the scene.*

A few miles farther on, Catlin visited the grave of Black Bird, an Omaha chief, on another "elevated bluff."

> *[T]his very noted chief, who had been on a visit to Washington City, in company with the Indian agent, died of the small-pox, near this spot, on his return home. And, whilst dying, enjoined on his warriors who were about him, this singular request, which was literally complied with. He requested them to take his body down the river to this his favorite haunt, and on the pinnacle of this towering bluff, to bury him on the back of his favourite war-horse.*

In this story from the Lakota people, an old wolf adds his melancholy lament to the old man's reveries. The story appeared in Prairie Smoke *by Melvin R. Gilmore (New York: Columbia University Press, 1929).*

❖❖❖

There is a story told among the people of the Dakota nation that once on a time an old man went out to be alone upon a high hill above the Missouri River to give himself to meditation and prayer. He chose this situation because of the grandeur and majesty of the view of the great sweep of the prairie plains and hills, one hill beyond another, away and away to the far horizon.

Below flowed the wonderful and mysterious river, whose waters came down from the mighty mountains at the west and rolled on and on past the villages of many different nations, finally reaching the Great Salt Water.

As the old man thus sat meditating and considering all the manifestations of life and power and mystery of earth and sky, he espied out upon the prairie a group of wolves trotting toward the river. When they reached the river, they plunged in and swam across to the other side, all but one old one who was now too enfeebled by age to dare try his strength against the swift and powerful current of the river.

This old wolf sat down upon the bank of the river and watched his companions as they swam across and trotted away out of sight on the other side. When they had disappeared from sight, he raised his muzzle toward the sky and mournfully sang in a man's voice the following song:

> All o'er the earth I've roamed,
> I've journeyed far and wide;
> My spirit haste and go,
> I'm nothing, nothing now,
> I'm nothing, nothing now.
>
> Missouri River, flow,
> Thou sacred water flow;
> My spirit haste and go,
> I'm nothing, nothing now,
> I'm nothing, nothing now.

After the old wolf had sung this song, he wearily made his way to the top of a hill and lay down in the warm sunshine, in the shelter of a rock, and there waited until his spirit went away.

And so now, when old men of the Dakota nation find the infirmities of age creeping upon them, and feel as though they had been left behind in life's march, they will often go out alone to the summit of some high hill overlooking the Missouri River and, sitting there in solitude, will muse upon their activities and noteworthy deeds in the past, of their companions of former days now long gone from them, and contrast all this with their present inactivity and loneliness. Then they will sadly and quaveringly sing this "Song of the Old Wolf."

THE WOLF RITUAL
Nootka

 IN this story, the legendary hero Ha-Sass creates "the pattern for individual excellence" to be followed by the people of the Northwest Coast. The author of The Wolf Ritual of the Northwest Coast *(Eugene: University of Oregon Press, 1952), from which this story is taken, noted: "[T]he warrior qualities of bravery, endurance, and wisdom, so desirable to the tribe or group, were personal and individual, and . . . must be gained by each man for himself, by his sole effort, and for the span of his single life. Each must wrest from the supernatural powers about him the secrets of power and strength needed for himself and others. But the power of the leader is also dangerous to others who have not also been 'renewed' by the Wolves. It must be hidden or veiled from sight; and it cannot be transmitted or given away." These virtues were fostered and taught to initiates through the Klukwana, the secret ceremony of the Wolf Ritual.*

Here are two versions of a tale about "the gray protector," "the silent warrior—'the bravest and fiercest of them all.'"

❖❖❖

[One origin story] tells in brief of four brothers, the only survivors of a tribe wiped out in warfare. Cast away on a small island near the edge of the sea, they were swimming out to a rocky fastness to save themselves from death. One of them said: "Surely if you train long enough, if you bathe and swim and fast, you can get power enough to overcome these people who have destroyed our tribesmen. You can get power from the Wolves." They knew the Wolves had this power. So the youngest of the brothers began stern training, bathing and swimming for many days to build up endurance. Finally, to gain access to the mountain home of the Wolves and obtain the desired secrets of their strength, he sewed himself into the skin of a hair seal and placed himself out on the beach with the other seals, which were carried away by the Wolves to their fastness. At last, reaching the House of the Wolves, he stayed there four days, listening to what they said. When, in return, they began to ask questions, promising to give him anything he wished, he chose out of a long list of possible objects which might bring power or skill to his tribe, a magic club which, when merely held up, caused the people who look at it to die. In the long run, too, he saw the Wolves dancing. They wore the masks of men, animals, and birds. They taught the young man all the dances and songs, and finally brought him back to his home. He now had the power to conquer all his enemies, and the Klukwana dances, songs, and masks (which he alone knew how to make) belonged in his family as its secret and ultimate possession. To his relatives he taught the secret ritual of Klukwana—which so originated. It has been handed down by them and transmitted to others; through marriage, warfare, and exchange its peculiar and striking ceremonial has spread to all parts of the Northwest Coast. But its aim was the rescue and survival of his tribe through bravery and endurance.

❖❖❖

Ha-Sass, the younger brother of the four mentioned, belonged to the tribe at It-tat'soo village, which in its long and bitter wars with a nearby tribe had been almost destroyed. They heard that the Wolves had in their possession something invincible to fight with (the Che-to'kh, a magic war club) and Ha-Sass decided he would go up to the Wolves' House far up in the mountain, to try to obtain this in order to save his tribe from extinction. The Wolves were very different in those times. Also in ancient times there was a hole at the foot of the mountain, and the Wolves went right through here. They did not climb the mountain. Ha-Sass, planning with his brothers how he could gain entrance to the House of the Wolves, decided he would drain his blood out, so they could not scent him as man. Finding a large flat stone on the beach, covered with barnacles, he lay down upon it and had his brothers pull him against the barnacles—four times, once on each side of his body, and his arms as well. He was bleeding all over, and finally, when enough blood had been let, he had his brothers sew him into the skin of a hair seal. They knew the Wolves ate the hair seal; so, after being sewed inside, he was carried by the brothers on a flat piece of wood over to the beach. Ha-Sass kept a small flat stone close upon his chest because he knew that, when the Wolves have a dead thing, they try to catch it on a sharp stick to make sure it is dead. The Raven, messenger of the Wolves, saw the hair seal on the beach and, flying over, took out its right eye as a sign to the Wolves that the Raven had been there. Raven does this with everything he finds on the beach: hair seal, sea lion, or what not. Ha-Sass' brothers were watching, to see which way the Raven went. He flew right up the mountain, but his house is not in the Wolves' House. Then the brothers saw many Wolves come down to the beach. These took up the hair seal, and all went away into the bush. The largest of the

Wolves is the Carrier Wolf (Ka-noh-pass'a). There is only one of these to each pack, and his back is different—it is wider for carrying things so they will not fall off. The others merely go along with him to help. It was the Carrier Wolf who took Ha-Sass in the hair seal skin upon his back, and after a time he said: "This creature feels warm. It must be alive. There must be a man alive in it." The Carrier Wolf, who is the main helper of the Wolf Chief, is also wiser than the common Wolves, and at this point the Carrier threw Ha-Sass from his back against the sharp sticks (o-sa-wuk'a-yuk) which lined the whole road to the Wolves' House, and against which they dash whatever they take, to make sure it has been killed. But the wary Ha-Sass was also watching, and, as he held the flat stone closely to his breast, he bounced off from these each time. Finally the Carrier Wolf took him on his back, and they went on their way.

They at last reached the secret fastness of the Wolves, very far up in the mountains, and entered the house of the Wolf Chief. All the wolves had gone along; for they, together with the Carrier Wolf, worked for the Wolf Chief, and when they got any food must take it to him. When they all came together in the Wolf Chief's home, the Carrier at once complained that he was tired, as what he had been carrying was very heavy. As soon as the hair seal was inside the house, they started to cut it into pieces, so that the Wolves could eat right away and make a feast. They had gathered into a circle for this, and when the Wolf Chief cut into the skin they found the man alive inside. Then they began asking him questions, for the Wolf Chief, who was wise beyond all others, knew that he would not have undergone the dangers of coming up there unless he had desired something. Admiring his courage, they promised him anything he wished. They were not afraid of the man. There was friendship with the Wolves, because this was after the woman had married the Wolf Chief. The Wolves first asked him if he would like something for catching whales, but he remained silent. Then they asked him if he wanted a comb, so he could have long hair, but again he did not answer. Next they asked him if he wanted teks-yah'pe, something which, if placed inside a dead body, would bring it back to life. Again he did not answer. Finally the wolves asked if he wanted Che-to'kh, and Ha-Sass at once replied that this was what he wanted. The Che-to'kh was a magic club which, held high, caused all who saw it to fall dead. It was never represented in carvings because people died when they saw it. Ha-Sass too died when he first saw it; but the Wolves brought him back to life again by putting teks-yah'pe upon his body. They brought him back to life four times. Then the Wolves called the man to come and get the death bringer, and he walked into the place indicated to receive it. This was in a distant secret room in the Wolves' House (it was kept always hidden), and here one of the Wolves handed it to him. Then the Wolves sent him back to his own house accompanied by a number of their pack. And they gave him also the small whistle held in the mouth during Klukwana. Ha-Sass kept this with him and, when he blew it on reaching home, everyone would look toward him. Then he would lift up the Che-to'kh during wartime, and kill the people in great numbers. At first, on reaching his own village, Ha-Sass tried the Che-to'kh on the geese, to be sure he had the power of killing things, and all the geese fell down dead. To test it further, he next moved to a place called Klits-holch', a high rocky cliff on the point. To climb this sheer precipice was in itself a feat of strength and skill. Though not painted, it was white. Having proved on the geese that he had "power" so much needed, he isolated himself here for a time. But the word soon spread to other tribes that the people at this village "had something" again, and they came in numbers to see what it was. Then Ha-Sass would blow his whistle, and they would look up to where he lived. The Che-to'kh had the same power of death for these outsiders.

Then everyone around was very much afraid of the people at It-tat'soo village, because they had something to kill with, and its owner became a great leader. When Ha-Sass received the death bringer from the Wolves, they told him not to give it to anyone when he died. It would kill this person. Ha-Sass had been brought to life again by the Wolves; others had not been thus resurrected, and the Wolves did not wish to trouble with them all. Ha-Sass was braver than any of his people, and for this reason the magic power was given to him by the Wolves. But the gift was dangerous. Ha-Sass was always afraid that someone would come and ask to see it (and thus die), and therefore he kept it hidden deep in the woods. So, when he himself died, no one knew where it was, and the Wolves got it again. The Wolves knew everything, for they were wise as well as brave.

EARLY EXPLORERS AND NATURALISTS

THE nine stories in this section cover the period from the 1740s to the 1830s. They reveal perspectives on wolves of some of the first Europeans and Americans who sought out America's wilderness. Some of this early exploration was done for commercial purposes, particularly to expand territories of the highly competitive fur companies. Some was practical in nature, to map lands newly acquired in the Louisiana Purchase or to seek useful native plants. And some had more scientific purposes, to identify the New World's plants and animals and to learn about its native people.

Despite the authors' presumed familiarity with wolves from the Eastern seaboard colonies and from Europe, these accounts share a general sense of eagerness and curiosity for discovery, and their attentive recording of detail brings lost worlds to life again for us. Some authors remarked on relations between wolves and native people ("Samuel Hearne, Arctic Explorer"), use of wolf skins in native dress ("Myths and Medicines"), and the role of wolves in the hideous smallpox epidemics that swept through native North America ("A Swedish Naturalist in America" and "Our Hearts Failed Us"). Wolf behavior and possible differences between European and American wolves interested the scientists who wrote "Flower Hunter Meets Black Wolf" and "On the Barren Grounds." Travelers to the Great Plains witnessed predation first-hand in "Buffalo and Wolves" and "The Rite of Life."

This rather select group of writers was not representative though. Side-by-side in early American life with curiosity and discovery was a Euro-American savagery toward wolves ("Pitting of Wolves"), born of an increasingly agricultural populace, increasingly disrupted wildlife dynamics, and an ancient European mythology about the character of the wolf. As the era of exploration ended, the prejudices of those who followed the explorers were the same ones that had held sway among European descendents for centuries.

A SWEDISH NATURALIST IN AMERICA
1748-51

 IN *the mid-eighteenth century, the Swedish Academy of Sciences was interested in finding useful plant and tree species from other northern lands that could be imported to Sweden and profitably grown there. As part of this effort, the Academy sent naturalist Peter Kalm to North America. Kalm, who had been a student of Carl Linnaeus, the famous botanist and taxonomist, journeyed to the British colonies from 1748 to 1751. He collected lots of seeds to send back to Sweden, as directed, but the real value of his travels historically was that, in response to his unbridled curiosity, he took copious notes on practically every facet of colonial life and natural history. Here are his findings on wolves as taken from the 1770 English translation of his reports* (Peter Kalm's Travels in North America, *edited by Adolph B. Benson, New York: Wilson-Erickson, Inc., 1937). As we can see, even at this early date, wolves had already been eliminated from some parts of North America.*

❖❖❖

There are two varieties of wolves here, which however seem to be of the same species. For some of them are yellowish, or almost pale gray, and others are black or dark brown. All the old Swedes related, that during their childhood, and still more at the arrival of their fathers, there were excessive numbers of wolves in the country, and that their howling and yelping might be heard all night. They also frequently tore in pieces sheep, hogs, and other young and small cattle. About that time or soon after, when the Swedes and the English were quite settled here, the Indians were attacked by the smallpox. This disease they got from the Europeans, for they knew nothing of it before. It killed many hundreds of them, and most of the Indians of the section, then called New Sweden, died of it. The wolves then came, attracted by the stench of so many corpses, in such great numbers that they devoured them all, and even attacked the poor sick Indians in their huts, so that the few healthy ones had enough to do to drive them away. But since that time they have disappeared, so that they are now seldom seen, and it is very rarely that they commit any disorders. This is attributed to the greater cultivation of the country, and to their being killed in great numbers. But further up the country, where it is less inhabited, they are still very abundant. On the coasts of Pennsylvania and New Jersey, the sheep stay all night in the fields, without the people fearing the wolves. However, to prevent their multiplying too much there is a reward of twenty shillings in Pennsylvania, and of thirty in New Jersey, for bringing in a dead wolf, and the person that brings it may keep the skin. But for a young wolf the reward is only ten shillings of Pennsylvania currency. There are instances of these wolves being made as tame as dogs.

SAMUEL HEARNE, ARCTIC EXPLORER
1769-72

 AS an employee of the Hudson's Bay Company, young English-man Samuel Hearne was sent on extensive explorations north and west of Hudson Bay, in the company's efforts to expand its control of the lucrative North American fur trade. Hearne was the first white man to reach the Arctic overland from Churchill, a trip he made with Indians only, dragging a small sled in winter and canoeing in summer. He was the first to provide clear accounts of the northern lands and their human and animal inhabitants. These early notes about wolves are from his journals, first published in 1795, A Journey from Prince of Wales's Fort in Hudson's Bay to the Northern Ocean, 1769, 1770, 1771, 1772 *(reprint, edited by Richard Glover, Toronto: Macmillan Company of Canada Ltd., 1958).*

❖❖❖

Wolves are frequently met with in the countries West of Hudson's Bay, both on the barren grounds and among the woods, but they are not numerous; it is very uncommon to see more than three or four of them in a herd. Those that keep to the Westward, among the woods, are generally of the usual colour, but the greatest part of those that are killed by the Esquimaux are perfectly white. All the wolves in Hudson's Bay are very shy of the human race, yet when sharp set, they frequently follow the Indians for several days, but always keep at a distance. They are great enemies to the Indian dogs, and frequently kill and eat those that are heavy loaded, and cannot keep up with the main body. The Northern Indians have formed strange ideas of this animal, as they think it does not eat its victuals raw; but by a singular and wonderful sagacity, peculiar to itself, has a method of cooking them without fire. The females are much swifter than the males; for which reason the Indians, both Northern and Southern, are of opinion that they kill the greatest part of the game. This cannot, however, always be the case; for to the North of Churchill they, in general, live a forlorn life all the Winter, and are seldom seen in pairs till the Spring, when they begin to couple; and generally keep in pairs all the Summer. They always burrow underground to bring forth their young; and though it is natural to suppose them very fierce at those times, yet I have frequently seen the Indians go to their dens, and take out the young ones and play with them. I never knew a Northern

Indian hurt one of them: on the contrary, they always put them carefully into the den again; and I have sometimes seen them paint the faces of the young Wolves with vermillion, or red ochre.

FLOWER HUNTER MEETS BLACK WOLF
1773-77

"FLOWER Hunter" was the name given to botanist William Bartram by the Seminoles who gave him permission to collect plants on their lands during one of the most productive exploratory expeditions of the colonial period. Bartram was one of America's foremost botanists as well as a highly regarded naturalist, artist, and scientist. For five years around the time of the American Revolution, he undertook an expedition from the Carolinas, through Georgia and Florida, and inland to the Mississippi. The book that resulted from this trip is a classic of American natural history, full of careful observations, lavish descriptions, wonderful imagery, explanations and philosophizing, and anecdotes of encounters with alligators, bears, Indians, and, of course, wolves. One biographer called Bartram a "painterly poet," and in fact his Travels influenced the poetry of Wordsworth, Shelley, and Coleridge (whose notebooks were filled with passages from it).

The "black wolf" of Florida was a black phase of the red wolf of the southeastern United States, which is a separate species from the gray wolf that inhabits the rest of North America and Eurasia. These excerpts are taken from The Travels of William Bartram; Naturalist's Edition, edited by Francis Harper (New Haven: Yale University Press, 1958).

❖❖❖

I drew up my light vessel on the sloping shore, that she might be safe from the beating waves in case of a sudden storm of wind in the night. A few yards back the land was a little elevated, and overgrown with thickets of shrubs and low trees, consisting chiefly of Zanthoxilon, Olea Americana, Rhamus frangula, Sideroxilon, Morus, Ptelea, Halesia, Querci, Myrica cerifera and others; these groves were but low, yet sufficiently high to shelter me from the chilling dews; and being but a few yards distance from my vessel, here I fixed my encampment. A brisk wind arising from the lake, drove away the clouds of musquitoes into the thickets. I now, with difficulty and industry, collected a sufficiency of dry wood to keep up a light during the night, and to roast some trout which I had caught when descending the river; their heads I stewed in the juice of Oranges, which, with boiled rice, afforded me a wholsome and delicious supper: I hung the remainder of my broiled fish on the snags of some shrubs over my head. I at last, after reconnoitring my

56

habitation, returned, spread abroad my skins and blanket upon the clean sands by my fire side, and betook myself to repose.

How glorious the powerful sun, minister of the Most High, in the rule and government of this earth, leaves our hemisphere, retiring from our sight beyond the western forests! I behold with gratitude his departing smiles, tinging the fleecy roseate clouds, now riding far away on the Eastern horizon; behold they vanish from sight in the azure skies!

All now silent and peaceable, I suddenly fell asleep. At midnight I awake; when raising my head erect, I find myself alone in the wilderness of Florida, on the shores of Lake George. Alone indeed, but under the care of the Almighty, and protected by the invisible hand of my guardian angel.

When quite awake, I started at the heavy tread of some animal, the dry limbs of trees upon the ground crack under his feet, the close shrubby thickets part and bend under him as he rushes off.

I rekindled up my sleepy fire, lay in contact the exfoliated smoking brands damp with the dew of heaven.

The bright flame ascends and illuminates the ground and groves around me.

When looking up, I found my fish carried off, though I had thought them safe on the shrubs, just over my head, but their scent, carried to a great distance by the damp nocturnal breezes, I suppose were too powerful attractions to resist.

Perhaps it may not be time lost, to rest awhile here, and reflect on the unexpected and unaccountable incident, which however pointed out to me an extraordinary deliverance, or protection of my life, from the rapacious wolf that stole my fish from over my head.

How much easier and more eligible might it have been for him to have leaped upon my breast in the dead of sleep, and torn my throat, which would have instantly deprived me of life, and then glutted his stomach for the present with my warm blood, and dragged off my body, which would have made a feast afterwards for him and his howling associates; I say would not this have been a wiser step, than to have made protracted and circular approaches, and then after, by chance, espying the fish over my head, with the greatest caution and silence rear up, and take them off the snags one by one, then make off with them, and that so cunningly as not to awaken me until he had fairly accomplished his purpose.

❖❖❖

Passing through a great extent of ancient Indian fields, now grown over with forests of stately trees, Orange groves and luxuriant herbage. The old trader, my associate, informed me it was the ancient Alachua, the capital of that famous and powerful tribe, who peopled the hills surrounding the savanna, when, in days of old, they could assemble by thousands at ball play and other juvenile diversions and athletic exercises, over those, then, happy fields and green plains; and there is no reason to doubt of his account being true, as almost every step we take over those fertile heights, discovers remains and traces of ancient human habitations and cultivation. It is the most elevated eminence upon the savanna, and here the hills descend gradually to the savanna, by a range of gentle, grassy banks. Arriving at a swelling green knoll, at some distance in the plains, near the banks of a pond, opposite the old Alachua town, the place appointed for our meeting again together; it being near night our associates soon after joined us, where we lodged. Early next morning we continued our tour; one division of our company directing their course across the plains to the North coast: my old companion, with myself in company, continued our former rout, coasting the savanna W. and N. W. and by agreement we were all to meet again at night, at the E. end of the savanna.

We continued some miles crossing over, from promontory to promontory, the most enchanting green coves and vistas, scolloping and indenting the high coasts of the vast plain. Observing a company of wolves (lupus niger) under a few trees, about a quarter of a mile from shore, we rode up towards them, they observing our approach, sitting on their hinder parts until we came nearly within shot of them, when they trotted off towards the forests, but stopped again and looked at us, at about two hundred yards distance; we then whooped, and made a feint to pursue them, when they separated from each other, some stretching off into the plains and others seeking covert in the groves on shore; when we got to the trees we observed they had been feeding on the carcase of a horse. The wolves of Florida are larger than a dog and are perfectly black, except the females, which have a white spot on the breast, but they are not so large as the wolves of Canada and Pennsylvania, which are of a yellowish brown colour. There were a number of vultures on the trees over the carcase, who, as soon as the wolves ran off, immediately settled down upon it; they were however held in restraint and subordination by the bald eagle (falco leucocephalus.)

❖❖❖

I have been credibly informed that the wolves here are frequently seen pied, black and white, and of other mixed colours. They assemble in companies in the night time, howl and bark altogether, especially in cold winter nights, which is terrifying to the wandering bewildered traveller.

❖❖❖

Early next morning, our guide having performed his duty, took leave, returning home, and we continued on our journey, entering on the great plains; we had not proceeded far before our people roused a litter of young wolves, to which giving chase we soon caught one of them, it being entangled in high grass, one of our people caught it by the hind legs and another beat out its brains with the but of his gun,—barbarous sport!—This creature was about half the size of a small cur-dog, and quite black.

OUR HEARTS FAILED US
1784-1812

"ONE of the greatest practical land geographers the world has ever known." That is the tribute of one twentieth century historian for explorer David Thompson. Thompson was indentured to the Hudson's Bay Company at the age of fourteen, and in his twenty-eight years in the West, he covered more than 50,000 miles on foot, horse, and canoe, from Churchill to the Rocky Mountains, throughout the Columbia Basin, to Lake Superior and south to St. Louis. He was an intelligent and resourceful frontiersman who is credited with initiating contact with several Indian nations, establishing new fur trading posts, and thus opening vast areas to the Canadian fur trade. More important though, he learned surveying early and left a legacy of some 1.7 million miles of precisely mapped routes in the U.S. and Canada!

One interesting historical note is that Thompson's employer, the Hudson's Bay Company, had forwarded his huge map of the West to a famous geographer in London, who used it to draw his own map without giving Thompson credit. It was this map, first published in 1795, that Thomas Jefferson used to plan the Lewis and Clark expedition of 1804-06.

But these were not the last of Thompson's contributions. He also kept detailed journals of his travels, "a rich and revealing narrative" that offered a more personal response to his experiences than most other early explorers. These two excerpts are from David Thompson's Narrative, 1784-1812 *(reprint, edited by Richard Glover, Toronto: The Champlain Society, 1962), with the spelling of the original maintained. Although wolves are not featured prominently in the second excerpt, their role in the grisly ecology of European disease in the New World is amply illustrated.*

❖❖❖

Of the three species of Wolf, only one is found in this stony region that I have described, and this species appears peculiar to this region; it is the largest of them, and by way of convenience is called the Wood, or Forest Wolf, as it is not found elsewhere; it's form and color [is] much the same as the others, of a dark grey, the hair, though not coarse, cannot be called soft and fine, it is in plenty, and with the skin makes warm clothing. It is a solitary animal. Two are seldom seen together except when in chase of some animal of the Deer species. Fortunately they are not numerous, they are very rarely caught in a trap, but redily take the bait of a set Gun, and [are] killed. The cased skin of one of these Wolves, came with ease over a man of six feet, two inches in height dressed in his winter clothing, and was ten inches above his head, yet powerful and active as he is, he is not known to attack mankind, except in a rare case of something like canine madness, and his bite does not produce hydrophobia. At least it never has been so among the Natives, and the dogs bitten by him, only suffer the pain of the bite. Foxes have sometimes this canine madness or something like it, but hydrophobia is wholly unknown. Two of these Wolves are a full match of either the Moose, or Rein Deer, the only two species found in this region. When they start one of these Deer, they are left far behind, but the Deer must stop to feed, they then come up to, and again start the Deer, and thus continue until the animal, harrassed for want of food and rest becomes weak and turns to bay in this state ready to defend itself with it's powerful feet. The wolves cautiously approach, one going close in front to threaten an attack, yet keeping out of the reach of it's fore feet. The other wolf goes behind, keeping a little on one side to be out of the direct stroke of the hind feet; and watching, gives a sharp bite to cut the back sinew of one of the hind legs, this brings on a smart stroke of the hind legs of the Deer, but the wolf is on one side, and repeats his bites until the back sinew is cut, the Deer can now no longer defend itself, the back sinew of the other hind leg is soon cut, the Deer falls down and becomes the easy prey of the Wolves; the tongue and the bowels are the first to be devoured. From the teeth of the old Wolves being sharp pointed, it does not appear they knaw the bones, but only clean them of the flesh, and in this state we find the bones. The Deer in summer sometimes takes to the water, but this only prolongs his life for a few hours. They are very destructive to the young deer; and their loud howlings in the night make the Deer start from their beds and run to a greater distance. When wounded, he will defend himself, but tries to get away, and dies as hard as he lived. There is something in the erect form of man, while he shows no fear, that awes every animal.

❖❖❖

[W]hen we came to them [the Indians], to our surprise they had marks of the small pox, were weak and just recovering, and I could not help saying, thank heaven we shall now get relief. For none of us had the least idea of the desolation this dreadful disease had done, until we went up the bank to the camp and looked into the tents, in many of which they were all dead, and the stench was horrid; Those that remained had pitched their tents about 200 yards from them and were too weak to move away entirely, which they soon intended to do; they were in such a state of despair and despondence that they could hardly converse with us, a few of them had gained strength to hunt which kept them alive. From what we could learn, three fifths had died under this disease; Our provisions were nearly out and we had expected to find ten times more than we wanted, instead of which they had not enough for themselves; They informed us, that as far as they knew all the Indians were in the same dreadful state, as themselves, and that we had nothing to expect from them.

We proceeded up the River with heavy hearts, the Bisons were crossing the River in herds, which gave us plenty of provisions for the voyage to our wintering ground.

When we arrived at the House instead of a crowd of Indians to welcome us, all was solitary silence, our hearts failed us. There was no Indian to hunt for us; before the Indians fell sick, a quantity of dried provisions had been collected for the next summers voyage, upon which we had to subsist, until at length two Indians with their families came and hunted for us. These informed us, that the Indians of the forest had beaver robes in their tents some of which were spread over the dead bodies, which we might take, and replace them by a new blanket and that by going to the tents we would render a service to those that were living by furnishing them with tobacco, ammunition, and a few other necessaries and thus the former part of the winter was employed. The bodies lately dead, and not destroyed by the Wolves and Dogs, for both devoured them, we laid logs over them to prevent these animals.

From the best information this disease was caught by the Chipaways (the forest Indians) and the Sieux (of the Plains) about the same time, in the year 1780, by attacking some families of the white people, who had it, and wearing their clothes. They had no idea of the disease and its dreadful nature.

From the Chipaways it extended over all the Indians of the forest to it's northward extremity, and by the Sieux over the Indians of the Plains and crossed the Rocky Mountains. More Men died in proportion than Women and Children, for unable to bear the heat of the fever they rushed into the Rivers and Lakes to cool themselves, and the greater part thus perished. The countries were in a manner depopulated, the Natives allowed that far more than one half had died, and from the number of tents which remained, it appeared that about three fifths had perished; despair and despondency had to give way to active hunting both for provisions, clothing and all the necessaries of life; for in their sickness, as usual, they had offered allmost every thing they had to the Good Spirit and to the Bad, to preserve their lives, and were in a manner destitute of everything. All the Wolves and Dogs that fed on the bodies of those that died of the Small Pox lost their hair especially on the sides and belly, and even for six years after many Wolves were found in this condition and their furr useless. The Dogs were mostly killed.

BUFFALO AND WOLVES
1804-06

 LIKE George Catlin in later years, America's best known explorers, Lewis and Clark, remarked on the close association of wolves with the vast herds of bison that roamed the plains. The abundance of wolves on the prairies seems to have impressed them: "a great number of wolves about us this evening" and "Great Many Wolves of Diffrent sorts howling about us" and "vast assemblages of wolves" and "Saw emence numbers of Elk Buffalow and wolves today." The herds of bison, elk, and pronghorns probably supported large concentrations of wolves, which contrasted noticeably with the Atlantic states, in many parts of which wolves had long since been exterminated. The animals' lack of ferociousness merited attention, too: "we saw a great many wolves in the neighborhood of these mangled carcases they were fat and extreemly gentle, Capt. C. who was on shore killed one of them with his espontoon [a short spear]." Other than that, they seemed to be mostly a nuisance to travelers who had to hunt to eat.

These excerpts are from the Original Journals of the Lewis and Clark Expedition, 1804-1806, *edited by Reuben Gold Thwaites (New York: Antiquarian Press, 1959). We have retained the original spelling and punctuation.*

❖❖❖

October 19, 1804

our hunters killed 4 Elk 6 Deer & a pelican, I saw Swans in a Pond & killed a fat Deer in my walk, Saw about 10 wolves. This day is pleasent

October 20, 1804

I observe near all large gangues of Buffalow wolves and when the buffalow move those animals follow, and feed on those that are killed by accident or those that are too pore or fat to keep up with the gangue.

December 7, 1804

many times (as I am told) a hunter who kills maney Buffalow in a chase only Gets a part of one, all meat which is left out all night falls to the *Wolves* which are in great numbers, always in [the neighborhood of] the Buffalows.

February 12, 1805

A little after dark this evening Capt. Clark arrived with the hunting party since they set out they have killed forty Deer, three buffaloe bulls, & sixteen Elk, most of them were so meager that they were unfit for uce, particularly the Buffaloe and male Elk the wolves also which are here extreemly numerous helped themselves to a considerable proportion of the hunt. if an anamal is killed and lyes only one night exposed to the wolves it is almost invariably devoured by them

April 22, 1805

Capt Clark informed me that he saw a large drove of buffaloe pursued by wolves today, that they at length caught a calf which was unable to keep up with the herd.

April 29, 1805

The Wolves distroy great numbers of the antilopes by decoying those animals singularly out in the plains and prosueing them alternetly, those antelopes are curious and will approach any thing which appears in motion near them &^{c}. . . .

The quantity of wolves appear to increase in the same proportion; they generally hunt in parties of six eight or ten; they kill a great number of the Antelopes at this season; the Antelopes are yet meagre and the females are big with young; the wolves take them most generally in attempting to swim the river; in this manner my dog caught one drowned it and brought it on shore; they are but clumsey swimers, tho' on land when in good order, they are extreemly fleet and dureable. we have frequently seen the wolves in pursuit of the Antelope in the plains; they appear to decoy a single one from a flock, and then pursue it, alturnately relieving each other untill they take it. . . .

The large woolf found here is not as large as those of the atlantic staes. they are lower and thicker made shorter leged. their colour which is not effected by the seasons, is a grey or blackish brown and every intermediate shade from that to a creen [cream] coloured white; these wolves resort [to] the woodlands and are also found in the plains, but never take refuge in the ground or burrow so far as I have been able to inform myself. we scarcely see a gang of buffaloe without observing a parsel of those faithfull shepherds on their skirts in readiness to take care of the mamed wounded. the large wolf never barks, but howls as those of the atlantic states do.

May 14, 1805

I felt an inclination to eat some veal and walked on shore and killed a very fine buffaloe calf and a large woolf, much the whitest I had seen, it was quite as white as the wool of the common sheep.

June 3, 1805

between the time of my A.M. and meridian Capt. C. & myself stroled out to the top of the hights in the fork of these rivers from whence we had an extensive and most inchanting view; the country in every derection around us was one vast plain in which innumerable herds of Buffalow were seen attended by their shepperds the wolves;

June 14, 1805

Sent the others to bring in the ballance of the buffaloe meat, or at least the part which the wolves had left us, for those fellows are ever at hand, and ready to partake with us the moment we kill a buffaloe; and there is no means of putting the meat out of their reach in those plains; the two men shortly after returned with the meat and informed me that the wolves had devoured the greater part of the meat

October 29, 1805

The robes of those Indians are of wolf deer elk, wild cats, some fox, & Deer

January 15, 1806

the quiver is usually the skin of a young bear or that of a wolf invariably open at the side in stead of the end as the quivers of other Indians generally are; this construction appears to answer better for the canoe than if they were open at the end only. . . . the deadfalls and snares are employed in taking the wolf the raccoon and fox of which there are a few only

February 15, 1806

The quadrupeds of this country from the Rocky Mountains to the pacific

Ocean [include] the large brown wolf, the small woolf of the plains, the large wolf of the plains

February 20, 1806

The large brown woolf is like that of the Atlantic States and are found only in the woody country on the Pacific Ocean imbracing the mountains which pass the Columbia between the great falls and rapids of the same. the large and small woolves of the plains are the inhabitants principally of the open country and the woodlands on their borders and resemble in their habits and appearance those of the plains of the Missouri precisely. they are not abundant in the plains of Columbia because there is but little game on which for them to subsist.

July 8, 1806

I killed a very large and the whitest woolf I have seen.

July 14, 1806

the hunters killed a couple of wolves, the buffaloe have almost entirely disappeared. saw the bee martin. the wolves are in great numbers howling around us and loling about in the plains in view at the distance of two or three hundred yards. I counted 27 about the carcase of a buffaloe which lies in the water at the upper point of the large island. these are generally of the large kind.

July 21, 1806

Saw several herds of buffalow Since I arived at this Camp also antelops, wolves, pigions, Dovs, Hawks, ravins, crows, larks, Sparrows, Eagles & bank martins &c. &c. The wolves which are the constant attendants of the Buffalow are in great numbers on the Scents of those large gangues which are to be Seen in every direction in those praries

July 22, 1806

last night the wolves or dogs came into our camp and eat the most of our dryed meat which was on a scaffold

August 8, 1806

. the night after the horses had been stolen a Wolf bit Serg^t. Pryor through his hand when asleep, and this animal was so vicious as to make an attempt to seize Windsor, when Shannon fortunately Shot him. Serg^t. Pryers hand has nearly recovered.

PITTING OF WOLVES
1812-14

 THIS vignette of frontier life by John James Audubon is one of the "Delineations of American Scenery and Manners" that were interspersed through his Ornithological Biography *(Edinburgh, 1835). In this five-volume set were the species descriptions for all the birds he depicted in his most famous work,* The Birds of America. *Audubon also included this account in his description of the "Black American Wolf" in* Quadrupeds of North America *(1851).*

One of his biographers put this rather famous story in context:

> *Bloody, cruel, and useless, wolf-baiting was nevertheless a popular sport on the frontier; hunters said it was necessary for training their dogs. Bearbaiting was another common game. A captured bear would be turned loose in the middle of a pack of dogs, while the spectators formed a ring around the fighting animals. Not only was the bear killed, several dogs were usually maimed or destroyed; and the greater the flow of blood, the greater the pleasure of the audience. Still another sport was gander-pulling. The participants would grease the neck of a live gander, then hang it by its legs from the limb of a tree just low enough to be within reach of a horseman. Taking turns, they would gallop underneath and try to wrench the bird's head off. Because of the grease and the toughness of the neck, this required considerable strength and dexterity; and the suffering bird would be subjected to one attempt after another until it finally died. The real trick was to snap the head off so quickly that the onlookers could hear the bird's breath still rushing through its headless windpipe. That feat always brought applause.*
>
> *Alexander B. Adams,* John James Audubon, a Biography *(London: Victor Gollancz Ltd., 1967.)*

❖❖❖

There seems to be a universal feeling of hostility among men against the Wolf, whose strength, agility, and cunning, which latter is scarcely inferior to that of his relative master Reynard [the fox], tend to render him an object of hatred, especially to the husbandman, on whose flocks he is ever apt to commit depredations. In America, where this animal was formerly abundant, and in many parts of which it still occurs in considerable numbers, it is not more mercifully dealt with than in other parts of the world. Traps and snares of all sorts are set for catching it, while dogs and horses are trained for hunting the Fox. The Wolf, however, unless in some way injured, being more powerful and perhaps better winded than the Fox, is rarely pursued with hounds or any other dogs in open chase; but as his depredations are at times extensive and highly injurious to the farmer, the greatest exertions have been used to exterminate his race. Few instances have occurred among us of any attack made by Wolves on man, and only one has come under my own notice.

Two young Negroes who resided near the banks of the Ohio, in the lower part of the State of Kentucky, about twenty-three years ago, had sweethearts living on a plantation ten miles distant. After the labours of the day were over, they frequently visited the fair ladies of their choice, the nearest way to whose dwelling lay directly across a great cane brake. As to the lover every moment is precious, they usually took this route, to save time. Winter had commenced, cold, dark, and forbidding, and after sunset scarcely a glimpse of light or glow of warmth, one might imagine, could be found in that dreary swamp, excepting in the eyes and bosoms of the ardent youths, or the hungry Wolves that prowled about. The snow covered the earth, and rendered them more easy to be scented from a distance by the famished beasts. Prudent in a certain degree, the young lovers carried their axes on their shoulders, and walked as briskly as the narrow path would allow. Some transient glimpses of light now and then met their eyes, but so faint were they that they believed them to be caused by their faces coming in contact with the slender reeds covered with snow. Suddenly, however, a long and frightful howl burst upon them, and they instantly knew that it proceeded from a troop of hungry, perhaps desperate Wolves. They stopped, and putting themselves in an attitude of defence, awaited the result. All around was dark, save a few feet of snow, and the silence of night was dismal. Nothing could be done to better their situation, and after standing a few minutes in expectation of an attack, they judged it best to resume their march; but no sooner had they replaced their axes on their shoulders, and begun to move, than the foremost found himself assailed by several foes. His legs were held fast as if pressed by a powerful screw, and the torture inflicted by the fangs of the ravenous animal was for a moment excruciating. Several Wolves in the mean time sprung upon the breast of the other Negro, and dragged him to the ground. Both struggled manfully against their foes; but in a short time one of them ceased to move, and the other, reduced in strength, and perhaps despairing of maintaining his ground, still more of aiding his unfortunate companion, sprung to the branch of a tree, and speedily gained a place of safety near the top. The next morning, the mangled remains of his comrade lay scattered around on the snow, which was stained with blood. Three dead Wolves lay around, but the rest of the pack had disappeared, and Scipio, sliding to the ground, took up the axes, and made the best of his way home, to relate the sad adventure.

About two years after this occurrence, as I was travelling between Henderson and Vincennes, I chanced to stop for the night at a farmer's house by the side of the road. After putting up my horse and refreshing myself, I entered into conversation with mine host, who asked if I should like to pay a visit to the wolf-pits, which were about half a mile distant. Glad of the opportunity I accompanied him across the fields to the neighbourhood of a deep wood, and soon saw the engines of destruction. He had three pits, within a few hundred yards of each other. They were about eight feet deep, and broader at bottom, so as to render it impossible for the most active animal to escape from them. The aperture was covered with a revolving platform of twigs, attached to a central axis. On either surface of the platform was fastened a large piece of putrid venison, with other matters by no means pleasant to my olfactory nerves, although no doubt attractive to the Wolves. My companion wished to visit them at evening, merely as he was in the habit of doing so daily, for the purpose of seeing that all was right. He said that Wolves were very abundant that autumn, and had killed nearly the whole of his sheep and one of his colts, but that he was now "paying them off in full;" and added that if I would tarry a few hours with him next morning, he would beyond a doubt shew me some sport rarely seen in those parts. We retired to rest in due time, and were up with the dawn.

"I think," said my host, "that all's right, for I see the dogs are anxious to get away to the pits, and although they are nothing but curs, their noses are none the worse for that." As he took up his gun, an axe and and large knife, the dogs began to howl and bark, and whisked around us, as if full of joy. When we reached the first pit, we found the bait all gone, and the platform much injured; but the animal that had been entrapped had scraped a subterranean passage for himself and so escaped. On peeping into the next, he assured me that "three famous fellows were safe enough" in it. I also peeped in and saw the Wolves, two black, and the other brindled, all of goodly size, sure enough. They lay flat on the earth, their ears laid close over the head, their eyes indicating fear more than anger. "But how are we to get them out?"—"How Sir," said the farmer, "why by going down to be sure, and ham-stringing them." Being a novice in these matters, I begged to be merely a looker-on. "With all my heart," quoth the farmer, "stand here, and look at me through the brush." Whereupon he glided down, taking with him his axe and knife, and leaving his rifle to my care. I was not a little surprised to see the cowardice of the Wolves. He pulled out successively their hind legs, and with a side stroke of the knife cut the principal tendon above the joint, exhibiting as little fear as if he had been marking lambs.

"Lo!" exclaimed the farmer, when he had got out, "we have forgot the rope; I'll go after it." Off he went accordingly, with as much alacrity as any youngster could shew. In a short time he returned out of breath, and wiping his forehead with the back of his hand—"Now for it." I was desired to raise and hold the platform on its central balance, whilst he, with all the dexterity of an Indian, threw a noose over the neck of one of the Wolves. We hauled it up motionless with fright, as if dead, its disabled legs swinging to and fro, its jaws wide open, and the gurgle in its throat alone indicating that it was alive. Letting him drop on the ground, the farmer loosened the rope by means of a stick, and left him to the dogs, all of which set upon him with great fury and soon worried him to death. The second was dealt with in the same manner; but the third, which was probably the oldest, as it was the blackest, shewed some spirit, the moment it was left loose to the mercy of the curs. This Wolf, which we afterwards found to be a female, scuffled along on its fore legs at a surprising rate, giving a snap every now and then to the nearest dog, which went off howling dismally with a mouthful of skin torn from its side. And so well did the furious beast defend itself, that apprehensive of its escape, the farmer levelled his rifle at it, and shot it through the heart, on which the curs rushed upon it, and satiated their vengeance on the destroyer of their master's flock.

ON THE BARREN GROUNDS
1819-22 and 1825-27

 PRIOR to seeking the fabled Northwest Passage, the British government sent Naval officer John Franklin on two overland expeditions in the 1820s to chart the northern coastline of Canada. John Richardson, author of this account about wolves, served as sort of a general "science officer" on both trips—that is, he was both surgeon (doctor) and naturalist. The first expedition was small and heavily dependent on the fur trade companies active in the area. But because the companies were engaged in fierce competition for control of the region's valuable fur resources, Franklin's first expedition ended up with inadequate provisions, worthless equipment, and a poor crew. Making slow progress and accomplishing little, they were finally forced—by food shortages and the onset of the bitter Arctic winter—to turn back. Half the crew died of starvation on the return trip, and one man was executed for murdering an officer and, it was suspected, cannibalizing him. The other members of the expedition survived only because they made contact with Indians who helped them. Franklin supplied the second expedition himself and had much better success.

Franklin, incidentally, is best remembered for the disappearance of his third Arctic expedition in 1845, a journey by sea to discover the Northwest Passage. A succession of rescue parties finally learned that his ships had been caught in the ice and that all had perished, but his records and his ships have never been found.

John Richardson, however, is best remembered for his scholarly tomes, Flora Boreali-Americana *and* Fauna Boreali-Americana *(respectively, The Plants of North America and The Animals of North America). This excerpt from* Fauna Boreali-Americana *(London: John Murray, 1829) is a fairly comprehensive account of the behavior and habits of the wolves of the north country, based on his own observations—collected, as we can imagine, amid enormous hardship—as well as information from others.*

❖❖❖

The Common Wolves of the Old and New World have been generally supposed to be the same species —the *Canis lupus* of Linnæus. The American naturalists have, indeed, described some of the northern kinds of Wolf as distinct; but it never seems to have been doubted that a Wolf, possessing all of the characteristics of the European Wolf, exists within the limits of the

United States. The Wolf to which these characters have been ascribed, seems to be the "large brown Wolf" of Lewis and Clark, and, according to them, inhabits not only the Atlantic countries, but also the borders of the Pacific and the mountains which approach the Columbia river, between the Great Falls and rapids, but is not found on the Missouri to the westward of the Platte. I have seen none of these *Brown Wolves*; but if their resemblance is so close to the European Wolf as Major Smith states it to be, I have no hesitation in saying that they differ decidedly from the Wolf which inhabits the countries north of Canada. While attached to the late expeditions, I passed through thirty degrees of latitude and upwards of fifty of longitude on the American continent, and in the course of seven years travelled upwards of twenty thousand miles, during the whole of which time I had almost daily opportunities of observing the form and manners of the wolves, but I saw none which had the gaunt appearance, the comparatively long jaw and tapering nose, the high ears, long legs, slender loins, and narrow feet of the Pyrenean Wolf. . . .

Wolves are found in greater or less abundance in different districts, but they may be said to be very common throughout the northern regions; their footmarks may be seen by the side of every stream, and a traveller can rarely pass a night in these wilds without hearing them howling around him. They are very numerous on the sandy plains which, lying to the eastward of the Rocky Mountains, extend from the sources of the Peace and Saskatchewan rivers towards the Missouri. There bands of them hang on the skirts of the buffalo herds, and prey upon the sick and straggling calves. They do not, under ordinary circumstances, venture to attack the full-grown animal: for the hunters informed me that they often see wolves walking through a herd of bulls without exciting the least alarm; and the marksmen, when they crawl towards a buffalo for the purpose of shooting it, occasionally wear a cap with two ears in imitation of the head of a wolf, knowing from experience that they will be suffered to approach nearer in that guise. On the Barren-grounds through which the Coppermine River flows, I had more than once an opportunity of seeing a single wolf in close pursuit of a rein-deer; and I witnessed a chace on Point Lake when covered with ice, which terminated in a fine buck rein-deer being overtaken by a large white wolf, and disabled by a bite in the flank. An Indian, who was concealed on the borders of the lake, ran in and cut the deer's throat with his knife, the wolf at once relinquishing his prey, and sneaking off. In the chase the poor deer urged its flight by great bounds, which for a time exceeded the speed of the wolf; but it stopped so frequently to gaze on its relentless enemy, that the latter, toiling on at a "long gallop," with its tongue lolling out of its mouth, gradually came up. After each hasty look, the poor deer redoubled its efforts to escape; but either exhausted by fatigue, or enervated by fear, it became, just before it was overtaken, scarcely able to keep its feet. The Wolves destroy many foxes, which they easily run down if they perceive them on a plain at any distance from their hiding places. In January, 1827, a wolf was seen to catch an Arctic fox within sight of Fort Franklin, and although immediately pursued by hunters on snow-shoes, it bore off its prey in its mouth without any apparent diminution of its speed. The buffalo-hunters would be unable to preserve the game they kill from the wolves, if the latter were not as fearful as they are rapacious. The simple precaution of tying a handkerchief to a branch, or of blowing up a bladder, and hanging it so as to wave in the wind, is sufficient to keep herds of Wolves at a distance. At times, however, they are impelled by hunger to be more venturous, and they have been known to steal provisions from under a man's head in the night, and to come into a traveller's bivouac, and carry off some of his dogs. During our residence at Cumberland House in 1820, a wolf, which had been prowling round the Fort, and was wounded by a musket-ball and driven off, returned after it became dark, whilst the blood was still flowing from its wound, and carried off a dog from amongst fifty others, that howled piteously, but had not courage to unite in an attack on their enemy. I was told of a poor Indian woman who was strangled by a Wolf, while her husband, who saw the attack, was hastening to her assistance; but this was the only instance of their destroying human life that came to my knowledge. As the winter advances and the snow becomes deep, the wolves being no longer able to hunt with success, suffer from hunger, and in severe seasons many die. In the spring of 1826 a large gray Wolf was driven by hunger to prowl amongst the Indian huts which were erected in the immediate vicinity of Fort Franklin, but not being successful in picking up aught to eat, it was found a few days afterwards lying dead on the snow near the Fort. Its extreme emaciation and the emptiness of its intestines shewed clearly that it died from inanition [starvation]. The skin and cranium were brought to England, and presented to the Museum of the Edinburgh University; and a drawing from it is to be engraved for Mr. Wilson's beautiful Illustrations of Zoology.

The American Wolf burrows, and brings forth its young in earths with several outlets like those of a fox. I saw some of their burrows on the plains of the Saskatchewan, and also on the banks of the Coppermine River. The number of young in a litter varies from four to five to eight or nine. In Captain Parry's and Captain Franklin's narratives, instances are recorded of the female Wolves associating with the domestic dog; and we were informed that the Indians endeavour to improve their sledge-dogs by crossing the breed with wolves. The resemblance between the northern wolves and the domestic dog of the Indians is so great, that the size and strength of the Wolf seems to be the only difference. I have more than once mistaken a band of wolves for the dogs of a party of Indians; and the howl of the animals of both species is prolonged so exactly in the same key, that even the practised ear of an Indian fails at times to discriminate them.

The following notices, by Captain Lyons, of the wolves of Melville Peninsula, are good illustrations of the strength and habits of the northern wolves in general:—"A fine dog was lost in the afternoon. It had strayed to the hummocks ahead without its master, and Mr. Elder, who was near to the spot, saw five wolves rush at, attack, and devour it in an incredibly short space of time: before he could reach the place the carcase was torn in pieces, and he found only the lower part of one leg. The boldness of the wolves was altogether astonishing, as they were almost constantly seen amongst the hummocks, or lying quietly at no great distance in wait for dogs. From all we observed, I have no reason to suppose that they would attack a single unarmed man, both English and Esquimaux frequently passing them without a stick in their hands; the animals, however, exhibited no symptoms of fear, but rather a kind of tacit agreement not to be the beginners of a quarrel, even though they might have been certain of proving victorious."—"The wolves had now grown so bold as to come alongside, and on this night they broke into a snow-hut, in which a couple of newly purchased Esquimaux dogs were confined, and carried them off, but not without some difficulty, for in the day-light we found even the ceiling of the hut sprinkled with blood and hair. When the alarm was given, and the wolves were fired at, one of them was observed carrying a dead dog in his mouth, clear of the ground, at a canter, notwithstanding the animal was of his own weight. Before morning they tore a quantity of canvass off the observatory, and devoured it."—"The Esquimaux wolf-trap is made of strong slabs of ice, long and narrow; so that a fox can with difficulty turn himself in it, but a wolf must actually remain in the position in which he is taken. The door is a heavy portcullis of ice, sliding in two well-secured groves of the same substance, and is kept up by a line, which, passing over the top of the trap, is carried through a hole at the furthest extremity: to the end of the line is fastened a small hoop of whalebone, and to this any kind of flesh-bait is attached. From the slab which terminates the trap, a projection of ice, or a peg of wood or bone, points inwards near the bottom, and under this the hoop is lightly hooked; the slightest pull at the bait liberates it, the door falls in an instant, and the wolf is speared where he lies."

MYTHS AND MEDICINES
1833-35

 TO explore and map, to observe and describe, to collect and classify—these were the goals of Europe's intellectual and scientific tradition when the New World was discovered. Among those engaged in such efforts was Prince Maximilian of Prussia, a scholarly ethnologist and naturalist who made expeditions to South America in 1815-17 and to North America in 1833-35. He met and stayed with several Indian peoples on the Upper Missouri, particularly the Mandans and Hidatsa. He seems to have earned the trust of some leaders, "worthy men," he called them, who facilitated his studies of their languages and cultures and became his friends.

These several observations on wolves, Indians' beliefs concerning wolves, and uses of wolves in their material cultures come from Travels in the Interior of North America, *v. 22-24 of the series* "Early Western Travels, 1748-1846," *(edited by Reuben Gold Thwaites, Cleveland: The Arthur H. Clark Co., 1906; first English translation published in 1843).*

❖❖❖

Of the genus *canis*, I met with five wild species in western North America. The changeable wolf (*Canis variabilis*), undoubtedly a distinct species, as Lewis and Clarke likewise affirm, is very common on the whole of the Upper Missouri. It is found to vary in colour from wolf grey to pure white. In winter these animals are nearly famished, and extremely lean. They closely follow the herds of buffaloes, and many sick, young, or weak animals become their easy prey; and when the hunters are abroad there is a rich harvest for the wolves. They even bite and devour each other, yet they did not meddle with the dead wolves which we left in the prairie; possibly they might not have been so ravenously hungry just then. They distinguish the report of a gun so well, that they hasten to the spot almost immediately after the shot has been fired. The same is the case with the ravens; and the Indian hunters affirm that the wolves watch these birds, in order to ascertain the direction in which the prey is to be found: if a poor animal has only been wounded, they are on the alert, and instantly pursue it, and it inevitably becomes their prey. In cold winters they are often so bold that they come into the villages, and approach the people's dwellings.

❖❖❖

When a young [Mandan] man, who has never performed an exploit, is the first to kill an enemy on a warlike expedition, he paints a spiral line round his arm, of whatever colour he pleases, and he may then wear a whole wolf's tail at the ankle or heel of one foot. If he has first killed and touched the enemy he paints a line running obliquely round the arms and another crossing it in the opposite direction, with three transverse stripes. On killing the second enemy he paints his left leg (that is, the leggin) of a reddish-brown. If he kills the second enemy before another is killed by his comrades, he may wear two entire wolves' tails at his heels. On his third exploit he paints two longitudinal stripes on his arms, and three transverse stripes. This is the exploit that is esteemed the highest; after the third exploit no more marks are made. If he kills an enemy after others of the party have done the same, he may wear on his heel one wolf's tail, the tip of which is cut off. . . .

Those who fast and dream, in order to perform an exploit, are entitled to wear a wolf's skin.

❖❖❖

Jesuit missionary Father de Smet found similar uses among the western Indians: "That he has killed an enemy on his own land is distinguished by having the tails of wolves tied on his legs" ("Early Western Travels, 1748-1846," *v. 27, p. 173).*

❖❖❖

The Manitaries are as superstitious, and have as much faith in their medicines, or charms, as the Mandans. Among these medicines are included every kind of wolf and fox, especially the former; and, therefore, when they go to war, they always wear the stripe off the back of a wolf's skin, with the tail hanging down over their shoulders. They make a slit in the skin, through which they put their head, so that the skin of the wolf's head hangs down upon their breast.

❖❖❖

I saw few lances among the Blackfeet, but many war clubs, most of which they had taken from the Flatheads. Many have thick leather shields, which are usually painted green and red, and hung with feathers and other things, to which some superstitious belief is attached. When they are going to battle, they twist the leather case of their gun round their head, like a turban. Wolf skins are then useful to them, especially when they want to observe the enemy. They wear them across their shoulders, and, when they wish to approach the enemy unperceived, they throw them over their head, and lie down behind an elevation, or rising of the ground, in such a manner as to have the appearance of a white wolf.

❖❖❖

At this spot 1000 or 1200 Sioux had attacked the united Mandans and Manitaries thirty years before, but lost 100 of their people. One of those Indians was afraid to proceed on this path, because he suspected that a wolf-pit, or trap, might be in the way; but the partisan, or chief, wishing to shame him, went before, and actually fell into such a pit, with sharpened sticks at the bottom, by which he was killed. . . .

We had here on opportunity of seeing the wolf pits, in which the Indians fix sharp stakes, and the whole is so covered with brushwood, hay, and dry grass, that it cannot be perceived.

❖❖❖

In a Mandan legend . . . The lord of life once told the first man, that if the Numangkake should go over the river they would be devoured by the wolves; on which they both crossed the river, and killed all the old wolves. They ordered the young wolves not to devour men in future, but to confine themselves to buffaloes, deer, and other wild animals. They threw the old wolves into the north ocean, where they became putrid, and their hair swam on the surface of the water, from which the white men originated.

THE RITE OF LIFE
1830s

AS early as the 1830s, American artist George Catlin prophesied the destruction of the vast herds of bison and its dismal repercussions for native people, white people, and even for "1,500,000 wolves, whom direst necessity will have driven from their desolate and gameless plains, to seek for the means of subsistence along our exposed frontier." He pleaded eloquently for a better way. Although Catlin is best known for his "gallery" of Native American portraits and scenes made during his travels on the prairies, he wished to be remembered for his vision of this future:

Yet this interesting community, with its sports, its wildnesses, its languages, and all its manners and customs, could be perpetuated, and also the buffaloes, whose numbers would increase and supply them with food for ages and centuries to come, if a system of non-intercourse could be established and preserved. But such is not to be the case . . . .

It is a melancholy contemplation for one who has travelled as I have, through these realms, and seen this noble animal [buffalo] in all its pride and glory, to contemplate it so rapidly wasting from the world, drawing the irresistible conclusion too, which one must do, that its species is soon to be extinguished, and with it the peace and happiness (if not the actual existence) of the tribes of Indians who are joint tenants with them, in the occupancy of these vast and idle plains.

And what a splendid contemplation too, when one (who has travelled these realms, and can duly appreciate them) imagines them as they might in future be seen, (by some great protecting policy of government) preserved in their pristine beauty and wildness, in a magnificent park, where the world could see for ages to come, the native Indian in his classic attire, galloping his wild horse, with sinewy bow, and shield and lance, amid the fleeting herds of elks and buffaloes. What a beautiful and thrilling specimen for America to preserve and hold up to the view of her refined citizens and the world, in future ages! A nation's Park, containing man and beast, in all the wild and freshness of their nature's beauty!

I would ask no other monument to my memory, nor any other enrolment of my name amongst the famous dead, than the reputation of having been the founder of such an institution.

These remarks on his experiences with wolves come from Catlin's book, Letters and Notes on the Manners, Customs, and Condition of the North American Indians, *2nd edition (New York: Wiley and Putnam, 1842).*

❖❖❖

The poor buffaloes have their enemy *man*, besetting and beseiging them at all times of the year, and in all the modes that man in his superior wisdom has been able to devise for their destruction. They struggle in vain to evade his deadly shafts, when he dashes amongst them over the plains on his wild horse—they plunge into the snow-drifts where they yield themselves an easy prey to their destroyers, and they also stand unwittingly and behold him, unsuspected under the skin of a white wolf, insinuating himself and his fatal weapons into close company, when they are peaceably grazing on the level prairies, and shot down before they are aware of their danger.

There are several varieties of the wolf species in this country, the most formidable and most numerous of which are white, often sneaking about in gangs or families of fifty or sixty in numbers, appearing in distance, on the green prairies like nothing but a flock of sheep. Many of these animals grow to a very great size, being I should think, quite a match for the largest Newfoundland dog. At present, whilst the buffaloes are so abundant, and these ferocious animals are glutted with the buffalo's flesh, they are harmless, and everywhere sneak away from man's presence; which I scarcely think will be the case after the buffaloes are all gone, and they are left, as they must be, with scarcely anything to eat. They always are seen following about in the vicinity of herds of buffaloes and stand ready to pick the bones of those that the hunters leave on the ground, or to overtake and devour those that are wounded, which fall an easy prey to them. While the herd of buffaloes are together, they seem to have little dread of the wolf, and allow them to come in close company with them. The Indian then has taken advantage of this fact, and often places himself under the skin of this animal, and crawls for half a mile or more on his hands and knees, until he approaches within a few rods of the unsuspecting group, and easily shoots down the fattest of the throng.

❖❖❖

From the above remarks [about the wanton slaughter of buffalo] it will be seen, that not only the red men, but red men and white, have aimed destruction at the race of these animals; and with them, *beasts* have turned hunters of buffaloes in this country, slaying them, however, in less numbers, and for far more laudable purpose than that of selling their skins. The white wolves, of which I have spoken in a former epistle, follow the herds of buffaloes as I have said, from one season to another, glutting themselves on the carcasses of those that fall by the deadly shafts of their enemies, or linger with disease or old age to be dispatched by these sneaking cormorants, who are ready at all times kindly to relieve them from the pangs of a lingering death.

Whilst the herd is together, the wolves never attack them, as they instantly gather for combined resistance, which they effectually make. But when the herds are travelling, it often happens that an aged or wounded one, lingers at a distance behind, and when fairly out of sight of the herd, is set upon by these voracious hunters, which often gather to the number of fifty or more, and are sure at last to torture him to death, and use him up at a meal. The buffalo, however, is a huge and furious animal, and when his retreat is cut off, makes desperate and deadly resistance, contending to the last moment for the right of life—and oftentimes deals death by wholesale, to his canine assailants, which he is tossing into the air or stamping to death under his feet.

During my travels in these regions, I have several times come across such a gang of these animals surrounding an old or a wounded bull, where it would seem, from appearances, that they had been for several days in attendance, and at intervals desperately engaged in the effort to take his life. But a short time since, as one of my hunting companions and myself were returning to our encampment with our horses loaded with meat, we discovered at a distance, a huge bull, encircled with a gang of white wolves; we rode up as near as we could without driving them away, and being within pistol shot, we had a remarkably good view, where I sat for a few moments and made a sketch in my note-book; after which, we rode up and gave the signal for them to disperse, which they instantly did, withdrawing themselves to the distance of fifty or sixty rods, when we found, to our great surprise, that the animal had made desperate resistance, until his eyes were entirely eaten out of his head—the grizzle of his nose was mostly gone—his tongue was half eaten off, and the skin and flesh of his legs torn almost literally into strings. In this tattered and torn condition, the poor old veteran stood bracing up in the midst of his devourers, who had ceased hostilities for a few minutes, to enjoy a sort of parley, recovering strength and preparing to resume the attack in a few moments again. In this group, some were reclining, to gain breath, whilst others were sneaking about the licking their chaps in anxiety for a renewal of the attack; and others, less lucky, had been crushed to death by the feet or the horns of the bull. I rode nearer to the pitiable object as he stood bleeding and trembling before me, and said to him, "Now is your time, old fellow, and you had better be off." Though blind and nearly destroyed, there seemed evidently to be a recognition of a friend in me, as he straightened up, and, trembling with excitement, dashed off at full speed upon the prairie, in a straight line. We turned our horses and resumed our march, and when we had advanced a mile or more, we looked back, and on our left, where we saw again the ill-fated animal surrounded by his tormentors, to whose insatiable voracity he unquestionably soon fell a victim. . . .

FRONTIER ENCOUNTERS, OLD WORLD ATTITUDES

THE period covered by these twelve stories is almost 200 years, from the 1750s to 1927. Throughout this extraordinary length of time, the prevailing attitudes toward wolves that had developed in Europe, particularly in England, persisted in America.

Part of this attitude came from farmers who saw predators as cruel thieves that wantonly killed defenseless livestock and thereby robbed them of their livelihood ("None But Monsters of the Desert"). In addition, throughout most of Christian Europe and America, wolves had long been associated with evil and the devil, as illustrated in the European tale "Why is the Wolf Ferocious?" The association with evil may have been partly an outgrowth of the elusive, watchful, and nocturnal habits of the wolf, which led the "Skater Chased by Wolves" to wonder if the sound he heard in the midnight forest was perhaps a fiend "more than mortal" and the young man who spent "One Night Among Wolves" to fear for his life. Another ancient association was the dread disease rabies ("Mad Wolf in Camp"), outbreaks of which must have seemed more terrible in wolves than in skunks or raccoons.

Several frontier travelers also made note of wolf behavior and made their own value-laden interpretations, including "Having Two Hearts," "A Hat Trick," and "Scenes in the Rocky Mountains." Simple lack of knowledge of wolves was clearly a factor in many people's reactions, as in "A Bushel of Fun," whose author lamented, "had I known then, what I learned by experience . . . , I would not have attempted a thing so fool-hardy." "Trading Along the Columbia" contrasts Euro-American attitudes toward wolves to native American views in the early fur trading days.

Finally, the old attitudes, which persist even today, were so deeply engrained and unconscious as to merit the term "racial memory." That to some was a source of shame ("An Encounter in India"), while to others it was a source of conceit and disparagement of wolves ("Wolves of the Plains"). Together, the many faces of this ancient and enduring attitude toward wolves enabled Americans to kill wolves with a ferocity unknown outside human warfare.

NONE BUT MONSTERS OF THE DESERT
1750s

 GENERAL Israel Putnam, who distinguished himself at the Battle of Bunker Hill during the Revolutionary War, had many other adventures in his long life. He was captured by Indians during the French and Indian War, survived a shipwreck during the British expedition against Havana in 1762, and fought against the Ottawa Chief Pontiac in 1763-64. His exploits, including his encounter with a wolf on his Connecticut farm, made him a hero to generations of American young-sters. Reference was made to Putnam's wolf tale—more than a hundred years after it happened—in "Wolves of the Plains" by Richard Irving Dodge. This ver-sion of the story is from the classic biography by David Humphreys, The Life and Heroic Exploits of Israel Putnam, Major-General in the Revolutionary War *(New York: Ezra Strong, 1835).*

❖❖❖

In the year 1749 he removed from Salem to Pomfret, an inland, fertile town, in Connecticut, forty miles east of Hartford; having here purchased a considerable tract of land, he applied himself successfully to agriculture.

The first years on a new farm, are not however exempt from disasters and disappointments, which can only be remedied by stubborn and patient industry. Our farmer, sufficiently occupied in building a house and barn, felling woods, making fences, sowing grain, planting orchards, and taking care of his stock, had to encounter, in turn, the calamities occasioned by drought in summer, blast in harvest, loss of cattle in winter, and the desola-tion of his sheepfold by wolves. In one night he had seventy fine sheep and goats killed, besides many lambs and kids wounded. This havoc was com-mitted by a she wolf, which, with her annual whelps, had for several years infested the vicinity. The young were commonly destroyed by the vigilance of the hunters, but the old one was too sagacious to come within reach of gunshot; on being closely pursued she would generally fly to the western woods, and return the next winter with another litter of whelps.

This wolf at length became such an intolerable nuisance, that Mr. Putnam entered into a combination with five of his neighbours, to hunt alternately until they could destroy her. Two by rotation, were to be constantly in pur-suit. It was known that, having lost the toes from one foot, by a steel trap, she made one track shorter than the other. By this vestige, the pursuers recognised, in a light snow, the route of this pernicious animal. Having followed her to Connecticut river, and found she had turned back in a direct course towards Pomfret, they immediately returned, and by ten o'clock the next morning the bloodhounds had driven her into a den, about three miles distant from the house of Mr. Putnam. The people soon collected with dogs, guns, straw, fire and sulphur, to attack the common enemy. With this apparatus several unsuccessful efforts were made to force her from the den. The hounds came back badly wounded, and refused to return. The smoke of blazing straw had no effect; nor did the fumes of burnt brimstone, with which the cavern was filled, compel her to quit the retirement. Wearied with such fruitless attempts, which had brought the time to ten o'clock at night, Mr. Putnam tried once more to make his dog enter, but in vain; he proposed to his negro man to go down into the cavern and shoot the wolf: the negro declined the hazardous service. Then it was that the master, angry at the disappointment, and declaring that he was ashamed to have a coward in his family, resolved to destroy the ferocious beast, lest she should escape through some unknown fissure of the rock. His neighbours strongly remonstrated against the perilous enterprise: but he, knowing that wild animals were intimidated by fire, and having provided several strips of birch-bark, the only combustible material which he could obtain, that would afford light in this deep and darksome cave, prepared for his descent. Having, accordingly, divested himself of his coat and waistcoat, and having a long rope fastened round his legs, by which he might be pulled back, at a concerted signal, he entered head foremost, with the blazing torch in his hand.

The aperture of the den, on the east side of a very high ledge of rocks, is about two feet square; from thence it descends obliquely fifteen feet, then running horizontally about ten more, it ascends gradually sixteen feet towards its termination. The sides of this subterraneous cavity are composed of smooth and solid rocks, which seem to have been divided from each other by some former earthquake. The top and bottom are also of stone, and the entrance, in winter, being covered with ice, is exceedingly slippery. It is in no place high enough for a man to raise himself upright, nor in any part more than three feet in width.

Having groped his passage to the horizontal part of the den, the most terrifying darkness appeared in front of the dim circle of light afforded by his torch. It was silent as the house of death. None but monsters of the desert had ever before explored this solitary mansion of horror. Cautiously proceeding onward, he came to the ascent, which he slowly mounted on his hands and knees until he discovered the glaring eye-balls of the wolf, who was sitting at the extremity of the cavern. Started at the sight of fire, she gnashed her teeth, and gave a sullen growl. As soon as he had made the necessary discovery, he kicked the rope as a signal for pulling him out. The people, at the mouth of the den, who had listened with painful anxiety, hearing the growling of the wolf, and supposing their friend to be in the most imminent danger, drew him forth with such celerity that his shirt was stripped over his head and his skin severely lacerated. After he had adjusted his clothes, and loaded his gun with nine buckshot, holding a torch in one hand and the musket in the other, he descended the second time. When he drew nearer than before, the wolf, assuming a still more fierce and terrible appearance, howling, rolling her eyes, snapping her teeth, and dropping her head between her legs, was evidently in the attitude and on the point of springing at him. At the critical instant he levelled and fired at her head. Stunned with the shock, and suffocated with the smoke, he immediately found himself drawn out of the cave. But having refreshed himself, and permitted the smoke to dissipate, he went down the third time. Once more he came within sight of the wolf, who appearing very passive, he applied the torch to her nose, and perceiving her dead, he took hold of her ears, and then kicking the rope, the people above, with no small exultation, dragged them both out together.

I have offered these facts in greater detail, because they contain a display of character; and because they have been erroneously related in several European publications, and very much mutilated in the history of Connecticut, a work as replete with falsehood as destitute of genius, printed in London.

TRADING ALONG THE COLUMBIA
1815

 IN an essay about the history of Western art, historian William Cronon wrote that "the frontier narrative was about the glory of movement and change, of ordinary people making history by the mere act of living their ordinary lives." One such ordinary person was fur trader Alexander Ross, who first journeyed to the Pacific Coast in 1810 with John Jacob Astor's expedition, and whose journals so well reveal the brief era of intercultural trade. After the first encounter of whites with native people and new lands, but before the eventual settlement and pastoralism, and finally "fulfilled civilization," there existed a time when people of two vastly different cultures met and learned each other's ways, a time of change and exchange spurred largely by the fur trade.

In this account we see the coming together of different views of wolves at a trading post along the Columbia River in 1815. These two excerpts are from Ross' book, The Fur Hunters of the Far West, *first published in 1855.*

❖❖❖

One day Ye-whell-come-tetsa, the principal Oakinacken chief, came to me about a similar circumstance, saying he had bad news to tell me: adding, "I fear you will not believe me, for the whites say that Indians have two mouths and often tell lies, but I never tell lies, the whites know I have but one word and that word is truth." I said, "I never doubt the words of a chief; but come let us hear, what is it?" "My son," said he, "has just arrived from below, and has reported and his report is always true. That there is a great band of strange wolves some hundreds in number and as big as buffaloes coming up along the river, and they kill every horse, none can escape them. They have already killed thousands; we shall all be ruined. They are so fierce that no man can approach them, and so strong and hairy that neither arrows nor balls can kill them. And you," said he to me, "will lose all yours also, for they travel so fast that they will be here in two nights." I tried to console the melancholy chief, gave him some tobacco, and told him not to be discouraged, that if the wolves came to attack our horses we should certainly kill them. That we had balls that would kill anything. With this opinion he seemed pleased and went off to circulate the opinion of the whites among his own people. I had heard of the report respecting the wolves some time before the chief had told me, for these things spread like wildfire; I was convinced some horses had been killed, it was a common assurance for not a year passes when the snows are deep, and often when there is no snow at all; but such things happen; but as to anything else, I looked upon it as mere fable.

On the third day after my parley with the chief, sure enough the wolves did come, and killed, the very first night, five of our horses. On discovering in the morning the havock the unwelcome visitors had made, I got a dozen steel traps set in the form of a circle round the carcass of one of the dead horses, then removing the others and keeping a strict guard on the livestock, we waited with anxiety for the morning, when taking a man with me and our rifles, we set out to visit the traps.

On reaching the spot we found four of them occupied. One of them held a large white wolf by the foreleg, a foot equally large was gnawed off and left by another, the third held a fox, and the fourth trap had disappeared altogether. The prisoner held by the leg was still alive, and certainly as the chief said, a more ferocious animal I never saw. From the moment we approached it, all efforts were directed towards us. It had marked and cut the trap in many places. It had gnawed and almost consumed a block of oak which held fast the chain, and in its fruitless efforts had twisted several links in the chain itself. For some time we stood witnessing its maneuvers, but it never once turned around to fly from us, on the contrary, now and then it sprang forward to get at us with its mouth wide open, teeth all broken, and its head covered with blood. The part which the trap held was gnawed, the bone broken, and nothing holding it but the sinews. Its appearance kept us at a respectable distance, and although we stood with our guns cocked, we did not consider ourselves too safe for something might have given way, and if so we should have regretted our curiosity. So we sent two shots and put an end to its suffering. Its weight was a hundred and twenty-seven pounds. And the skin which I gave to the chief was considered a valuable relic. "This," said he, holding up the skin in one hand, "is the most valuable thing I ever possessed." The white wolf skin in season is esteemed an article of royalty, it is one of the chief honours of the chieftainship and much used by these people in their religious ceremonies, and the kind of wolves are not numerous. "While I have this," exclaimed the chief, "we have nothing to fear, strange wolves will kill no more of our horses, and I shall always love the whites." Leaving the chief in a joyful humour, the man and myself followed the faint traces of the lost trap which occasionally appeared upon the crust of the snow. Having proceeded for some miles, we at length discovered the wolf with the trap at his heels, making the best of his way over rugged and broken surface of rocks, ravines, hills and dales, sometimes north, sometimes south, in zig zag courses to suit his escape and deceive us: he scampered along at a good trot, keeping generally about a quarter of a mile ahead of us. We had not been long in pursuit, however, before the man I had with me, in his anxiety to advance, fell and hurt himself and had to return home; I, however, continued the pursuit with eagerness for more than six hours until I got a shot; it proved effectual. Had any one else done it I would have praised him for the act, for at the distance of one hundred and twelve yards, when nothing but its head appeared, my faithful and trusty rifle arrested his career and put an end to the chase, after nearly a whole day's anxious pursuit.

Some idea of the animal's strength may be conveyed to our readers from the fact that it had dragged a trap and chain weighing eight and a half pounds by one of its feet or claws the distance of twenty-five miles, without appearing in the least fatigued. The prize lay at my feet, when another difficulty presented itself; I took no knife with me and the skin must have. Taking therefore, according to Indian habit, the flint out of my gun, I managed to do the business, and home with the skin and trap I hied my way, no less fatigued, but pleased with the successful result.

There we succeeded in destroying the three ringleaders of the destructive game which had caused so much anxiety and loss to the Indians, nor were there more it would appear than three of the large kind in the troop; for not another horse was killed during the season, in all that part of the country; whenever several of the large wolves associated together for mischief, there is always a numerous train of small ones who follow in the rear and act as auxiliaries in the work of destruction. Two large wolves such as I have mentioned are sufficient to destroy the most powerful horse, and seldom more than two ever begin the assault, although there may be a score in the gang. And it is no less curious than amusing to witness their ingenious mode of attack. If there is no snow or but little on the ground, those two approach in the most playful and caressing manner, lying, rolling, and frisking about until the too credulous and unsuspecting victim is completely off his guard by curiosity and familiarity. During this time the gang squatted on their hindquarters, looking on at a distance. After some time spent in this way, the two assailants separate; when one approaches the horse's head, the other his tail, with a slyness and cunning peculiar to themselves. At this stage of the attack their frolicksome approaches become very interesting, it is in right good earnest, the former is a mean decoy, the latter is the real assailant and keeps his eyes steadily fixed on the hind strings or flank of the horse. The critical moment is then watched, the attack is simultaneous; both wolves spring at their victim the same instant, one to the throat, the other as stated, and if successful, which they generally are, the hind one never lets go his hold till the horse is completely disabled, for instead of springing forward or kicking to disengage himself, he turns round and round without attempting to defend himself. The one before now springs behind, to assist the other. The sinews are cut, and in half the time I have been telling it, the horse is on his side, his struggles are fruitless, the victory is won. At this signal the lookers on close in at a gallop, but the small fry of followers keep at a respectful distance until their superiors are gorged, then they take their turn unmolested. The wolves, however, do not always kill to eat; wasteful hunters, they often kill for the pleasure of killing, and leave the carcasses untouched. The helplessness of the horse when attacked by wolves is not more singular than its timidity and want of action when in danger by fire. When these animals are assailed by fire, in the plains or otherwise, their strength, swiftness and sagacity are of no avail. They never attempt to fly but get bewildered in the smoke, turn round and round, stand and tremble until they are burnt to death, which often happens in this country in a conflagration of the plains.

No wild animal in this country stands less in awe of man than the wolf, nor is any other animal that we know so fierce. The bear on most occasions tries to fly from man, and is only bold and ferocious when actually attacked, wounded, or in defence of her young. The wild buffaloes are the same; but the wolf to the contrary has often been known to attack man, and at certain seasons of the year, the spring for instance, it is man's wisdom to fly from them. Some time ago a gang of seventeen in a band forced two of our men to take shelter for several hours in a tree, and although they had shot two of the most forward of them before they got to the tree for protection, the others instead of dispersing kept close at their heels. Wolves are as ferocious among themselves as they are voracious. I have more than once seen a large one lay hold of a small one, kill it on the spot, and feast on the smoking carcass.

When the Indians are apprehensive of an attack from them they always contrive to light a fire.

❖❖❖

Wolf hunting as well as bear hunting occasionally occupies the attention of the natives. In these parts both species are numerous. The former is an inhabitant of the plains, the latter of the woods. Wolves and foxes are often run down on horseback, hunted with the gun or caught in traps. With all the cunning of the fox, however, the wolf is far more difficult to decoy or entrap, being shy, guarded and suspicious.

During the winter we are speaking of, a good many wolves and foxes were caught by the whites with hook and line as we catch fish, with this difference however that the one is taken in water, the other on dry land. For this purpose, three cod hooks are generally tied together back to back, baited, and then fixed with a line to the branch of a tree so that the hooks are suspended in the air at the distance of four or five feet from the ground. To get hold of the bait the animal has to leap up, and the moment the hooks catch their hold it finds itself either in a standing or suspended position, which deprives the animal of its strength, neither can it in that posture cut the line; it is generally caught, sometimes dead, sometimes alive.

The catching of wolves, foxes or other wild animals by the whites was however the work rather of leisure hours. In these parts as well as in many others the wolves kept prowling about night and day, having their favourite haunts on hillocks or other eminences on which they would stand to rest or look about them for some time. We therefore used to scatter bones or bits of meat as decoys to attract them and in the interval kept practising ourselves in shooting at these frequented spots, taking different elevations with the gun until habit and experience had brought us to hit a small object at a very great distance, and with as much precision as if the object had been near to us.

A band of Indians happening to come to the fort one day and observing a wolf on one of the favourite places of resort, several of them prepared to take a circuitous turn to have a shot at the animal. Seeing them prepare, I said: "And kill it from where you are." The Indians smiled at my ignorance. "Can the whites," said the chief, "kill it at that distance?" "The whites," said I, "do not live by hunting or shooting as do the Indians or they might." "There is no gun," continued the chief, "that could kill at that distance." By this time the wolf had laid hold of a bone or piece of flesh and was scampering off with it at full speed to the opposite woods. Taking hold of my gun, "If we cannot kill it," said I, "we shall make it let go its prey." "My horse against your shot," called out the chief, "that you do not hit the wolf." "Done," said I; but I certainly thought within myself that the chief ran no great risk of losing his horse, nor the wolf of losing its life; taking an elevation of some fifteen or sixteen feet over it, by chance I shot the rascal in his flight! To the astonishment of the chief as well as all present, who clapping their hands to their mouths in excitement, measured the distance by five arrow shots! and nothing but their wonder could exceed their admiration of this effect of fire arms.

When the ball struck the wolf it was in the act of leaping, and we may judge of its speed at the time from the fact that the distance from whence it took the last leap to where it was lying stretched measured twenty-four feet! The ball struck the wolf in the left thigh, and after passing through the body, the neck and head, I cut it out of the lower jaw with my pen knife. The chief on delivering up his horse, which he did cheerfully, asked me for the ball, and that ball was the favourite adornment of his neck for years afterwards. The horse I returned to its owner. The Indians then asked me for the skin of the dead wolf and to each of the guns belonging to the party was appended a piece, the Indians fancying that the skin would make them in future to kill animals at a great distance.

HAVING TWO HEARTS
1830-35

 THIS brief tale, which captures so well the behavior of a wolf, comes from Warren Angus Ferris' Life in the Rocky Mountains; a Diary of Wanderings on the Sources of the Rivers Missouri, Columbia, and Colorado, 1830-1835 *(reprint, edited by Leroy R. Hafen, Denver: The Old West Publishing Company, 1983). This narrative is considered to be the earliest and best in-depth account of the fur trade in the central Rockies, and its accompanying map is comprehensive and accurate. John Richardson, in "On the Barren Grounds," also notes that "the simple precaution of tying a handkerchief to a branch, or of blowing up a bladder, and hanging it so as to wave in the wind, is sufficient to keep herds of Wolves at a distance."*

❖❖❖

On the 14th April, having placed a rag at the extremity of a stick, planted in the ground near camp, to prevent the wolves from rifling it, we all set out to combat a grizzly bear that had buried the carcass of an animal, some distance up, near the margin of the river, and had put Blackface to flight last evening whilst heedlessly approaching his prey. We reached the spot after riding four miles, and opening a little mound of fresh earth, discovered and disinterred the entire carcass of a large elk, recently killed. We remained some time awaiting the appearance of the bear, but our numbers probably deterred him from leaving the thicket in which we supposed he was concealed, being but a few paces from his charge, and from which his traces led to and fro. However, we returned disappointed to camp, where every thing remained as we had left it, though a large grey wolf sat upon his haunches a short distance off, having evidently (as an Indian would express it) two hearts, *for* and *against*, helping himself to some of the fresh elk meat that lay exposed to view with perhaps for him the same attractions, that a roast pig would have had for one of us. His cogitations on the propriety or expediency of charging up to the luscious store, and committing larceny, in open defiance of the fearful banner waving over it, being interrupted by our approach, his thoughts immediately turned into a new channel, and he came at once to the sage conclusion, with wonderful alacrity and sagacity, that—

> "He who coolly runs away,
> May live to steal another day,"

and proceeded to put the decision into practice, without unnecessary delay.

A HAT TRICK
1831-40

 JOSIAH Gregg's Commerce of the Prairies, *which includes this encounter with a wolf in the Southern Plains, has been considered a classic almost since its first publication in 1844. The author spent nine years crossing the Plains with "merchant caravans," trading American goods for Mexican along the Santa Fe Trail. He kept copious notes on practically everything he encountered in his travels, from plants to politics. Although he was a self-taught naturalist, his excellence as an observer and a frontiersman and his love of the prairies produced an unparalleled account of a particular time and place in American history. He developed these into a "masterpiece [of] prairie lore and human adventure" that continues to delight readers today.*

This story comes from a reprint of Commerce of the Prairies *(Max L. Moorhead, ed., Norman: University of Oklahoma Press, 1954).*

❖❖❖

We forded the Arkansas without difficulty, and pursued our journey to the Missouri border with comparative ease; being only now and then disturbed at night by the hideous howlings of wolves, a pack of which had constituted themselves into a kind of 'guard of honor,' and followed in our wake for several hundred miles—in fact to the very border of the settlements. They were at first attracted no doubt by the remains of buffalo which were killed by us upon the high plains, and afterwards enticed on by an occasional fagged animal, which we were compelled to leave behind, as well as by the bones and scraps of food, which they picked up about our camps. Not a few of them paid the penalty of their lives for their temerity.

❖❖❖

American hunters, as well as Indians, to butcher the buffalo, generally turn it upon the belly, and commence on the back. The hump ribs, tender-loins, and a few other choice bits being appropriated, the remainder is commonly left for the wolves. The skin is chiefly used for buffalo rugs, but for which it is only preserved by the Indians during fall and winter (and then rarely but from the cows and bullocks), when the hair is long and woolly. I have never seen the buffalo hide tanned, but it seems too porous and spongy to make substantial leather. Were it valuable, thousands of hides might be saved that are annually left to the wolves upon the Prairies.

Although the buffalo is the largest, he has by no means the control among the prairie animals: the sceptre of authority has been lodged with the large *gray wolf.* Though but little larger than the wolf of the United States, he is much more ferocious. The same species abound throughout the north of Mexico, where they often kill horses, mules and cattle of all sizes; and on the Prairies they make considerable havoc among the buffalo.

Many curious tales are told of the wiles and expedients practised by these animals to secure their prey. Some assert that they collect in companies, and chase a buffalo by turns, till he is fatigued, when they join and soon dispatch him: others, that, as the buffalo runs with the tongue hanging out, they snap at it in the chase till it is torn off which preventing him from eating, he is reduced by starvation, and soon overpowered: others, that, while running, they gnaw and lacerate the legs and ham-strings till they disable him, and then he is killed by the gang. Be this as it may, certain it is that they overcome many of the largest buffaloes, employing perhaps different means of subduing them, and among these is doubtless the last mentioned, for I have myself seen them with the muscles of the thighs cruelly mangled—a consequence no doubt of some of these attacks. Calves are constantly falling victims to the rapacity of these wolves; yet, when herds of buffalo are together, they defend their offspring with great bravery.

Though the color of this wolf is generally a dirty gray, it is sometimes met with nearly white. I am of opinion, however, that the diversity of color originates chiefly from the different ages of the hair, and the age and condition of the animal itself. The few white wolves I have seen, have been lean, long-haired, and apparently very old. There are immense numbers of them upon the Prairies. Droves are frequently to be seen following in the wake of caravans, hunting companies, and itinerant Indian bands, for weeks together—not, like the jackal, so much to disinter the dead (though this they sometimes do), as to feast upon the abandoned carcasses of the buffalo which are so often wantonly killed and wasted. Unless in these cases, they are rarely seen, except in the neighborhood of buffalo; therefore, when the hungry traveller meets with wolves, he feels some assurance that supplies of his favorite game are at hand.

I have never known these animals, rapacious as they are, [to] extend their attacks to man, though they probably would, if very hungry and a favorable opportunity presented itself. I shall not soon forget an adventure with one of them, many years ago, on the frontier of Missouri. Riding near the prairie border, I perceived one of the largest and fiercest of the gray species, which had just descended from the west, and seemed famished to desperation. I at once prepared for a chase; and, being without arms, I caught up a cudgel when I betook me valiantly to the charge, much stronger, as I soon discovered, in my cause than in my equipment. The wolf was in no humor to flee, however, but boldly met me full half-way. I was soon disarmed, for my club broke upon the animals head. He then 'laid to' my horse's legs, which, not relishing the conflict, gave a plunge and sent me whirling over his head, and made his escape, leaving me and the wolf at close quarters. I was no sooner upon my feet than my antagonist renewed the charge; but, being without weapon, or any means of awakening an emotion of terror, save through his imagination, I took off my large black hat, and using it for a shield, began to thrust it towards his gaping jaws. My *ruse* had the desired effect; for, after springing at me a few times, he wheeled about and trotted off several paces, and stopped to gaze at me. Being apprehensive that he might change his mind and return to the attack, and conscious that, under the compromise, I had the best of the bargain, I very resolutely—took to my heels, glad of the opportunity of making a drawn game, though I had myself given the challenge.

MAD WOLF IN CAMP
1833

 HERE are passages from the writings of three fur traders about an incident that took place at the fur traders' rendezvous on the Green River in Wyoming in 1833: a rabid "wolf" entered several camps, biting both men and beasts. None of these accounts described the animal, however, in enough detail to confirm that it was a wolf, a dog, or a hybrid. It was likely that, in the panic of the attack in the middle of the night, no one got a close look at it.

One of the oldest recorded infectious diseases, rabies was dreaded throughout Europe and Asia from ancient times for the horrible and certain death it caused in humans and livestock. All warm-blooded animals are susceptible to the ravages of the virus, which attacks the central nervous system and is transmitted by biting. Outbreaks of the disease, which can occur when a species' population is dense enough to ensure easy transmission, have been known in domestic dogs, foxes, skunks, coyotes, raccoons, and many other species. Its appearance in wolf populations very likely intensified fear of wolves in Europe. In North America, very few wolves and coyotes have been known to carry the disease. Louis Pasteur developed a vaccine in 1885, but before that time, dread and loathing filled people who had been bitten and waited for the onset of the symptoms.

These excerpts are from Charles Larpenteur, Forty Years a Fur Trader on the Upper Missouri *(Elliott Coues, ed., New York: Francis P. Harper, 1898); Washington Irving,* The Adventures of Captain Bonneville, U.S.A., in the Rocky Mountains and the Far West *(reprint edited by Edgeley W. Todd, Norman: University of Oklahoma Press, 1961); and Warren Angus Ferris,* Life in the Rocky Mountains; a Diary of Wanderings on the Sources of the Rivers Missouri, Columbia, and Colorado, 1830-1835 *(reprint edited by Leroy R. Hafen, Denver: The Old West Publishing Company, 1983).*

❖❖❖

LARPENTEUR

A day or so later we learned that a mad wolf had got into Mr. Fontenelle's camp about five miles from us, and had bitten some of his men and horses. My messmates, who were old hands, had heard of the like before, when men had gone mad. It was very warm, toward the latter end of July; we were in the habit of sleeping in the open air, and never took the trouble to put up the tent, except in bad weather; but when evening came the boys set up the tent. Some of the other messes asked, "What is that for?" The reply was, "Oh, mad wolf come—he bite me." When the time came to retire the pack saddles were brought up to barricade the entrance of our tent, the only one up in camp, excepting that of the boss. After all hands had retired nothing was heard in the camp except, now and then, the cry of "All's well," and some loud snoring, till the sudden cry of, "Oh, I'm bitten!"—then immediately another, and another. Three of our men were bitten that night, all of them in the face. One poor fellow, by the name of George Holmes, was badly bitten on the right ear and face. All hands got up with their guns in pursuit of the animal, but he made his escape. When daylight came men were mounted to go in search, but nothing could be seen of him. It was then thought that he had gone and was not likely to return, and no further precaution was taken than the night before. But it seems that Mr. Wolf, who was thought far away, had hidden near camp; for about midnight the cry of "mad wolf" was heard again. This time the animal was among the cattle and bit our largest bull, which went mad afterward on the Big Horn, where we made the boats. The wolf could have been shot, but orders were not to shoot in camp, for fear of accidentally killing some one, and so Mr. Wolf again escaped. But we learned afterward that he had been killed by some of Mr. Fontenelle's men.

As well as I can remember it was the first week in August when we were ordered to take final leave for the Horn. . . . Two days before reaching the Horn one of our bulls commenced to show some symptoms of hydrophobia by bellowing at a great rate, and pawing the ground. This scared my poor friend Holmes, who was still in our party, but not destined to reach the Yellowstone. He was a young man from New York, well educated, and we became quite attached to each other on our long journey. The poor fellow now and then asked me if I thought he would go mad; although thinking within myself he would, being so badly bitten, I did all I could to make him believe otherwise. When he said to me, "Larpenteur, don't you hear the bull—he is going mad—I am getting scared," I do believe I felt worse than he did, and scarcely knew how to answer him. The bull died two days after we arrived at the Horn, and I learned, some time afterward, from Mr. Fontenelle, that Holmes had gone mad. For some days he could not bear to cross the small streams which they struck from time to time, so that they had to cover him over with a blanket to get him across; and at last they had to leave him with two men until his fit should be over. But the men soon left him and came to camp. Mr. Fontenelle immediately sent back after him; but when they arrived at the place, they found only his clothes, which he had torn off his back. He had run away quite naked, and never was found. This ended my poor friend Holmes.

❖❖❖

IRVING

During this season of folly and frolic [at the annual rendezvous of trappers, Indians, and traders], there was an alarm of mad wolves in the two lower camps. One or more of these animals entered the camps for three nights successively, and bit several of the people.

Captain Bonneville relates the case of an Indian, who was a universal favorite in the lower camp. He had been bitten by one of these animals. Being out with a party shortly afterwards, he grew silent and gloomy, and lagged behind the rest as if he wished to leave them. They halted and urged him to move faster, but he entreated them not to approach him, and, leaping from his horse, began to roll frantically on the earth, gnashing his teeth and foaming at the mouth. Still he retained his senses, and warned his companions not to come near him, as he should not be able to restrain himself from biting them. They hurried off to obtain relief; but on their return he was nowhere to be found. His horse and his accoutrements remained upon the spot. Three or four days afterwards a solitary Indian, believed to be the same, was observed crossing a valley, and pursued; but he darted away into the fastnesses of the mountains, and was seen no more.

Another instance we have from a different person who was present in the encampment. One of the men of the Rocky Mountain Fur Company had been bitten [Holmes]. He set out shortly afterwards in company with two white men on his return to the settlements. In the course of a few days he showed symptoms of hydrophobia, and became raving toward night. At length, breaking away from his companions, he rushed into a thicket of willows, where they left him to his fate!

❖❖❖

FERRIS

About this time we learned that two persons, who were bitten by a wolf, at last rendezvous, had died or disappeared suddenly. The circumstances during the hurry and bustle of business of rendezvous were by mistake not recorded in my journal, though they produced great excitement at that time. They were as follows: whilst we were all asleep, one night, an animal, supposed to be a dog, passed through camp, bit several persons as they lay, and then disappeared. On the following morning considerable anxiety was manifested by those who were bitten, under the apprehension that the animal might have been afflicted with the hydrophobia, and several of them took their guns and went about camp, shooting all *suspicious looking* dogs; but were unable to determine that any one was positively mad. During the day information came from the R.M.F. Co. [Rocky Mountain Fur Company], who were encamped a short distance below us on the same side of the river, that several men were likewise bitten in their camp during the night, and that a wolf supposed to be rabid, had been killed in the morning. The excitement which this affair originated, however, gradually subsided, and nothing more was heard of mad-dogs or wolves. In the fall subsequent, one [of] the persons who had been bitten, a young Indian brought from the council Bluffs by Mr. Fontenelle, after having given indications of the hydrophobia, disappeared one night from camp and was heard of no more. The general impression being, that he wandered off while under its influence, and perished. Another individual [Holmes] died of that horrible malady, after having several violent spasms, while on his way from the mountains to St. Louis, in company with two others. Whether there have been any more instances of the kind, I am not informed.

SCENES IN THE ROCKY MOUNTAINS
1836-47

 RUFUS B. Sage was an energetic young New Englander who moved out West—Ohio, that is—in 1836 and worked at a variety of jobs, mostly in the newspaper business. In 1841, he conceived of a plan to travel to the Far West with the intention of writing a book about his experiences and observations. He left Independence, Missouri, that autumn with a party of traders headed for the Platte River country and, during the next three years, traveled widely. His book, "Scenes in the Rocky Mountains and in Oregon, California, New Mexico, Texas, and the Grand Prairies," published in 1846, was eagerly read by Easterners hungry for information about the little known open country west of the United States.

These excerpts are taken from Rufus B. Sage, His Letters and Papers, 1836-1847, with an annotated reprint of his Scenes in the Rocky Mountains and in Oregon, California, New Mexico, Texas, and the Grand Prairies *(LeRoy R. Hafen and Ann W. Hafen, eds., 2 v., Glendale, California: The Arthur H. Clark Company, 1956). They show Sage as a sharp observer of animal behavior. Very minor corrections have been made in the text.*

❖❖❖

[T]he dismal howlings of the half-starved wolves, that gathered by scores upon every hill-top and renewed, in more piteous accents, their ceaseless concert;—all these united to invest the scene, so magnificent in itself, with a savage wildness, at once incitive of terror and admiration. . . .

Our night slumbers were disturbed by the quick discharge of firearms, which instantly brought every man to his feet, rifle in hand. The cause of this alarm was the appearance of a mad wolf among the caravan animals, and several shots were fired before the guard could despatch him. He proved one of the largest of his species, and looked fearful as his blood-red eyeballs and foaming mouth were exposed by the camp-fire.

In the morning it was ascertained he had bitten nine head of horses and cattle.

The buffalo range affords every variety of wolves, common to the mountains and regions still further west. Of these there are five distinct classifications, viz: The big white or buffalo wolf; the shaggy brown, the black; the gray, or prairie wolf; and the cayeute, (wa-chunka-monet,) or medicine-wolf of the Indians.

The white and brown wolves are the most numerous, and follow the buffalo in bands by hundreds, subsisting upon the carcases of such as die of themselves or are slaughtered as their necessities demand.

These wolves behave with great sagacity in their predatory operations, and appear to exercise a perfect understanding and concert of action with each other on such occasions. First, stationing themselves by files at given distances along the course their intended victim is expected to run, two or more of them enter the herd of unconscious buffalo, and, singling out the fattest one, drive it to the track at which their companions await to take part in the grand race. This done, the victim is made to run the gauntlet between two rows of wolves. As it advances, others join their fresh numbers to the chase, till at length, tired down and exhausted in strength, the ill-fated animal falls ready prey to their greediness. The poor creature is first hamstrung to prevent its escape, and then literally devoured alive!

The black wolf is seldom met with in these parts. It nearly equals the white and brown in size, and is fully as large as the common cur-dog.

The prairie wolf is not more than half the size of the above mentioned, and much less ferocious. Its color is of a dark gray, and its fur quite soft and fine.

The cayeute or medicine-wolf compares with the common feist [a small dog], and is of a grayish color, much like that of the wild rabbit of the States. Its fur is fine and thick, and might be turned to good account for the manufacture of caps, muffs, &c.

❖❖❖

Our intended evacuation of the post was postponed till the week following, and, meanwhile, the few customers, that still hung on, were careful to improve the passing opportunity of steeping their senses in liquor.

Another general drunken frolic was the consequence, ending as usual in a fight and still further attempts upon the life of our trader.

Soon after this, our catalogue of disasters was increased by the death of two horses, which fell a prey to wolves.

The case was an aggravated one, and provoking in the extreme. Both of them were "buffalo horses," and the fleetest and most valuable in our possessions,—in fact, they were the only ones of which we ventured to boast. We had others of little worth, so poor and feeble they could oppose none resistance to magpies, and much less to the rapacity of wolves.

But, no. These blood-thirsty depredators, desirous of a feast of fat things, were determined to have it, reckless of cost,—and, the encrimsoned tracks, coursing the snowy plain in every direction where passed the swift chargers in vain effort to escape, proved that they won their supper at an enormous expense of leg-wear.

❖❖❖

A pack of hungry wolves, attracted by the scent of camp, were our regular nocturnal visitors, and proved a constant source of annoyance. On one occasion they carried off a bake-kettle to a distance of several hundred yards;—at another time, they took away a tin-pan, which we never afterwards recovered;—and, stranger yet, one night these piratical pests stole a fur cap from off my head while I was sleeping, and in the morning, after a diligent search, no trace of it could be found.

❖❖❖

Our horses being quite enfeebled from the fatigue of travel, we gladly availed ourselves of the presence of buffalo to prolong our stay at Cherry creek some ten days, and meanwhile found no difficulty in procuring a continued feast of good things from the dense herds that thronged the country upon every side.

The severe weather and frequent snows of the past two months, had driven these animals from the open prairie into the creek bottoms and mountains, whose vicinities were completely blackened with their countless thousands.

The antelope, too, seemed to have congregated from all parts, and covered the country in one almost unbroken band. Their numbers exceeded anything of the kind I ever witnessed before or since. We amused ourselves at times in shooting them merely for their skins, the latter being superior to those of deer or even sheep in its nicity of texture and silky softness.

One day, as was my custom, I left camp for the above purpose, and had proceeded but a short distance, when, happening upon a large band of antelope, a discharge from my piece brought down one of its number.

Before reaching it, however, my supposed victim had rejoined his companions, and the whole throng were lost to view almost with the speed of thought.

The profuseness of blood that marked its trail through the snow, induced me to follow it in expectation of soon obtaining the object of my pursuit; but in vain.

At length, after travelling four or five miles, I began to despair of success, and, feeling weary, sat down upon the point of a small hill that commanded a view of the surrounding prairie. While here an unusual stir among the wolves attracted my attention, and I amused myself by watching their movements.

Upon a neighboring eminence some fifty or a hundred of these insatiate marauders were congregated, as if for consultation. Adjoining this, two parallel lines of low hills led out from the river bottom into the prairie, for five or six miles, defining a narrow valley, at the extremity of which a large band of antelope were quietly grazing.

The chief topic of the wolfine conference seemed to have particular reference to this circumstance; for, in a very short time, the council dispersed, and its members betook to the hills skirting the valley before described, and, stationing themselves upon both lines at regular intervals, two of them commenced the attack by leisurely approaching their destined prey from opposite directions, in such a manner as to drive the whole band between the defile of hungry expectants. This done, the chase began without further preliminary.

Each wolf performed his part by pursuing the terrified antelope till relieved by his next companion, and he by the succeeding one; and so on, alternately; taking care to reverse their course at either extremity of the defile—again and again to run the death-race, until, exhausted by the incessant effort and crazed with terror, the agile animals, that were wont to bid defiance to the swiftest steed, and rival the storm-wind in fleetness, fell easy victims to the sagacity of their enemies.

I watched the operation until several of them yielded their lifeless carcases to appease the appetite of their rapacious pursuers, when I returned to camp with far more exalted ideas of the instinctive intelligence of wolves (savoring so strongly of reason and calculation) than I had previously entertained.

Two or three severe snow-storms occurred shortly after our arrival; but having constructed commodious shantees in regular mountain style, with large fires in front, we were both dry and comfortable.

These occasions, too, afforded their own amusement. Snugly stowed away in bed, with our rifles at hand, whenever a straggling wolf ventured within gun-shot, in fond hopes of a deserted camp, he was almost sure to fall a victim to his own temerity.

Bands of five or ten would frequently approach almost to the camp-fire, totally unsuspicious of danger till the sharp crack of a rifle told the fall of some one of their number.

❖❖❖

A person in the enjoyment of good health and a quiet mind, generally sleeps sound. In proof that such was the case with our party, I need only advert to a circumstance which here occurred.

Having awoke one moonshiny night, and observing an unusual number of wolves in the vicinity of camp, I seized my rifle and shot one of them; soon after I improved the opportunity to lay another prostrate, and in a few minutes subsequent a third fell in like manner; all at three several shots.

A continuation of the sport seemed likely to detract too much from the hours of sleep, and so, placing the victims in front of the camp-fire, I addressed myself to repose.

A light snow fell in the interval, and sunrise found us all in bed, patiently waiting to see who would have the courage to rise first. At length, one man jumped up and turned to renew the fire. On noticing the wolves before it he wheeled for his rifle, in his eagerness to secure which he fell sprawling at full length.

"Hello!" says one; "what's the matter, my boy. Is that a sample of the *ups* and *downs* of life?"

"Matter?" exclaimed our hero, gathering himself up in double-quick time, and rushing for his gun; "matter enough! The cursed wolves have grown so bold and saucy, that they come to the fire to warm themselves! Only look! A dozen or more of 'em are there now, in broad day-light! Get up, quick! and let's kill 'em!"

Aroused by this extraordinary announcement, the whole *posse* were instantly on their feet to repel the audacious invaders; when, lo! the cause of alarm proved three dead carcases.

But, where did they come from? When were they killed? Who placed them there? These were questions none were able to solve, and in regard to which all were profoundly ignorant. Finally, the circumstance occasioned quite an animated discussion, which was soon merged into angry dispute; and, after amusing myself awhile at their expense, I unravelled the mystery, to the surprise of all.

"Can it be possible!" was the general exclamation,— "can it be possible that we should have slept so sound as not to hear the report of a rifle fired three times in succession, and under our very ears, at that!"

"This reminds me," said one, "of dreaming that somebody fired during the night. But it seemed so much like other dreams I had forgotten it till now."

"Well," retorted a second, "we are a pretty set of customers to live in a dangerous country! Why, a single Indian might have come into camp and killed the whole of us, one after another, with all the ease imaginable!"

The above incident induced the narration of a circumstance, happening to an individual of my acquaintance two or three weeks previous.

He had been into the mountains after deer, and was on his return to the Fort for a fresh supply of ammunition, and, having occasion to camp out at night, like a genuine mountaineer, he took his saddle for a pillow. This, being covered with raw hide, excited the cupidity of a marauding wolf.

The hungry beast felt ill-disposed to let slip an opportunity thus favorable for appeasing his appetite with a dry morsel, and so, gently drawing it from beneath the head of the unconscious sleeper, he bore off his prize to devour it at his leisure.

In the morning our hero awoke minus saddle, and nothing save a number of wolf-tracks at his head furnished clue to the mystery of its disappearance; and, after spending several hours in fruitless search, neither hide or hair of it could be found.

❖❖❖

In our excursions after game, the remains of an Indian fort had been discovered in a small grove, a short distance below camp, which received the honor of our subsequent occupancy. A few hours devoted to repairs rendered it a complete shelter from either wind or rain; and, still farther to enhance its conveniences, we succeeded in digging a small well adjoining the entrance, thus securing a most welcome supply of cool water. Here revelling in the midst of plenty, with nothing to think of or care for but our own personal comforts, we had no mind to exchange our situation for the fatigues of war and the drudgery of camp-duty.

Several incidents also occurred in the interim to enliven the scene and relieve its otherwise dull monotony. On one occasion a strolling wolf, venturing too near camp, received the contents of my rifle and instantly fell. Supposing the shot to be a fatal one, I advanced and seized him by the tail with the design of taking his skin.

But the creature, having been only stunned by a neck wound, now re-
vived in full strength, and, enraged at his rough treatment, called into exercise the utmost tension of his energies to afford a bitter sample of the fierceness of wolfine vengeance. Here was a quandary—to relinquish the hold
would have been to invite a doubtful collision—to allow him an instant's
time for turning upon, must have proved equally perilous;—the only resource
was to retain my grasp with twofold energy, and run backwards as fast as
possible, which I did, pulling the struggling beast after me,—now twisting
this way, now that way, in vain effort to attack,—and growling and snapping
this teeth with all the ferocity of his savage nature.

What would have been the result of this strange adventure, it is hard to
tell, were it not that one of my camp-mates hastened to the rescue, and with
a club despatched his wolfship. At any rate I had no curiosity to submit the
question to a further test.

ONE NIGHT AMONG WOLVES
1839-40

THE young author of this story, Darius B. Cook, was forced by ill health in November of 1839 to leave his post at the Kalamazoo Gazette. His doctor told him, "You want fresh air and exercise. Go live with the Indians, sleep in their wigwams on a bed of leaves, hunt in the forests, live as they live, and the chances are you will recover." So he rounded up a fellow adventurer, eight large wolf traps, rifles and ammunition, and other provisions, and set out in an ox-drawn cart for the wilderness about 30 miles north of Kalamazoo. Of his first night in the woods, he wrote: "Sleep, there was little. The snuffing and growling of hungry wolves until day light, no pen can describe.

> *'Twas if a thousand fiends of hell*
> *Were sending forth the battle yell."*

In 1889, Mr. Cook published his memoirs of his sojourn, Six Months Among Indians, Wolves and Other Wild Animals, in the Forests of Allegan County, Mich., in the Winter of 1839 and 1840 (Niles Mirror Office, Niles, Michigan). Prior to its publication, he traveled again to his old hunting grounds of fifty years earlier. Where in 1839 there had been dense forests, numerous Indian villages, Indian men old enough to have witnessed the death of Tecumseh in 1813, and widely scattered pioneer cabins, there was in 1889 the thriving town of Wayland. The changes to the American landscape in the nineteenth century were enormous.

We have made a few very minor corrections. Throughout this account, incidentally, the author refers to himself as "we."

❖❖❖

"Captain, there are fresh deer tracks between here and the spring," said I early one morning as we returned with a pail of water, "and I propose to get one before breakfast," seizing our rifle. "Yes, but I'll have breakfast in half an hour or so," said the Captain. "I'll be here on time, and if you hear me shoot come out and help me drag one in," said I, jokingly. "Yes, yes," said the Captain laughing.

Out we went, and in less than thirty rods we saw a fine doe lying down, and she was shot dead in her bed. But a few steps off a fine buck jumped up, and ere we could load was out of reach. By a cautious pursuit we got in a shot at long range, but drew blood freely and followed on, but knowing we would be late to breakfast we retraced our steps for the doe, and much to our surprise there was nothing left but a small piece of skin which we took back for a cushion to the shaving horse. The wolves had carried it all off. This could not be believed until the Captain examined the ground.

Breakfast being over we resolved to pursue the wounded buck. Taking the track, the blood showed he had a serious wound, and we had not gone far ere he sprang up and dashed off, getting a second, but it seems not a fatal shot. Thus we pursued this wounded buck far off from our lodge until the shadows of night began to set in, and we saw there was danger of not getting to our lodge. The day was cloudy and we had no idea how far we were from our camp. Our compass told us which way to steer our course to strike Rabbit river, and we hastened on as speedy as possible. But darker and darker it grew. Old Jim [a local resident wolf] set up his great bass howl in the same place he always did, and we knew we must be a long distance off for he was between us and the lodge. If we could reach Rabbit river before dark we were safe for we knew of an Indian encampment up that river, but the distance to it seemed too great. Coming to a tamarack swamp we made up our mind our only salvation was to strike a fire, for the wolves were on our track and when darkness fairly set in an attack was certain. We gathered a lot of dry tamarack poles and kindlings but to our sorrow we could not find a match. Every pocket was searched in vain. We tried rubbing dry sticks together, but could not succeed in getting any thing but sparks. We determined to discharge our rifle and load with powder and tow [coarse flax, hemp, or jute fibers], which we had in our game bag, which would set the tow on fire. After doing so and taking the tow out of the bag a solitary match dropped from it into the snow which we seized with the utmost care. Preparing well for a fire we lit the match, set the tow on fire and the dry bark and sticks were soon going, and as darkness fairly set in we had a fire which illuminated the wilderness for a long distance. We listened for the signal gun in vain, we were beyond hearing it. Every short time we would fire our own gun, but it was useless. The wolves surrounded us in large numbers, but the fire was our protector. Sometimes when it became a little dim they would approach nearer. Their howls and growls were terrific. They would often have a fight among themselves, and their clear voices would ring for miles around. When their eyes were turned towards us they would glisten by the light of the fire, and occasionally we would shoot as near as possible between them. The noise of a rifle would still them but for a moment when a louder and more terrific howling would be set up. Thus all the long night we worked to keep up the fire, and dry tamarack near us was getting scarce. To venture out too far was certain food for them. On one occasion, one wolf more daring than the rest, while we were procuring a dead tree four or five rods from the fire, came so near we heard him snuff. Turning around we saw his glaring eyes not over three rods off. Dropping our pole we took good aim at his eyes and he fell dead, but we did not know it then. He was apparently crouched for a spring when we shot. We only knew the eyes disappeared. It was a cold and dreary night. We had fixed a place to sit down, and in a minute we fell asleep and fell off. This awakened us and we dare not sit down again. A few frozen roasted potatoes were found in our pocket, which we thawed out and ate, which were refreshing. Daylight dawned at last, and as it grew lighter the pack drew off and their noise was hushed. We went to see the effect of our shots and found the venturesome wolf dead in the snow. Those farther off had been hit, as seen by blood, but not fatally. All around and within eight rods and less the snow was completely tread down, and here and there blood and hair, caused either by their fights or bullets, by bullets we imagined, for we sent not less than ten in their direction.

It was a night of terror, long and dreary. Almost ready to surrender to fatigue we pursued our northern course slowly and sadly, for even then we began to think we must perish alone in the forest. At last we struck the river and took new courage. Here there was a half beaten Indian trail and our steps were quickened. Onward we pressed and at last we beheld one of the most beautiful pictures the eye could imagine. It was smoke curling up among the trees. It was an Indian encampment and we were greeted with a hearty welcome. . . . We told them our story, and two young bucks started for the wolf with ponies, and in less then an hour he was brought in.

They feasted us on their best—boiled muskrat, corn bread and potatoes. They brought up their best ponies and one strapped the wolf on, took the lead, and in an hour we reached our lodge. It was about 10 a.m. and the Captain had taken our track, but a shot from our rifle was answered near a mile off and he speedily returned and it was a joyful meeting for he never expected to see us alive. We remained in camp three days before we recovered sufficiently to be out.

❖❖❖

The bait for wolves on the shanty came down and was dragged about three-fourths of a mile into a black ash swamp and left by a fallen tree. Three traps were set near it. To them a chain was attached and a heavy clog to the chain. Visiting the traps the next morning, two were gone and one was sprung, evidently by a piece of bark falling from the log. Not a vestige of the bait was left. Both were found. The clogs had caught against little trees, and the wolves had wound the chains around them and twisted their feet out, leaving the balls and claws in the traps.

We supplied bait the next night with the head of a deer and caught others, but they would twist out in the same manner. We found it was useless to catch them in this way, for so powerful were they no trap we had would hold them. We invented a plan to

SAVE THEM.

A huge grape vine ran far up into the limbs of a tree, and both of us pulled it down and tied it to the roots of a tree with moose bark. We then cut it off and attached the chain of the trap to the vine, and the bait near the trap surrounding it in such manner that an animal must step over into the trap to get it. In this way we saved our first wolf. He was caught by the forepaw. He leaped and broke the bark, the vine sprung up and Mr. wolf was jerked two feet from the earth. At our appearance he could only kick at air and turn his head fiercely. Throwing a cord around the vine we could swing him thirty feet each way, and in this amusement we participated for some time, his feet touching the snow as he came down from his long sweep. A bullet through his head as he was swept up put an end to the sport.

SKATER CHASED BY WOLVES
1844

WOLF researcher L. David Mech points out in his 1970 book, Wolves: The Ecology and Behavior of an Endangered Species, *that numerous historical descriptions of wolves' hunting behavior have generally made "fascinating, although fanciful, reading." Yet, even in a fear-ridden story such as this, one can sometimes detect an element of true wolf behavior. What was a nerve-shattering pursuit for this ice skater was actually a predictable sequence in the normal hunting behavior of wolves. Mech says "the rush" at the prey is stimulated in wolves by the flight of the prey, and in fact, "a nonmoving creature seems to inhibit the rush response." Little consolation to the hapless skater whose midnight dash triggered this innate response!*

"Skater Chased by Wolves" was published by C. W. Webber in The Hunter-Naturalist; Romance of Sporting; or, Wild Scenes and Wild Hunters *(Philadelphia: J. W. Bradley, 1851).*

❖❖❖

Everybody has read the remarkable adventure with the wolves on the ice, related by Mr. Whitehead. The story has made so strong an impression upon me, that I cannot resist the temptation of preserving it here, along with the previous narrative, as incidental to our "Wild Scenes," entirely legitimate here. I present it with an illustration, as one of the most effective stories ever given about wolves.

During the winter of 1844, being engaged in the northern part of Maine, I had much leisure to devote to the wild sports of a new country. To none of these was I more passionately addicted than to skating. The deep and sequestered lakes of this State, frozen by the intense cold of a northern winter, present a wide field to the lovers of this pastime. Often would I bind on my skates, and glide away up the glittering river and wind each mazy streamlet that flowed beneath its fetters on toward the parent ocean, forgetting all the while time and distance in the luxurious sense of the gliding motion—thinking of nothing in the easy flight, but rather dreaming, as I looked through the transparent ice at the long weeds and cresses that nodded in the current beneath, and seemed wrestling with the wave to let them go; or I would follow the track of some fox or otter, and run my skate along the mark he had left with his dragging tail until the trail would enter the woods. Sometimes these excursions were made by moonlight; and it was on one of these occasions that I had a rencontre which even now, with kind faces around me, I cannot recall without a nervous looking-over-my-shoulder feeling.

I had left my friend's house one evening just before dusk, with the intention of skating a short distance up the noble Kennebec, which glided directly before the door. The night was beautifully clear. A peerless moon rode through an occasional fleecy cloud, and stars twinkled from the sky and from every frost-covered tree in millions. Your mind would wonder at the light that came glinting from ice, and snow-wreath, and incrusted branches, as the eye followed for miles the broad gleam of the Kennebec, that like a jeweled zone swept between the mighty forests on its banks. And yet all was still. The cold seemed to have frozen tree, and air, and water, and every living thing that moved. Even the ringing of my skates echoed back from the Moccasin Hill with a startling clearness, and the crackle of the ice as I passed over it in my course seemed to follow the tide of the river with lightning speed.

I had gone up the river nearly two miles, when coming to a little stream which empties into the larger, I turned into it to explore its course. Fir and hemlock of a century's growth met overhead, and formed an archway radiant with frost-work. All was dark within; but I was young and fearless, and, as I peered into an unbroken forest, that reared itself on the borders of the stream, I laughed with very joyousness; my wild hurrah rang through the silent woods, and I stood listening to the echo that reverberated again and again, until all was hushed. Suddenly a sound arose—it seemed to me to come from beneath the ice; it sounded low and tremulous at first, until it ended in one wild yell. I was appalled. Never before had such a noise met my ears. I thought it more than mortal; so fierce, and amidst such an unbroken solitude, it seemed as though a fiend had blown a blast from an infernal trumpet. Presently I heard the twigs on shore crack as though from the tread of some brute animal, and the blood rushed back to my forehead with a bound that made my skin burn, and I felt relieved that I had to contend with things earthly, and not of spiritual nature—my energies returned, and I looked around me for some means of escape.

The moon shone through the opening at the mouth of the creek by which I had entered the forest, and considering this the best means of escape, I darted towards it like an arrow. 'Twas hardly a hundred yards distant, and the swallow could scarcely excel my desperate flight; yet, as I turned my head to the shore, I could see two dark objects dashing through the underbrush at a pace nearly double in speed to my own. By this great speed, and the short yells which they occasionally gave, I knew at once that these were the much dreaded gray wolves.

I had never met with these animals, but from the description given of them, I had but little pleasure in making their acquaintance. Their untameable fierceness, and the untiring strength which seems part of their nature, render them objects of dread to every benighted traveller.

> "With their long gallop, which can tire
> The deer-hound's hate, the hunter's ire,"

they pursue their prey—never straying from the track of their victim—and as the wearied hunter thinks that he has at last outstripped them, he finds that they but waited for the evening to seize their prey, and falls a prize to the tireless animals.

The bushes that skirted the shore flew past with the velocity of lightning, as I dashed on in my flight to pass the narrow opening. The outlet was nearly gained; one second more and I would be comparatively safe, when my pursuers appeared on the bank above me, which here rose to the height of ten feet. There was no time for thought, so I bent my head and dashed madly forward. The wolves sprang, but miscalculating my speed, fell behind, while their intended prey glided out upon the river.

Nature turned me towards home. The light flakes of snow spun from the iron of my skates, and I was some distance from my pursuers, when their fierce howl told me I was still their fugitive. I did not look back, I did not feel afraid, or sorry, or glad; one thought of home, of the bright faces awaiting my return, and of their tears if they never should see me, and then every energy of body and mind were exerted for escape. I was perfectly at home on the ice. Many were the days that I spent on my good skates, never thinking that at one time they would be my only means of safety. Every half minute an alternate yelp from my fierce attendants made me but too certain that they were in close pursuit. Nearer and nearer they came; I heard their feet pattering on the ice nearer still, until I could feel their breath and hear their snuffing scent. Every nerve and muscle in my frame was stretched to the utmost tension.

The trees along the shore seemed to dance in an uncertain light, and my brain turned with my own breathless speed, yet still they seemed to hiss forth their breath with a sound truly horrible, when an involuntary motion on my part, turned me out of my course. The wolves, close behind, unable to stop, and as unable to turn on the smooth ice, slipped and fell, still going on far ahead; their tongues were lolling out, their white tusks glaring from their bloody mouths, their dark, shaggy breasts were fleeced with foam, and as they passed me, their eyes glared, and they howled with fury. The thought flashed on my mind, that by this means I could avoid them, viz: by turning aside whenever they came too near; for they, by the formation of their feet, are unable to run on ice except in a straight line.

I immediately acted upon this plan. The wolves, having regained their feet, sprang directly towards me. The race was renewed for twenty yards up the stream; they were already close on my back, when I glided round and dashed directly past my pursuers. A fierce yell greeted my evolution, and the wolves, slipping upon their haunches, sailed onward, presenting a perfect picture of helplessness and baffled rage. Thus I gained nearly a hundred yards at each turning. This was repeated two or three times, every moment the animals getting more excited and baffled.

At one time, by delaying my turning too long, my sanguinary antagonists came so near that they threw the white foam over my dress as they sprang to seize me, and their teeth clashed together like the spring of a fox-trap. Had my skates failed for one instant, had I tripped on a stick, or caught my foot in a fissure of the ice, the story I am now telling would never have been told.

I thought all the chances over; I knew where they would first take hold of me if I fell; I thought how long it would be before I died, and then there would be a search for the body that would already have its tomb; for oh! how fast man's mind traces out all the dread colors of death's picture, only those who have been near the grim original can tell.

But I soon came opposite the house, and my hounds—I knew their deep voices—roused by the noise, bayed furiously from the kennels. I heard their chains rattle: how I wished they would break them! and then I should have protectors that would be peers to the fiercest denizens of the forest. The wolves taking the hint conveyed by the dogs, stopped in their mad career, and after a moment's consideration, turned and fled. I watched them until their forms disappeared over a neighboring hill, then taking off my skates, wended my way to the house, with feelings which may be better imagined than described. But even yet I never see a broad sheet of ice in the moon-shine, without thinking of that snuffing breath and those fearful things that followed me so closely down the frozen Kennebec.

A BUSHEL OF FUN
1852

 IN 1852, Origen Thomson took his family over the Oregon Trail. His account of the trip was published decades later as Crossing the Plains, Narrative of the Scenes, Incidents and Adventures attending the Overland Journey of the Decatur and Rush County Emigrants to the "far-off" Oregon, in 1852 *(Greensburg, Indiana: Orville Thomson, Printer, 1896). This story is excerpted from "Mr. McCoy's Story, His Buffalo Hunt, and Battle with Mountain Wolves," one of several appendices to Thomson's fascinating journal.*

Sutherland McCoy was one of the young single men in the wagon train of 111 that made its way from Indiana to Oregon. While the group was camped for a day of rest in eastern Wyoming, he and an older companion named Brown slipped away from the other travelers and set off in search of antelope or buffalo. Ten miles from camp, they spotted a herd of bison and crept to within firing range on their hands and knees. When several shots failed to bring an animal down, Brown decided to return to camp. McCoy kept on, determined to get his buffalo.

❖❖❖

When I came up with the buffalo there were a great many white wolves, (or "buffalo" wolves, as they were called,) attracted, I suppose, by the smell of blood, following after him, and when they would come very close he would charge upon them; and after getting several shots, at rather long range, I succeeded in killing him. All this time the wolves had been increasing in numbers, and when the buffalo fell I made a charge—yelling and shooting with my revolver, and so managed as to be first to reach the carcass. In an instant, however, I was surrounded, and used my rifle at short range, and with deadly effect.

Then opened a scene I had never before witnessed: wolves devouring their own dead and wounded; and, in some instances, those not wounded would be seized by two or three wolves at each end, who jerking in opposite directions would tear them asunder and devour them almost as quickly as I have been describing it. With hair standing on end, and legs rather shaky, I carved into the carcass for a small portion of meat to carry back to camp; (but had I known then, what I learned by experience long before I reached there, I would not have attempted a thing so fool-hardy). Cutting a strip off its hide and stringing the meat on it across my shoulder, in the manner I would carry my canteen, I started for camp. It seemed then that the hungry devils be-grudged me the small morsel I took, as they raised a terrific howl, and seemed on the point of charging on me.

I quickly decided that my time was *now or never*; and with revolver in one hand and gun in the other, firing as fast as I could, charged through their lines. They merely opened their ranks sufficiently to let me out. Then fol-lowed a scene that baffles human language to adequately describe .... With one simultaneous rush the entire pack was on the carcass, snarling, and fight-ing, and piling on top of each other. Feeling somewhat grateful to them for allowing me free passage through their ranks, after having me in such close quarters, I could not resist the temptation to turn and fire at the seething mass, which seemed but to increase their fury .... Then I began to congratu-late myself, thinking surely there can be no more white wolves within a ra-dius of at least twenty miles, as they were certainly all in at the feast; but after footing it at a rapid gait, and covering several miles in the direction of camp, I was horrified to hear the long-drawn-out howl of the white wolf off to my left, in the direction from which the wind was blowing, and soon the howl was answered by another, and then another, and then I knew they had scented me.

My first inclination was to throw down my meat, and let them have it; then again I thought that, at the speed I was traveling, if I could hold out, I certainly would reach camp before night overtook me; and did not think a fresh pack would be fool-hardy enough to attack me in daylight for a small piece of meat. By this time—the time it takes me to tell it—their numbers had, and were yet rapidly increasing, and their howl was almost continuous. How I scanned the horizon, hoping to come in view, even at a distance off, of our covered wagons; and what fun it would be to the boys in camp to see me coming in at a break-neck speed, pursued by a pack of hungry wolves.

The sun went down, and no wagon train in sight, but myriads of wolves in my wake and on either side; and, having sighted their victim, their voices changed. (I have learned since then, that while away in the distance their howl is long-drawn-out and mournful, when they sight their game it is shorter and sharper, and, to my ear, it is much more blood-curdling.) As the sun was now down and the shades of night coming on, I concluded to halt and shoot a few of them, as they were in short range, hoping they would stop to devour the dead and wounded and ease up on me,—shooting a few times with deadly effect. On stopping I unloaded my buffalo meat, to give my shoulders a rest, but when I came to take it up it seemed so heavy that I decided to divide with them, retaining only a few pounds.

About this time I discovered a lone tree, on the summit of a very steep hill, and somewhat out of the direction I was traveling, and at once decided to run for it, which I did with all the speed I could command. The hill was so steep I had to come down to a walk; and, to my horror, on reaching it I found it was almost surrounded by wolves, as they were crowding closely in the rear and running in two parallel lines with me. It had begun to look as though they would surround, and take me in, before I could reach the tree; and as some were within a few steps of me I turned, and with my revolver fired a few shots into them, and while they were devouring the wounded succeeded in reaching the tree, which proved to be a cedar, possibly eight inches in diameter. I could just reach the lower limbs, and, shoving my gun up into them, by almost super-human effort drew myself up after it.

From my perch in the tree I could see the Emigrant camp-fires, a mile or two away, and had the wind been blowing from their direction they must have heard the baying of the wolves and my firing quite distinctly. Trimming out a few small branches and seating myself,—thinking to rest pretty comfortably in the tree until morning, or until the wolves should leave me, and feeling that I did not want to do any more running that night, (all the while the hungry devils snarling, snapping and fighting below me,) I thought to change the exercises and have some circus acting in connexion with that menagerie . . . so taking a long-bladed knife that I carried in my belt, and trimming off the ends of the limb, so that the wolves could have a fair view of the meat, which was hung on the limb, and bracing myself securely, with a good grip on it with the left and the knife in the right hand, all was in readiness for opening the performance. The jumping exercise began as soon as they saw the meat,—or, rather, they would stand upright on their hind legs and spring at the bait, but hardly high enough for me to reach them with the knife. Finally one big fellow who had been snarling around considerably, and acting as though he was the master of ceremonies, drew back some distance and, with a warning snarl that caused the others to open a way for him, his eyes shining like gas jets, bounded forward and crouching to the ground made a leap that excelled anything of the kind I had ever witnessed. His aim was not exactly true, or he would have got the meat, for his great jaws cracked together almost in my face. I lost no time in pulling in the meat and climbing higher in the tree.

Whether or not I made a thrust at him with the knife I could not tell, as I was so astonished I hardly knew anything just then. I had then climbed about as high as I could, the tree beginning to bend under my weight, when, to my horror, I discovered the brutes were gnawing it down. Their biting and jerking kept the top in a constant quiver, which caused cold chills to creep up and down my spinal column, and most serious thoughts were rushing through my mind. One was that my fate would never be known, for if the tree was gnawed down I would be devoured alive; another, and the one uppermost in my mind, was what a fool I had been in slipping off from the boys that morning, and how acceptable the company of a few of them would have been from the time the wolves first made their appearance. And while thus deploring my condition the thought occurred that I might be better engaged—in shooting the wolves.

As they stood on their hind legs, chawing the tree, their eyes glared at me like coals of fire. I still had a few rounds left for my revolver, and as soon as I commenced shooting the fighting and devouring of the wounded commenced. Whenever a wolf began to gnaw at the tree I shot at his head. This did not last a great while until, to my great relief, they began to disappear. After remaining some time in the tree, I came down and, to my great relief, there were no *live* wolves in sight. I presume they had satisfied their hunger by feasting upon their fellows; and, as I stood among the bones and carcasses of the dead that were strewn around the tree, how thankful I was to the—*Allen Revolver*—that had saved my life; for, on examination of that tree, I found it was half eaten down.

—Now let me say to the reader, this incident occurred *forty-four years ago*, and yet my recollection of that night is as vividly before my mind as if it had occurred yesterday, and yet I can never describe my feelings. One short hour before I thought my fate sealed; and such a fate . . . too horrible to contemplate. Imagine a condemned culprit standing in the presence of his executioner, who is ready prepared to carry out the sentence of death, when suddenly a commutation is granted, and you have it.

—A walk of about two miles brought me to camp, a-half mile from which I was met by several of the boys, who had started out to look me up. My old friend Brown had returned to camp late in the afternoon, had laid down in his tent to rest, and fallen asleep, and not waking until after night was very much alarmed about my safety, and was heading the party that met me. I shall never forget his salutation. Seizing me by the hand he thanked God that they had found me alive, for—as he said—"I expected the indians had got your scalp." He knew, from the way I had out-footed him every time we had retreated that day, that no wounded buffalo could catch me on the run.

—I told him I was sorry he could not have stayed with me, as I had a bushel of fun shooting wolves,—which the same was not *strictly true*, however.

WOLVES OF THE PLAINS
1876

 RICHARD Irving Dodge was a U.S. Army officer whose long military career was spent almost entirely in the Great Plains. Extensive travels and a broad range of official duties, as well as his favorite pastime—hunting—provided him with a wealth of firsthand knowledge about the land, its native people, and its wildlife. In the early 1870s, a friend, impressed with Dodge's knowledge and storytelling ability, strongly encouraged him to write a book. The result, The Plains of North America and their Inhabitants, *was quickly recognized as an authoritative source about a region that was still dismissed as the Great American Desert despite decades of exploration, fur trapping, emigration, surveying, homesteading, and railroads. But as one editor pointed out, and as Dodge himself anticipated in the last paragraph of this selection, the Old West was changing so rapidly that, within a decade, Dodge's book of "observations, anecdotes, and opinions" had lost its currency and become merely historical in significance.*

Dodge lamented the passing of "the silent mysteries of the plains." It's not clear if he counted the wolf among those mysteries, but from our vantage point 120 years later, we most certainly do.

The Plains of North America and their Inhabitants *was first published in 1876. These selections are from a new edition edited by Wayne R. Kime (Newark: University of Delaware Press, 1989).*

❖❖❖

There is scarcely a portion of the prairie that can be traversed by the hunter, on which he will not see wolves. These are of two kinds.

The buffalo wolf, as tall as an ordinary greyhound, lean, gaunt, and hungry looking; the prairie wolf (miscalled coyote on the middle and northern plains) about halfway in size between the fox and the buffalo wolf. The coyote proper I have never seen except in Texas and Mexico. It is a miserable little cur of an animal scarcely larger than a fox.

All of these wolves are exceedingly cowardly, one alone, not possessing courage enough to attack even a sheep. When in packs and very hungry they have been known to muster up resolution enough to attack an ox or cow, if the latter be entirely alone. Writers of all ages have linked the name of the wolf with hypocrisy, with famine, with ferocity, until we have come to regard the animal as the incarnation of all that is mean, treacherous, blood thirsty and dangerous. What American boy but has felt the glow of enthusiasm or tremor of terror, on reading the exploit of the heroic young Putnam? It is not a grateful office to divest the imagination of ideas imbibed from childish story books, or to show the absurdity of long cherished beliefs, but truth compels me to assert that of all the carnivorous animals of equal size and strength, he is the most harmless to beast and the least dangerous to man. He will not even attack when wounded, and though he will snap at attacking dogs in self defense, he never follows up the advantage which his sharp teeth and powerful jaws give him, but takes to flight the moment he can do so.

The wolf is marvellously acute in all his senses, so that it is only in places remote from the route of hunters that a good shot can be had at him. He furnishes splendid sport when hunted with hounds, though he is so fleet and long winded, that, no ordinary pack can overtake him. It is usual to have in each pack one or more greyhounds, to overrun and bring him to bay and thus enable the slower hounds to come up.

❖❖❖

In the late fall when the antelope are in great herds, the Utes and other Indians of the foot hills make surround and kill great numbers of the panic stricken animals.

Antelope possess very great vitality and carry off more lead in proportion to their size, than any other animal. They possess too, remarkable courage; and under ordinary circumstances do not trouble themselves to get out of the way even of the large buffalo wolves. A single antelope will bravely face a single wolf and successfully beat off his attack, and a herd does not fear the attack of any number of wolves. Wherever the antelope are plenty, will generally be found plenty of wolves, who lie around the herds at a little distance, watchful and ready to take advantage of any accident in their favor, now pouncing upon one which has strayed from the protection of the herd, and making a prompt meal of any one which should happen to be sick or get hurt in any way.

I once wounded a large doe from a herd which ran past me. I saw she was badly hurt, shot through the body, and wished to give her time to lie down. Mounting my horse I rode slowly in the direction taken by the herd. After proceeding half a mile I saw her standing faced partly towards me, and very much on the alert, and in a moment discovered that she was in the heat of a combat with a large wolf. The wolf circled round, trying to get at her flanks and rear, and made many feints of springing upon her, but in spite of the advantage of his sharp teeth, he was too cowardly to come to close quarters. The little antelope bravely faced her foe, and continually charged, striking viciously with her fore feet, and would certainly have beat off her assailant, but that the smell of blood made him unusually pertinacious. I watched the fight for more than five minutes with the greatest interest. At last the antelope in making a charge, slipped probably from weakness. In an instant the wolf had her by the throat, threw her on the ground and worried her like a dog. I wanted the wolf to kill her, and waited for some time until she was perfectly quiet and I believed dead. I then rode up slowly. The wolf took to his heels on my approach, and to my very great surprise, the antelope sprung to its feet, and went off in another direction, at as great a rate of speed as before. I ran her with my horse for a long distance and finally brought her to bag with another shot. The wolf, though a large one had only scarified the throat, and though he would eventually have killed and eaten her, he had done her no serious injury, though he had had her unresisting in his jaws, and had been worrying her for several minutes.

Very different was the result when a pack of wolves got after a wounded antelope. On the same hunt as in the last case (and during which I saw more wolves than ever before or since in the same time) a friend and I had got several shots into a herd, bagging four or five, several of which though mortally wounded, ran off to greater or less distances. Leaving the dead we went off at once after the wounded, securing after some little time and trouble all but one. When we got near the place where he had been last seen, we started a pack of six or eight wolves, and going to the spot found our antelope, its throat lacerated, its ham strings cut, its flanks torn open and half the viscera already devoured.

❖❖❖

Indians say that wolves not unfrequently go mad, rush into their villages and do great damage. The following most interesting and perfectly authenticated facts are taken from the records of the Hospital at Fort Larned on the Arkansas River.

"On the 5th August at 10 o'clock P.M. a rabid wolf of the large grey species came into the post and charged round furiously. He entered the Hospital and attacked Corpora — who was lying sick in bed, biting him severely in the left hand and right arm. The left little finger was nearly taken off. The wolf next dashed into a party of ladies and gentlemen sitting in the moonlight on Colonel ——'s porch and bit Lieut. —— severely in both legs. Leaving there he soon after attacked and bit Private —— in two places. This all occurred in an incredibly short space of time and although those above mentioned were the only persons bitten, the animal left the marks of his presence in every quarter of the garrison. He moved with great rapidity, snapping at everything within his reach, tearing tents, window curtains, bed clothing &c. in every direction. The sentinel at the guard house fired over the animal's back while he ran between the man's legs. Finally he charged upon a sentinel at the hay stack, and was killed by a well directed, most fortunate shot. He was a very large wolf and his long jaws and teeth presented a most formidable appearance.

The wounds were thoroughly cauterized with nitrate of silver on the plan recommended by Mr. Youatt.

The Indians are still camped in the vicinity of the post in very large numbers. I have taken particular pains to question them as to their experience with regard to rabid wolves. They say that the appearance of mad wolves in their village is not unfrequent, that the time of year at which they are most often seen is in the months of February and March; that, once having entered a village the wolf will make no attempt to leave it, but will rush furiously from place to place until he is disabled, and that in no instance have any of them ever known a person to recover after having received the smallest scratch from the rabid animal's teeth.

They make no attempt at treatment and one or two instances were related where an Indian on being affected with the hydrophobial spasms threw himself into the water and was drowned.

September 9th Corporal —— showed signs of commencing hydrophobia on the evening of the 6th instant. The symptoms were as usually described, were well marked and very characteristic. He died on the morning of the 9th. No treatment was attempted after the symptoms commenced. His wounds had been well cauterized with lunar caustic from time and time and washed with alkali washes, and had he allowed the finger to be removed at first, there would have been a greater probability of his recovery. A large Newfoundland dog which had been seen fighting with the wolf has also just died with marked symptoms of hydrophobia.

The wounds have healed in the other two persons, and they appear to be in perfect health."

The officer bitten is now (1875) in perfect health, having never experienced any ill effects beyond the ordinary pain of the wounds.

The evidence as to frequency of rabies in wolves, comes entirely from Indians, and, with all due respect and consideration for their veracity, I doubt it. For nearly thirty years the Army has been as constant a resident of the plains as the Indians themselves, and with equal opportunity for witnessing all the phenomena of plains life, yet the instance given above is the only one on record. Rabies is not a plains malady.

No description of life on the plains can now be given which will be more than a special record of a particular time and place. But a few years ago, the journey across the plains was the work of a whole summer. From the time of leaving the Missouri River, the party was lost to the world, and lived only in and for itself, no mails, no news, no communication of any kind with civilization. Surrounded on all sides by treacherous savages, by danger of every kind each man became a host in himself.

To the fascination of a life of perfect freedom from all conventional restraints, of constant adventure, was added that other fascination, far stronger to many natures, the desire to penetrate the unknown.

Now all is changed. There is no longer an unknown. Rail Roads have bared the silent mysteries of the plains to the inspection of every shop boy. Civilization, like a huge cuttle fish, has passed its arms of settlements up almost every stream, grasping the land, killing the game, driving out the Indian, crushing the romance, the poetry, the very life and soul of the "plains," leaving only the bare and monotonous carcass.

AN ENCOUNTER IN INDIA
1927

 HERE is a tale not from frontier America, but from half a world away in twentieth-century British colonial India. Yet the Old World fears persist unshaken, no matter what the land, the century, the sophistication, or the technology. This story appeared in The Spectator, *September 3, 1927, under the title "An Encounter"; the author signed it only as "C. G. C. T."*

❖❖❖

All the day long I had expected something, known that every dreary furlong of my hundred-and-twenty mile drive across that Central Indian upland of thin grass and bare rock and stark, burnt earth brought me nearer to some adventure of a flavour hitherto untasted, and here it was! For as the car swung slowly over the crest of an undulation differing in no particular from the uncounted undulations left in my wake, They rose to their feet and faced me, four on my right, three on the road itself—Wolves!

Never before in my life had I seen these beasts in the open, and my childhood memory of wolves behind bars was lifeless and dim. Perhaps twenty, perhaps thirty years had passed since I had even thought of a wolf. The heavy jungles and sodden rice country where my work had lain till then do not hold them. But neither the startled mutter of the man at my side—"*Varri!*" nor his hurried, backward glance into the body of the car, where the guncase and its contents lay buried under a pile of miscellaneous bundles and trunks, were necessary for my enlightenment. I knew them at once, as a man would recognize a Unicorn, or a Mermaid, or Apollyon himself out of the illustrated *Pilgrim's Progress* of his nursery days. They were not jackals, nor big, whitish-grey village dogs, nor did they even suggest a likeness to those animals. They were the real thing, high as three-month calves, gaunt in their hot-weather coats, big-headed and ruffed at the neck. Their jagged lower jaws hung open in the heat and their tongues were very long and red. They were wolves.

Involuntarily I slowed the engine to avoid a collision with the three on the road, and these, without a glance at the car, walked leisurely aside and joined their companions. All seven of them paced uneasily up and down, leering at me sidelong, about fifteen paces away, panting and smelling the ground. Out of bravado—one feels so much braver in a car than galloping by moonlight through a Russian forest in a three-horse sleigh—I shouted at them. Then they left off their aimless pacing and lowered their heavy jowls almost to the ground, and clamped their hanging jaws together, and looked at me.

I belong to that eccentric class of persons who have no natural desire to kill every large wild beast that crosses their path. I would not walk a hundred yards to shoot a tiger which meant no harm to me, or, within reason, to the cattle of the villagers under my charge. And it has so fallen out that in the past quarter of a century I have very frequently—more frequently, perhaps, than most men with similar chances—met such animals, face to face and unexpectedly, on the march at dawn, or in the cool of an evening stroll. We have invariably parted without ill-feeling or excitement, after a momentary and mutual acknowledgment of each other's presence. So, the mere fact of a large carnivorous animal going peaceably about his business is not alarming to me, even if his eyes happen to meet mine. But under the malignant stare of those seven pairs of eyes set close together above the long, raking jaws (I had seen what was inside those jaws) I felt fear, the numbing fear of the child who wakes in the dark and knows there is a bear under his bed. It is not pleasant, it is positively indecent, to experience this emotion when one is on the wrong side of forty. I am sickeningly afraid of my dentist, and shall be until after the extraction of my last tooth, but that is quite a lawful kind of fear, with nothing in it humiliating or obscene.

Therefore, jamming the pedal into bottom gear, the car being a Ford, I whimpered to myself: *"They are following us, following us at their great padding pace which will quicken to a spring, and then, suddenly, my man and I will be smothered beneath their rank, hot bodies, and their long jaws will snap and worry at our necks and arms—a horrid death, but I will* not *release the clutch until the car has run twenty yards, according to the Book of the Ford."*

A quarter of a mile further on three villagers met us, grey-beards all, trampling mournfully to heaven knows where, two of them with iron-shod staves, and one had an ancient six-foot matchlock on his shoulder. Very brave and indifferent, I hailed them: *"Varri,"* said I, "seven of them, just round the next corner; if you hurry you may get a shot at them." But I could have wished that my voice had been steadier.

And straightway those three old men, for babble and excitement, became like men transfigured. One pulled a smouldering crust of dried cow-dung from his turban, blowing on it till it roared softly, and lit the other's match till it roared too. Right manfully the third swung his "lathi," and in a moment all of them were hurrying forward to the encounter like boys to catch a sight of hounds. "This State pays a reward of two rupees on every wolf's head," explained my man. "One will aim the matchlock, and when he gives the word another must put the match to the vent. There is no trigger or hammer to that gun. Let us stop here and listen for their shot."

But I opened the throttle all the wider, for the car now held a third passenger whose name was Shame, and he was in haste, "And yet," thought I bitterly, "what do those old men know of Little Red Riding Hood, or the fate of the Lamb at the brook, or how the howling wolf-pack closes in on the doomed sleigh when the ammunition is all spent and the trace-horse cut loose and left to his fate, and the devoted footman (Ivan is his name) has given his life for the lovely fur-clad Countess and her sleeping child? What is a werewolf to them? Or that grim, prowling monster of the privy paw, the terror of the sheepfolds? Nor have they so much as heard of that other ghoulish brute on whom my fellow-countrywoman laid the Ban in her noble Lament for the Forests of Ulster:—

> "'The great grey wolf with scraping claw, lest he
> Lay bare my dead for gloating foes to see,
> Lay bare my dead who died, and died for me.'"

As a good European, I inherit a whole huddle of dark neolithic fears which the poets and magicians and schoolmasters of my tribe have sedulously kept alive through the safe, comfortable centuries. I am not to blame. From my cradle have I been bidden, enjoined, commanded to fear the wolf. He tears you to pieces alive and digs you up when you are dead, and before the maid has time to run to your frantic ringing he pulls you down on your own threshold; between the pillarbox and the front-door he pulls you down, in the dark, after tea. No, I am not to blame.

But all that night, as I tossed, sleepless, under a glaring moon on the roof of the Dak bungalow, that uninvited companion of my drive sat by the bed. "The stature of my soul" had been shortened for ever by three old men, and Asiatics at that, with two sticks and a crazy matchlock between them.

WHY IS THE WOLF FEROCIOUS?
Romania

 TWO old fables from Europe are included here because, like the preceding story from India, they illustrate an aspect of Old World attitudes toward wolves that strongly influenced encounters in North America. In addition, these tales from Eastern Europe are particularly interesting because they are little known compared to so many familiar childhood stories. Like fables throughout the world, including some of the Native American stories given earlier, these tales are metaphysical in nature, explaining how and why the world is as it is. As the translator/editor wrote, "The wolf is dreaded as the most savage beast, and could therefore only be conceived by the popular imagination as the creation of the devil." These fables come from Rumanian Bird and Beast Stories, *rendered into English by M. Gaster (London: Sidgwick & Jackson, Ltd., 1915).*

❖❖❖

Once upon a time God was walking with St. Peter. On the way they met a dog who came close to them and frolicked round them, and God stroked the animal. St. Peter looked at God questioningly, and God said, "I know what is in thy mind, but since thou art he who keeps the key of heaven it is meet that thou shouldst know everything, and I will therefore tell thee the story of the dog and the wolf, for thou must know whom to let into heaven and whom to shut out. Thou seest, Peter, what that brother of mine—"

"You mean the devil?" interposed St. Peter.

"Yes," said God, "I mean him. You see what he has done to me with Adam and Eve, and how he made me drive them out of Paradise. What was I to do? When the poor man was starving I had to help him, so I gave him the sheep to feed him and to clothe him. But dost thou think the devil will give them peace?—no, not he!"

"Yes," said Peter, "all very well, but what about the dog? I know all that about Adam and Eve."

"Do not be in such a hurry," replied God, "I will tell thee everything; bide thy time."

"Now, where was I? It was when I made the sheep, and the devil then must again try and do something to hurt Adam, so he is now making the wolf, who will destroy the sheep and bring Adam and Eve to grief. For that

135

reason I have made the dog, and he will drive the wolf away and protect the flocks of sheep, and will be friendly to man, whose property he will guard with faithfulness."

St. Peter said, "I know that in thy goodness thou art going again to help the devil, as thou hast done aforetime."

The devil had made many things aforetime, but could not give them life or movement, and it was always God who helped and completed the work. Thus the devil made a car, but built it inside the house, and did not know how to take it out and use it until God widened the door and took it out, and as the devil was pulling away at it he broke the hind wheels, so God took the first part of the car and put it in the heavens, and it forms the constellation known as the Great Bear (in Rumanian, the Great Car).

Then the devil made the mill, but he could not start it, so God did. Then he made a house, but put no light into it, so God had to make the windows. Then the devil made a fire, but did not know how to kindle it.

He was now working away at moulding the wolf from clay. He worked so hard that the perspiration ran down his face. Scratching his head, he pulled out three hairs, but would not throw anything away—they were much too precious—so he stuck them in the head of the wolf between the eyes.

When he thought he had finished, he turned to God and said, "See what I have done."

"Yes," replied God, "I see, but what is it?"

"Thou shalt know more about it soon," replied the devil; and, turning to the wolf, which lay there lifeless, he said, "Up, wolf, and go for him." But the wolf never stirred.

Then God turned to St. Peter and said, "Just wait and see how I will pay him out," and, waving his hand over the wolf, he said, "Up, wolf, and go for the devil."

The devil can run fast, but never ran faster than on that day when the wolf jumped up and ran after him. In running he jumped into the lake. He dipped under the waters and saved himself from the fangs of the wolf. And ever since that time, the wolf has power over the devil: when he catches him, he eats him up. All the year round the devils are hiding in pools and bogs, but, from the night of St. Basil (1st January) until the Feast of Epiphany, the waters are holy, being sanctified through the Baptism. The devil can no longer stay in the water, and he must get on to the land, where the wolf lies in wait for him, and woe unto the devils who get too near the wolf.

When God and St. Peter saw the flight of the devil, they laughed until the tears ran down their cheeks. Then God turned to St. Peter and said to him, "I give these wolves now into thy care." Poor St. Peter trembled from head to foot when he heard the charge that was given to him, but God reassured him and said, "Never fear, Peter, they will not harm thee; on the contrary, they will follow thee and listen to thy command, as if they were friendly dogs." And so it has remained. Once every year, on the day of the Feast of St. Peter, in the winter-time, all the wolves come together to an appointed place to meet St. Peter. Thither he comes with a huge book in his hand, in which are written the names of all the persons who had given themselves over to the devil, and he tells the wolves whom they are to eat.

The three hairs which the devil had put on the wolf are of a green colour, and make the wolf look ferocious, for they are the devil's hairs, and it is from them that the devil's fire got into the wolves' eyes, which are lit up by it.

❖❖❖

[And in another tale,] the devil went to God and said to him, "O Lord, thou hast created man and so many other creatures, but thou has not yet created the wolf." And God replied, "Very well," and, showing him a huge boulder near a forest, told him to go and say to the stone, "Devil, eat the stone." The devil went and said, "Stone, eat the wolf." The boulder did not move. The devil went to God and said, "The stone does not move." "What didst thou say?" "Stone, eat the wolf." "But thou must say, 'Devil, eat the stone.'" The devil went again to the stone and said, "Stone, eat the devil." Whereupon the stone moved and ate the devil, and in its place there stood a wolf with the face of the devil. Since then there are no more devils in the world, but wolves too many.

SERIOUS KILLING

THE eleven stories in this section cover the period from 1859 to 1931. Although by 1859 wolves had been long since been eliminated from many Eastern states, their populations were still relatively healthy in the West. It was there that the killing of wolves became a deadly serious business, and it was there that in the 1920s and '30s the few "renegade" wolves that escaped extermination became legends. This section begins with an extraordinary two-part history of "The War on the Wolf" that provides a chilling overview of this "lurid chapter" in the story of humans and wolves.

The question that lingers, even as we debate current issues of wolf management, is, Why kill wolves? "Hatred" is one simple, ready, and cumulative answer, but individually and collectively these stories reveal more particular reasons as well as a more generalized pattern of thinking. Wolves meant money to the authors of "A Very Profitable Business" and "Bidden to a Feast," so millions of strychnine-laden meatballs were scattered over the prairies to kill wolves without damaging their precious hides. Speed, strength, endurance, and intelligence were the attributes that also made wolves a grand game animal for sportsmen—as described in "Wolf Coursing." But it was the Western ranching community's view of wolves (and, we might say, their definition of the "wolf problem") that ultimately overshadowed all other perspectives. "Badlands Billy" chronicles the fight of one ranch to protect its livestock from wolves, and "The Home Life of the Big Wolves" explains the federal government's support of ranchers' interests. "The Wolf Tracker," "Last Stand of the Lobos," and "Ghost Wolf of the Little Belts" all detail the intensity with which wolves were eventually hunted and hated.

At the end of this period, even conservationists such as William T. Hornaday, renowned for his efforts to save the American bison, claimed, "The gray wolf should always be killed. No danger of his extermination." And the hatred was certainly well developed, as in "Old Three Legs," but it was accompanied, very curiously, by an antithetical admiration and pride that may have contributed in part to the emergence of a contrary view of wolves.

THE WAR ON THE WOLF—PART I
1942

 STANLEY P. Young was, like Ernest Thompson Seton, incurably fascinated with wolves. He had extensive field experience with the species, camping in their habitat and observing their ways—both as a scientist and as a "wolfer" who killed them to control their depredations on livestock. He believed in the necessity of killing wolves, but harbored enormous admiration for the animal. "Isn't it a pity the old boy can't change his ways so as to be more tolerated by man? But, on the other hand, if he did so, he just would not be a wolf." This lament is from Young's book, The Last of the Loners, *(New York: Macmillan, 1970), which describes some of the famous and final renegade stock-killers of the Western plains and the "virile hard-working" men who hunted them down.*

This is the first of a two-part history of America's wolf-extermination efforts that appeared in the November and December 1942 issues of American Forests. *It is an awesome and awful reflection of our relationship with nature. Part I covers the period from antiquity through the American colonial period; Part II brings the reader up to World War II.*

❖❖❖

From the beginning of recorded history, the peoples of many races inhabiting the greater part of the world have been at war with *Canis lupus*, more familiarly known as the big, bad wolf. When this conflict first began is buried in the dust of the ages, but the chances are that when man and wolf first met on the early hunting grounds it was war at first sight. For at least 2700 years the practice of mankind to reward wolf killers has been more or less continuous. Indeed, no other mammal over such a long period of time has been the object of so many legal acts stipulating tribute for its extirpation.

What this centuries-old conflict has cost man is incalculable. It is conservatively estimated that bounties paid for predatory animal control, including the wolf, in the United States, Canada and Mexico exceed $100,000,000. But this is insignificant when compared with the economic and social disruptions caused by wolf depredations. For example, it has been stated that wolves held back the development of the sheep industry in Virginia for the better part of the seventeenth century. Certainly their devastating raids seriously affected the expansion of livestock westward across the prairies. All told,

America's wolf problems have been so great and so threatening during the past 300 years it is safe to say that in no other country, in such a comparatively short time, have laws for the riddance of wolves been passed in such numbers or amended so frequently. Everything from hogs and tobacco to rum and gun powder, along with American, English and Mexican money, have figured in the items employed at various times to reward the killer of a wolf.

A long and costly Old World background in wolf control set the stage for the conflict which began almost as soon as the first settlers set foot on the North American continent—a conflict which has continued in one form or another up to the present day. In the beginning, the wolf and the puma, commonly called the panther, were the animals against which the pioneers pooled their efforts. Later, as development swept inland and westward, bobcats, coyotes and bears were added to the predators to be dealt with. But, up until recent years, *Canis lupus,* the big bad wolf, was the great and real enemy, not only directly to human life, but to human economic interests as well.

From what can be gleaned from available records, it was in ancient Greece that the wolf first had a price placed on his head. Or at least it was there that the wolf bounty plan is believed to have originated. It was in this early land, it will be recalled, that perfection in speed, strength, skill and endurance was rewarded by the payment of certain tributes. This was particularly true in the Isthmian and other games. The great range of the wolf as it foraged for food, compared with the small size of land areas in ancient Greece, plus a large wolf population, placed the Greeks in constant conflict with the animal. Tribute payment, being in vogue for many decades, was the most likely plan for controlling wolves.

Old Italy, too, had a reward or bounty plan for wolf killing, but it is recorded that it was seldom paid by the government. Instead, the hunter carried a wolf skin, proof of his prowess, from door to door, and, according to Douglas in *Old Calabria,* received a small present, "half a cheese or a glass of wine," from each householder.

Edgar, King of England, in effecting a treaty of peace with the King of North Wales in 965, levied a tribute of 300 wolves yearly to be paid him. King Henry III, during the half century following 1216, in an effort to rid portions of England of wolves, made grants of land to individuals who would work toward their destruction. This land donation was in reality a bounty for hunting wolves. Two centuries later, during the reign of Henry IV, land was given for the blowing of a horn to frighten wolves, as well as for chasing them.

In Scotland, during the twelfth century reign of William the Lion, the Monks of Melrose made a practice of setting wolf traps. A bounty of two shillings was given by James I in 1427 for the slaying of a wolf in a barony, payable by the baron. Thus the baron became a sort of head wolf hunter.

Ireland had its share of wolf infestations and depredations, which led to the breeding of the Irish wolf hound. The employment of these dogs, coupled with bounty payments, dealt the wolf population in that country a staggering blow. These excellent hounds became so proficient in hunting down wolves that by 1652 Oliver Cromwell issued an order forbidding their removal to the Continent, where they were much in demand.

With bounty plans of one kind or another in effect for so many centuries in Europe and the British Isles, it was to be expected that similar plans would be instituted in the early colonial possessions of the mother countries. Many of the colonists in North America were fully versed in the operations of bounty schemes, and they lost little time putting them into effect when livestock was introduced. It is recorded that in 1609, two years after the founding of Jamestown Colony, horses, cattle, sheep and swine were brought over from England. The cattle multiplied rapidly, largely because of legislation prohibiting their slaughter, but sheep suffered from the ravages of wolves. The same situation prevailed in the Plymouth Colony in Massachusetts, where the wolf was quickly and thoroughly outlawed. So thoroughly, in fact, that the colonial lawmakers of Massachusetts adopted the first bounty law in America—a law designed to exterminate the wolf. This was in 1630, two years before Virginia legalized payments for wolf killing. After Virginia, bounties were adopted by New York and Pennsylvania. The laws of these four states were subsequently used as models for the various wolf bounty acts adopted throughout North America.

Pennsylvania, under the governorship of William Penn, employed professional wolf hunters, probably the first in America. George Washington, desiring to increase and improve the American brand of sheep, expressed the viewpoint, to which Thomas Jefferson subscribed, that the eastern United States could never be a great sheep country because of the heavy infestation of wolves "which cannot be extirpated." In this he was partly right, for in the final analysis it was not the bounty killing of wolves that effected their final elimination so much as it was the destruction of their habitat.

The Massachusetts wolf bounty law was promulgated by "A Court of Assistants, holden att Boston, November 9th, 1630," whereby "It is ordered, that any Englishe man that killeth a wolfe in any pte within the lymitts of this pattent shall have allowed him ld (one penny) for euy beast & horse, & ob. (a half penny) for euy weaned swyne & goate iu euy plantacons. . . ."

This ingenious attempt to assess the bounty tax according to the number of domestic animals on a "plantacon" [plantation] was repealed in 1632. New laws followed, however, providing for an increase in bounty and giving encouragement to the killing of wolves by dogs. "Every man that kills a wolfe with hounds," ruled the General Court in 1640, "shall have 40s alowed him, & whosoever kils a wolfe with trap, peece, or other engine, shall have 10s alowed him, to bee paid by that towne where the wolfe is killed, & if hee bee kiled out of any towne bounds, it shalbee paid by the Treasurer."

This regulation remained in operation only eight months, chiefly, it appears, because of general dissatisfaction over the fact that any keeper of suitable hunting dogs was exempted from taxation for bounty payments.

A special inducement was offered Indian hunters in 1644 in the form of a bounty of one bushel of corn or three quarts of wine for each wolf killed, payable by the town constable, provided the Indian could prove that the wolf was taken within the town limits. The word *town*, of course, referred in those days to a geographical area that might contain several villages and many farms.

Apparently corn and wine were not too attractive to the Indian, for in 1645 it was observed that "great losse and damage doth befall ye comon wealth by reason of wolues." Therefore, it was ordered that any person "either English or Indian" be paid ten shillings for a wolf hide. At the same time various schemes were tried in sharing payment between the towns and the colony, or "county." In some cases, the treasurer of the colonial government paid the whole amount, in others the town was responsible, and under still another plan the responsibility was divided, the town paying two-thirds of each bounty.

The Indian, however, shared equal bounty privileges only for a short time. By 1648 the amount allowed the white man for each wolf was increased to thirty shillings; the red man was given but twenty. At the same time the Court provided for wolf dogs to be kept at public expense—probably the first authorization of its kind in North America. In this the selectmen of the towns were authorized to purchase with public funds as many wolfing dogs as they might choose. The authorities were to "impose the keeping of them" on whatever citizens they saw fit. No other dogs were to be allowed in town except by the selectmen's permission. An interesting provision was added that no magistrate could be compelled to give up his dog, nor could he be forced to harbor any of the wolf hounds.

The variety of these enactments tried out in the first eighteen years of the existence of the General Court, give ample evidence of wolf depredations in the early days of the Massachusetts Bay Colony. Twelve separate pieces of legislation relative to bounty payments were adopted during this period in an effort to destroy the wolves. And more were to follow. In fact, bounty laws on wolves remained in effect almost continuously for more than two centuries after 1661.

The reward for each grown wolf increased to $15 for most of the sixty-year period from 1780 to 1840. Payment was made to claimants by the towns, which were reimbursed by the treasurer of the province. Under the law of 1817, this state bounty could be supplemented by additions from the treasury of any town through action of the voters at regular town meetings.

The Massachusetts code of 1860 provided that towns might vote such sums as "they judge necessary . . . for encouraging the destruction of 'noxious animals.'" This permissive regulation is included also in the code of 1882, after which date the nuisance of "noxious animals," including wolves, seems to have declined to the point where legislation was no longer necessary.

Virginia lawmakers, comparable to those of Massachusetts, changed the wolf bounty act many times as the colony increased in population, as well as in numbers of its livestock. Of all the states, including also all of the Canadian provinces, Virginia has had wolf bounties upon its statute books for the longest time—from 1652 to 1939—a period of 308 years.

The original wolf bounty laws for the Virginia colony are unique. The first, enacted by the Grand Assembly on September 4, 1632, at James City, as present-day Jamestown was known, provided that "Noe man shall kill any wild swyne out of the forrest or woods . . . without leave or lycense from the Governor. But it is thought convenient that any man be permitted to kill deare or other wild beasts or fowls in the common woods, forrests, or rivers in regard that thereby the inhabitants may be trained in the use of theire armes, the Indians kept from our plantations, and the wolves and other vermin destroyed. And for encouragement to destroy the wolves, it is thought that whosoever shall kill a wolfe, and bringe in his head to the commander, it shall be lawfull for such person or persons for every wolfe soe kild, to kill also one wild hogg and take the same for his owne use."

In these early days of the Jamestown Colony hogs and other livestock ran wild, receiving no special care. They were considered community property and only under certain conditions or when times were particularly hard were they permitted to be taken for essential meat. Therefore, the right to kill one wild hog from this livestock sanctuary as compensation for killing a wolf played an important part in the Virginia bounty scheme—for a time.

In 1646, the colonists either lost their taste for pork or meat generally was plentiful, for the Assembly was moved to order that "Whereas many losses are lately received by the inhabitants by reason of wolves which do haunt and frequent their plantations; for the better prevention and for the destroying of them, it is inacted that what person soever shall after publication hereof kill a wolfe and bring in the head to any commissioner upon certificate of the said commissioner to the county court he or they shall receive one hundred pounds of tob'o. for soe doeing to bee raysed out of the county where the wolf is killed."

Since tobacco was by far the most widely used currency in Virginia at that time, it would seem that its use in payment for wolf killing was effective, for it continued in use for a century and a half. Not until 1744 was a cash payment offered—six shillings for an old wolf and two shillings, six pence for a young one. The tax to meet these awards could be collected in money or in grain. A bounty payable in dollars does not appear until 1798, when seven counties were permitted to offer $4 for an old wolf, $2 for a young one, and eight other counties were allowed bounties of $10 and $5.

Another plan tried in Virginia was an assessment or order on the Indians to capture a specified number of wolves during the year. Seventeen groups of Indians, estimated to have 725 hunters, were "enjoyned and assessed to bring..." 145 wolves annually for a reward of 100 pounds of tobacco a wolf. This scheme was adopted in 1668, but was discarded the following year since it had "not produced the effects as were hoped and desired." No statement is included as to whether the red men resented the compulsion or were just not interested in the hopes and desires of the colonists.

On more than sixty different occasions, over a period of three centuries, Virginia legislators passed laws looking to the extermination of wolves. Twenty-six of these were enacted during the colonial era, and the others after statehood was attained. In numerous instances the regulations were set up for particular counties or groups of counties. During the last hundred years, as one would suppose, the bounties applied chiefly to the western parts of the state in the Blue Ridge and Allegheny regions.

Though special regulations for different counties were common, in 1810 the legislature decided that it should "be lawful for every county to allow such reward as the necessity of the case may require." Thus permissive bounties became statewide. Except for one seven-year period, the expense of bounty payments was borne by the county where the wolf was taken.

It was in 1683, a half century after Massachusetts and Virginia had legally organized against wolf depredations, that New York and Pennsylvania adopted bounty plans. New York began by offering twenty shillings for each wolf killed on Long Island, though other sections were soon included and the tribute increased. From 1683 to 1898, regulations regarding bounty payments on wolves were adopted by the State legislature or the Colonial Assembly on sixty different occasions. At least twenty-five such laws were given trial by the Colony before 1776, the amounts offered for each wolf varying from six shillings to $40.

Attempts at fraud and trickery in connection with bounty payments were frequent, not only in New York but in the other colonies as well. As an example of this, one authority writes:

"A man by the name of Ellsworth once made a pit-fall with a bait or decoy upon it. . . . On the morning of a town-meeting he found in it a she-wolf with six whelps, supposed to have had their birth after the bitch had fallen in. He left them where he found them and went to the town-meeting, where he made an animated discourse upon the mischievous depredations of these animals; stated in glowing colours the losses and the terrors of the farmers and finished by proposing a bounty such as might encourage some enterprising spirits to devote themselves entirely, and with zeal, to their destruction. His eloquence was popular and successful. The bounty was doubled; next morning he went with a neighbor to examine his pitfall and taking the seven scalps claimed and received for each, the augmented recompense."

Pennsylvania, under William Penn, offered a bounty of ten shillings for a dead wolf, but it is evident that this action was not sufficient to cope with their depredations. As a consequence, in 1705, twenty-four years after Pennsylvania became a colony, the early lawmakers legalized the employment of professional wolf hunters, their fee to be raised by taxation of the people. This is believed to be the first such provision in North America.

These hunters, many of whom were picturesque characters, devoted all of their time to wolf killing as required by the law. Their efforts during the seventy-odd years their employment was provided for had much to do with the wolf's eventual elimination from that state.

Thus during the crucial pioneering period along the Atlantic seaboard, did the North American wolf war get under way in earnest. It continued into the early part of the twentieth century with thirty-nine states and territories sanctioning bounty laws. By 1937 only Alaska and twelve states offered tribute for wolf killing, mainly because the animal had disappeared from much of its original habitat. Canada, in 1940, also repealed the wolf bounty in the Northwest Territories, although most of the provinces still have bounty laws, as do several of the Mexican states.

But between 1705, when Pennsylvania employed the first wolf hunter, and 1937, when the wolf was becoming a rare creature, there is a long and bloody trail—a trail that led across the Mississippi onto the Great Plains, over the Rocky Mountains and finally into the domain of the Far West. It is a trail blazed with rifles and set guns, wolf pens and pits, wooden and steel traps, snares and strychnine—particularly strychnine. And it is a trail littered with the bleaching skeletons of sheep and cattle, for the wolf, grown more wary as hunters, trappers and poison crews pressed him on every side, fought back savagely to the bitter end.

THE WAR ON THE WOLF—PART II
1942

 ALTHOUGH he adequately conveyed the enormity of America's wolf extermination efforts in this two-part magazine account, Stanley P. Young also wrote two exhaustive accounts of the subject, massively researched and documented. The Wolf in North American History *(Caldwell, Idaho: Caxton Printers, 1946) is a very readable examination of the wolf in colonial, frontier, and Old West America, as well as various control measures and government involvement.* The Wolves of North America *(New York: Dover, 1944) is a 600-page tome that covers "history, life habits, economic status, control, and classification" of wolves. Young, a senior biologist with the U.S. Fish and Wildlife Service, was well qualified to produce these books, which have become classics.*

This is the second part of the history of the war on the wolf that appeared in American Forests *in 1942; it covers the period from the mid-1800s to World War II, which Young calls "one of the strangest and most lurid chapters in the history of killing mammals."*

❖❖❖

For more than three centuries North American wolves have taken a heavy toll of livestock. George Washington, as previously noted, felt their depredations so keenly that he believed they could not be extirpated. Many years later, Theodore Roosevelt, with his eyes on the great range country of the West, termed the wolf "a veritable scourge to the stockman." And during this period of America's development, from its first to its twenty-sixth president, the costly and bloody North American wolf war raged unabated across the continent.

Driven beyond the Mississippi River not so much by the guns and traps of man as by the destruction of its habitat, the wolf met the trailblazing trapper and stockman at the edge of the prairie. There, also, it met strychnine—in vast quantities. As a ready weapon in the hands of profit-seeking pelt hunters and enraged stockmen, it was this deadly fruit of an East Indian tree, *Nux vomica*, which in the end had much to do with defeating the wolf. It also caused great losses in the ranks of other wildlife, the chief victims being coyotes, foxes and skunks, though many birds, particularly hawks, eagles and ravens, likewise fell before the strychnine onslaught. Indeed, it was through the unrestricted use of this poisonous drug that conservation suffered one of its early blows in the Great Plains region.

The use of strychnine as a means of killing noxious mammals and birds did not, of course, originate with the American trapper or stockman. Its toxic properties in eliminating so-called unwanted animals were known and used in the Old World several decades after the first colonial settlements in North America. According to one authority, *nux vomica*, also known as the Quaker or bachelor button, poison nut, dog button, or vomiting bean, was primarily used in England at that time to kill dogs and cats and also "crowes, ravens and other suchlike troublesome birds that by their noyse disquiet mans sleepe or studies."

To what extent it was imported and used for poisoning mammals in colonial America is not definitely known. Carney, one of the few authorities to shed light on the subject, believes the drug was used extensively. Another authority writes that in Pennsylvania "many wolves were poisoned by stuffing the hide of a lamb with lard, in which was hidden *nux vomica*." Whatever the extent of its use, it was insignificant when compared with that phase of the wolf war which began on the edge of the prairie. By 1860 strychnine was being employed in many and devious ways on Canadian as well as United States territorial lands from Texas to the Arctic.

Unlike the early days along the Atlantic seaboard, it was the value of wolf pelts and not the depredations of the animals that in the beginning accounted for the great number killed on the prairie. The trapper, trekking westward ahead of the stockman, turned to wolf skins when the beaver supply diminished and found, much to his surprise, a ready market for them. For the first time in the history of the western fur trade, wolf skins became valuable and in great demand—chiefly for robes and as overcoats for soldiers. With a market thus established, trappers set out to increase their kill, well armed with strychnine, then readily available.

With this began one of the strangest and most lurid chapters in the history of killing mammals such as wolves, not to mention the lesser animals. It seems unlikely that it was ever exceeded in North America unless by the slaughter that took place in the case of the buffalo and the antelope. Not only was the former trapper of beaver enabled to make a fair living at this new vocation, but, from 1860 to 1885 when the killing of wolves was at its peak, he was joined by others. The homesteader tried his hand, as did soldiers mustered out of service at western army posts. Still others were attracted to wolf poisoning because they considered it a thrilling game. All were given a free hand in this pursuit for, apparently, no western state or territory forbade the use of strychnine in destroying wild animals.

Some conception of the kills made with strychnine may be found in the volume *The Life and Adventure of George W. Brown*. In this it is recorded that from one poisoned buffalo carcass on the Kansas plains "thirteen big gray wolves, fifteen coyotes and about forty skunks" were taken in one night.

The killing of buffalo to bait *Canis lupus* seems to have been the rule on the prairie. Webb records the story of two conductors of mail from Independence to Santa Fe who did a thriving winter business in taking wolves for their pelts. "They would kill a buffalo," he wrote, "and cut the meat in small pieces, which were scattered in all directions a half mile or so from camp, and so bait the wolves for about two days. Meanwhile, all hands were preparing meat in pieces about two inches square . . . putting a quantity of strychnine in the center. When a sufficient amount was prepared, and the wolves were well baited, they would put out the poisoned meat. One morning after putting out the poison they picked up sixty-four wolves, and none of them over a mile and a half from camp. The proceeds from that winter's hunt were over four thousand dollars."

During the winter of 1861, three soldiers mustered out of the Army in Colorado Territory moved over into Kansas and, with the aid of strychnine, took more than 3,000 wolves, coyotes and swift foxes. The entire kill netted them $2,500—the value of the wolves being $1.25 a pelt, the coyotes seventy-five cents, and the foxes twenty-five cents a skin.

But the bag of these early westerners, great as it may seem, was small when compared with the kill of professional wolf poisoners, better known as "wolfers." These successors to the fur trapper were tough, capable, fearless,—plying their hazardous trade in a manner that was ruthless, spreading death over the width and breadth of the prairie country. Unlike the non-professionals—the ex-soldiers, homesteaders and thrill-seekers—they applied the strychnine sulphate crystals with great efficiency and with considerable more effect. Quite often it was mixed in water to the consistency of loose paste and poured under the skins of slain buffalo or antelope. The results were ghastly. Even birds, such as the junco or horned lark, were killed and used for bait, the super-saturated solution of strychnine inserted beneath the skin along the breast-bone. These morsels of death were then scattered along wolf runways.

Perhaps no better description of this picturesque character of the early West is found than that given by Taylor.

"With a full knowledge of his game," he wrote, "the wolfer rigs up an outfit similar to that of the hunter or the trapper with the exception of traps and baits. In place of these, he supplies himself liberally with strychnine poison. If it was in the autumn, he moved slowly in the wake of a buffalo herd, making open camp, and shooting down a few of the beasts. . . . After ripping them open, saturating their warm blood and intestines with from one to three bottles of strychnine to each carcass . . . he makes a camp in a ravine or coulee and prepares for the morrow.

"With the first glimmer of light in the eastern sky, he rises, makes his fire, and cooks his coffee, then hitches up, if he has a team, or saddles up if with packs, and follows his line to the finish. Around each buffalo carcass will probably be from three to a dozen dead wolves."

The most frequented winter grounds of the professional wolfers on the southern plains were described as along the Republican and Smoky Hill rivers of western Kansas, and "the country about the neighborhood of the Staked Plains in Northern Texas." The northern wolfers found their best grounds "along the Milk Musselshell and Judith rivers, and around the Bear Paw Mountains of Montana, and the Peace River country in Manitoba."

The northern wolfers had the "business well systemized," Taylor wrote, "and while many lost their lives by Indian hostility, and the exposure incident to that kind of life, yet many of them made small fortunes at times, but an infatuation born of the calling held them as in a serpent's charm until some reverse in his affairs left him where he began—in vigorous poverty."

The Indians had an especial antipathy to the wolfers, he stated. "Poisoned wolves and foxes in their dying fits often slobber upon the grass, which becoming sun dried holds its poisonous properties a long time, often causing the death months or even years after of the pony, antelope, buffalo or animals feeding upon it. The Indians losing their stock in this way feel like making reprisals, and often did."

A dramatic example of the wolf kills that took place is given by Fouquet who records visiting near Sun City, Kansas, at the mouth of Turkey Creek, a little cave village of buffalo and wolf hunters that was in existence during

1871. He states: "Not far above this cave village was a road going through the swampy creek valley, about seventy-five yards wide, and this had been artistically and scientifically paved with gray wolf carcasses and I drove over this bone road several times."

Batty, who was an official hunter and taxidermist connected with the Hayden Government Surveys, was of the opinion that these wolfers "are Yankees and half-breeds, and are brave and courageous beyond expression. . . . Remote from civilization, deeply drifted in with snow, they can scarcely travel, and often wonder how life will be sustained for the winter; but their pluck seems to keep them alive until spring dawns on them and their half-starved ponies."

The prowess of the professional wolfer, ably assisted by the non-professional, had by 1885 reduced the wolf population in many prairie regions. Also, there was modification of the former wolf habitat, due chiefly to farming and fencing as the lands came into private ownership. But the stockman had his wolf troubles and for more than a quarter century employed every means at his command, including strychnine, to rid the range of this menace.

Indeed, the conflict between the wolf and livestock never ceased after the first herds were brought to Jamestown in 1609. Before the advent of the wolfer, herds being driven along the western trails and livestock raised in the vicinity of the early trading posts and forts, were raided almost daily by the gaunt, savage animals. Eye-witness accounts of these early attacks, these first skirmishes of the western phase of the North American wolf war, are vividly given by early writers.

For example, Theodore Talbert, while in Wyoming in 1843 recorded: "We surprised a pack of large white wolves who had just succeeded in hamstringing a fine Durham bull. The poor fellow fought manfully, but numbers had overpowered him. This sagacious mode by which the wolves disable their prey has been frequently discredited, but here we saw an undoubted proof of its truth."

Audubon, on his voyage up the Missouri River during the same year observed that wolves were "extremely abundant" and "troublesome to the farmer who owned sheep, calves, young goats, or any other stock on which these ravenous beasts fed. . . . They will pursue and kill mules and colts even near a trading post, always selecting the fattest. The number of tracks or rather paths made by the wolves from among and around the hills to that station are almost beyond credibility, and it is curious to observe their sagacity in choosing the shortest course and most favorable ground in travelling."

Edwin Brant, following the immigrant trails to the Far West, made the following observation: "Oxen when footsore or exhausted by fatigue, are left by the immigrants, and immediately become the victims of wolves . . . Domesticated animals unprotected cannot resist the attacks of wolves, urged on as they are by their appetites and conducting their warfare with all the skill of instinct sharpened often by famine. The deer and antelope are compelled frequently to shelter themselves from the attacks of these animals under the strong protection of buffalos and antelope grazing together."

During this same period, Daniel W. Jones, coming east from Salt Lake City, "to render succor and aid" to a party of Mormons that was stranded on the immigrant trail, gives further evidence of early wolf peril. On reaching the party, he discovered that the cattle being driven westward were in poor shape, more than 200 head having already died. Their carcasses led "droves of prairie wolves into our camp," he recorded, "and it was almost impossible to keep them off from the cattle in the daytime . . . Once in the daytime a small bunch was taken and run off in spite of the efforts of the herders to stop them. In fact, it became dangerous to chase these wolves—they were at times almost ready to attack men. We soon found it impossible to save the cattle, and it was decided to kill them, some fifty head."

Thus, even in the beginning of the western livestock industry when herds were few and often well guarded, wolves were taking a heavy toll. The professional wolfer, beginning his era around 1860, helped considerably for a quarter century, but during this period the industry became firmly established, reaching out to the far corners of the grass country. Historic cattle trails, among which was that known in plains history as the Chisholm Trail, came into prominence. And with every new drive, with every new range opened up, the wolf, now driven westward and northward, fought back ferociously.

When the buffalo was eliminated from the grassland, bringing the wolf into direct competition with the producers of prairie cattle, it became a war to the bitter end. Every known means at the livestock producer's disposal—guards, guns, traps, poison, bounties, and enclosures—were employed as defense against wolf depredations. This vengeance on the wolf was due in the main to a psychological twist so noticeable among many of the western cattlemen. Disease could decimate his flocks and herds, or drought or severe winters could result in starvation or extreme loss by death, but none of these factors aroused his resentment and determination to kill as did the raiding of livestock corrals by wolves or kills made on the open range. And perhaps there was justification, for these losses by the cattlemen were among the most severe with which the open range industry had to contend during its development. The wolf, of course, seeking a substitute for its buffalo diet, quite naturally turned to beef cattle, bringing all of its killing traits into play.

In the heat of battle, the use of strychnine for wolf control became a major scheme of defense. A sort of range law was adopted whereby no ranch man would knowingly pass up a dead carcass without first inserting a goodly dose of strychnine, in hopes of eventually killing a wolf or two. The hazard of such a plan to other forms of wildlife was not apparent to the stock interests at the time. The predominating thought was to get the wolf at any and all means possible. Coincidental with this was the development of many wolf coursing dogs. Theodore Roosevelt wrote of these greyhounds and deerhounds, "One of the most famous packs in the West was that of the Sun River Hound Club of Montana, started by the stockmen of Sun River to get rid of the curse of wolves which infested the neighborhood and worked very serious damage to the herds and flocks."

With many of the cattle interests, particularly toward the close of the nineteenth century and the early 1900's, lack of profits in keeping with the investments made, seems to have given greater impetus to wolf control. Stock associations, state and county wolf bounties began to appear. Also some counties offered strychnine free to all who would use it. As a consequence, many, including a great number of cowboys, entered into the scheme of poisoning wolves.

Losses to the sheep industry from wolves were in many cases just as severe as in the cattle industry. In the former, however, coyotes supplemented the depredations by wolves. Dr. T. S. Palmer estimates that in 1892, in New Mexico, where sheep were valued at $4,556,000, such losses varied from three to seven per cent; in Nebraska the value of sheep was about $2,000,000, while the losses amounted to five per cent; and sheep owners in central Texas suffered losses to the extent of from ten to twenty-five per cent.

One of the foremost among those versed in the livestock problem at the time was the late Senator Thomas B. Kendrick of Wyoming. Commenting on the wolf menace, he said, "Between the time of the breeding season of one year and the spring roundups of the next season, even with a mild winter, and where there were infinitesimal losses from other sources, the grey wolf destroyed sometimes as high as fifty per cent of the calf crops within those months.

"I have never yet been quite able to estimate the number of cattle that a grey wolf will destroy within the period of a year's time. Neither have I ever been able to estimate the price that a ranchman could afford to pay for the destruction of a grey wolf.

Recently I have received quite a few letters from university people insisting, as I recall, on moderate action in connection with the extermination of predatory animals, but I am unable to conceive of anyone making that plea who had a personal acquaintance with either the terrific disaster wrought upon herds and flocks by wolves and coyotes or with the method employed by these animals in connection with the destruction of their prey. It is the most barbarous thing imaginable. No doubt, the motives of these people are the best, but I believe they are uninformed of the extent of the depredations.

"Nothing in my opinion has ever been imposed—I mean no injurious influence—upon the stockmen of the West that is equal to the destruction of the grey wolf and the coyote."

The clash that was increasing in volume during the late 90's and early 1900's between livestock interests and the predator problem brought demands to the Biological Survey (now Fish and Wildlife Service) for investigations that would ultimately bring some system of definite predator control into being. Practically all of the western states and many of the counties by this time had tried bounties—some with disastrous financial results—and it was felt that this plan was far from adequate.

Field naturalists of the Survey made investigations of the problem in connection with both the livestock and wild game angle of predator depredations, particularly with regard to the wolf. These investigations led to a number of published reports by the Department of Agriculture, one of which, "Key to Animals on Which Wolf and Coyote Bounties are Often Paid," issued in 1909, was later used to aid the states in reducing some of the fraud apparent in bounties, where all sorts of scalps from other than wolves and coyotes were being submitted for payment. At this time the Biological Survey also found losses from wolves and other predators could be prevented only by intelligent and concerted action throughout the predator-infested livestock country. It was revealed that in early spring the breeding dens of wolves could be located and the young destroyed at small expense. The application of this discovery in connection with scent baits for trapping adult wolves on the livestock ranges and other information obtained in previous field work, resulted in an immediate saving of stock valued at $1,000,000.

Further impetus was given wolf control when fees were collected by the government for the privilege of grazing stock on western national forests. The stock interests felt and so forcibly expressed the sentiment that it was unfair to collect a grazing fee when a forest area was heavily infested with wolves and other predators, that the Forest Service ordered its field officers, particularly the forest rangers, to carry on wolf trapping operations. These measures afforded some means of relief but there still remained large areas of public domain upon which no wolf control was attempted or if so, only in a haphazard manner. Consequently, on many national forests the effective wolf control that was done by the rangers afforded only temporary relief, due to wolf reinfestation from the surrounding lands.

Between 1907 and 1914, state and county bounties were continued, privately employed trappers took to the field, using every known method, including much poison, and finally national recognition of the predator problem was achieved. This recognition, and the fact that the federal government had a large interest in the problem, caused Congress to lend an ear to the financial pleadings of western stockmen.

Consequently, on July 1, 1915, the first appropriation specifically providing federal funds to assist in organizing predator control was made. This appropriation of $125,000 also provided for correlation of agencies at work on the problem.

Throughout the intervening years, many of the states have repealed their bounty laws, so by 1938 few remained upon the statute books. In lieu of these, the states have made modest appropriations through legislation directing cooperation with the federal government. These cooperative measures have been further supplemented by direct assessments of livestock associations and contributions from private stockmen and farmers, either in the way of cash or donated labor and material. The promiscuous and oft-times ill use of poison by the stock interests in predator control has practically become a thing of the past, due mainly to the hazards that were involved in its earlier unwise and unscientific application. Improvement in trapping technique has brought many worth-while humane devices for capture—a direct aid to conservation.

The wolf has been definitely brought under control, and exists today in North America as a very minor problem affecting man's interests, with the possible exception, at times, of portions of Texas, Arizona, New Mexico, Oklahoma, Missouri, Louisiana, Alaska, and the Canadian North. Where not in conflict with human interests, wolves may well be left alone. They form one of the most interesting groups of all mammals, and should be permitted to have a place in North American fauna.

Fortunately, wolves still exist in many areas where there is no conflict with human interests. Such areas, it is believed, will perpetuate the existence of these interesting mammals, unless they are crowded out by further development. This will not be for a long time to come, if ever.

A VERY PROFITABLE BUSINESS
1859

 JAMES R. Mead's first enterprise when he arrived in Kansas in 1859 was trading wagon loads of goods to the Indians and poisoning wolves to sell their pelts. Within a few years, this energetic young entrepreneur became one of the founders of Wichita, "encouraging immigration, developing the townsite, promoting the cattle trade, establishing banks, luring railroad companies, encouraging newspapers, and building bridges, sawmills, grain mills, hotels, and fine homes." Like others of his era, he realized later in life that "he had been part of something that was gone forever." This excerpt about poisoning wolves is from his "reminiscences of frontier life," Hunting and Trading on the Great Plains, 1859-1875 *(Schuyler Jones, ed., Norman: University of Oklahoma Press, 1986).*

Poison, an old remedy for predators, came west with the first white people. Anthropologist Richard K. Nelson says that Alaska's Chalkyitsik Kutchin Indians "seem to fear and despise it because poison is extremely dangerous for user and animal alike. In the words of one old man, 'Poison never dies.' Any animal that eats a poisoned bait will die; scavengers which feed on animals killed by the poison will be killed in turn, and so on, until hundreds of animals may eventually die from one poison set." But its use in the frontier West proliferated. Just as beaver pelts had been valuable in the 1820s, other furs, including wolf, brought the most money in the 1860s; wolf pelts were used as robes and overcoats for soldiers, according to Stanley P. Young's "The War on the Wolf." Thus the fur trade continued its crucial impact on the North American landscape, building commercial empires, extending white settlement, strangling Native American cultures, and devastating wildlife populations.

❖❖❖

In the Autumn of 1863, I outfitted from my trading post at Towanda a number of Butler County citizens and sent them out on hunting expeditions. I furnished them with arms, provisions, ammunition, and whatever else they lacked—which was nearly everything—and they paid me on their return out of furs and skins they secured on the trip. I also supplied their families during their absence with any provisions which they might need. The parties I equipped for wolf hunting mostly came back empty.

The buffalo did not winter on the unprotected treeless plains which extended further than our knowledge. Their trails led to the Southwest to some country unknown to us, and with the advent of Winter, they departed after the fashion of wild geese. The wolves, of course, went with them. As our hunters did not feel safe in venturing more than fifty miles West of the Arkansas into the apparently limitless, blizzard-swept, Indian haunted, inhospitable plains they found nothing. I was impatient at their lack of success. My curiosity as to where the buffalo went was aroused and I began to have the hunting fever which usually came on after I had been home a month or two. I had unlimited confidence in my ability to find game and put to shame the fellows I had sent out. . . .

We started out in January, 1864, following the Osage Trail to the Arkansas. . . .

We halted on a high bank while I rode across into the timber to select a suitable camping ground. Dismounting with the bridle on my arm, I had gone but a few steps in the brush when I saw a dozen fine deer looking at me not a hundred feet distant. I raised my rifle, fully expecting to kill two or three of them, as they were so close together. Just as I pulled the trigger, my pony jerked my arm and the bullet flew wide of the mark. We had hardly driven across the river and unhitched when four big gray wolves came out on the high bank about a hundred yards distant and leisurely inspected camp, curious to know what this strange intrusion into their country meant, and they found out in a day or two. We did not wish to disturb them. . . .

I returned to camp satisfied that we had found the winter home of the game we were in search of—a country unknown to white hunters and seldom occupied by Indians. Riding a short distance below camp to the junction of the rivers, I shot two big buffalo bulls and, splitting them open to attract the wolves, left them as they lay, taking only that choicest bit of all, the tongues. I scattered about a few baits for the benefit of the coyotes that are always on hand when an animal has been killed.

That night we sat round our camp fire well-pleased with the prospect: plenty of game, no Indians, no hunters to bother us, and a new and unknown country to explore. Even the rivers we had discovered had no place on the map. None of us smoked—the fire did enough of that—nor drank, except coffee. We were happy and content. Fulton and Carter were then in the prime of life, full of energy and fire, and as pleasant, genial companions as could be wished.

In the morning after breakfast I rode down to see how my two bulls were getting along and to my astonishment found them gone. Where they had been were two bunches of chewed grass about the size of a bushel basket. On looking around I saw a head some distance off, but all else—legs, hide, bones—and all, were gone. A short distance away were sand hills and on these were gangs of gray wolves lying down enjoying the warm morning sun. My two bulls were inside them; they had good appetites as well as we. The half dozen coyotes my bait had killed were torn to pieces and eaten by eagles and ravens. On riding toward the gray wolves, they lazily trotted off South on the prairie. I counted forty in one string. That was an interesting sight under any circumstances, but especially so as I knew their pelts would all be in our possession within two or three days.

I immediately returned to camp and we soon arranged our plan of action. Fulton went up the creek a couple of miles and killed three bulls. Carter went up the river and killed two, while I went down the river two or three miles and out on the bare prairie South of the river shot five buffalo. Returning to camp we prepared our "medicine," using eight dram bottles of strychnine, which should make 240 baits. A bait for wolves, such as we used, is a small piece of meat—two or three ounces—on which is rubbed one thirtieth of a dram of strychnine. At dusk each man went to his carcasses. The ravens would pick them up if put out before they had gone to roost, and the coyotes that came first would get them all if too easily found. So we hid them about in various places, some in and some under the dead buffalo in order that the big grays might have a show when they came round later.

That night we went to bed with great anticipations which were fully realized on the morrow. By daylight each man was on the way to his carcasses, leaving the camp to take care of itself. On reaching my baits, I saw dead wolves scattered over the prairie in all directions. Tying my pony to a buffalo head, I rapidly stripped off the hides. While at work, the coyotes, with their usual curiosity, came trotting up close. I shot five of them as I worked, scarcely delaying me five minutes. Towards noon I packed on my pony all the skins he could carry and led him to camp. No sign of Fulton or Carter, which was good evidence that they too were busy. I ate a hasty dinner and went back to "wolfing," finishing with another pony load.

I hunted up, skinned, and packed to camp that day 34 wolves, while Fulton and Carter came in with enough to make our number 72 for one day's killing. Next in order was to dry our skins, which was done by pegging them out on the ground, stretching them as tight as a drum. As each skin required 24 pegs there were from this day's work 1,728 pegs to be made and driven through an equal number of holes in the edge of the skins. We put our baits out and killed 20 or 30 more that night. . . .

[A few days later] we moved camp down to the mouth of the big sand creek near two bulls I had killed. At dusk Fulton and I went to put out baits, wading through the loose sand. On approaching the bulls there was such a gang of gray wolves at work that we could not see the carcasses until the wolves had trotted off. One big fellow, that was all inside except his tail, was too busy to notice us. As I stepped close to him he backed out, pulling at some choice bit he had hold of, and backed almost against me. With one stroke of my hunting knife I split him nearly in two lengthwise. He whirled, snapped at his assailant, ran a short distance and fell dead. We put out our baits and in the morning found fifty gray wolves lying about, some of them nearly buried by the drifting sand.

At the end of ten days' hunting we found that the grain for our horses was about gone. Big American horses could not live on the range like Texas or Indian horses and oxen. We did not care to tempt fortune further. We had 302 wolves, some buffalo, and other skins—all our team could conveniently haul—so we started for Towanda, taking a bee-line across the country . . . . Our furs reached market at a time of exceptionally high prices, and we realized $70 for each day spent on the hunting ground.

BIDDEN TO A FEAST
1876

FROM Brooklyn, L. S. Kelly penned this letter to the editor of Forest and Stream, *who published it on February 20, 1897. He recounts experiences he had in Montana some twenty years earlier—an era of widespread slaughter of wildlife in the West.* Forest and Stream, Field and Stream, Hunter-Trader-Trapper, *and other outdoor magazines of the time provided informative articles for sportsmen and a forum for readers to share their experiences. These widely read journals also helped generate game laws and disseminate a code of ethics for hunters, trappers, and anglers.*

❖❖❖

In days long gone by I have watched the large gray wolves that follow bands of buffalo, and their actions while on the move so closely resemble the fashion of a war party of wild Indians marching across the breaks of a rolling prairie country that the sight has more than once afforded me entertainment. There was little amusement, however, in watching a war party, but more of concern and anxiety.

The wolf will trot along the sheltered edge of a ridge or swell of land, pausing now and then to peer about him and survey the country, his companions meanwhile (and I have seen them in packs of fifty or more) trotting noiselessly on in advance, with uplifted heads in movement of wild grace that was significant of the roving habit, fixed with the remorseless craving to satisfy the inner wolf.

The "Okshena Duta"—red boys of the plains—imitative by instinct, utilize professionally the sly proclivities of the wolf, fox and panther.

I once came suddenly upon two gray wolves at a buffalo carcass. They instantly broke away in opposite directions, paused a moment at the exact distance to take a wild look at me, then disappeared in the gulches.

At another time we were pursuing "bad" Indians, who had counted *coup* on Custer and his men. The pursuit had reached the Yellowstone River, and Bull Eagle, with most of his tribe, was on the opposite side. Our half-breed interpreter, Billy, had managed to parley with three or four wild-eyed Sioux braves, who had been hanging on the flank of the column, and three of us rode up in a friendly way toward them. In response to Billy's promises they waited for us, but when we were almost close enough to shake hands the wild instinct of the savage nature, never in repose, flashed out on a sudden, and they broke away in the same manner as the wolves, only they kept their eyes on us as their swift ponies carried them away. Our commander was a little bit mad, thinking an important conference had been interrupted; but it turned out all right.

At that day—1876—wolves had become very scarce in Montana, and, as a consequence, the buffalo and other game increased in numbers. In the few years that followed the cessation of active hostilities, the buffalo had disappeared before the accurate aim of the professional skin hunters, who came into that country from the South.

It is in stormy weather that the wolf appears to be in his element; the unearthly chorus, ringing all the changes of the gamut, startles the hunter in camp or the traveler by night. A wolf delights in getting on some point of rock in a storm and howling in unison with the blast that sweeps through the gulches or cañons of the foothills. The wild dogs that infest Indian camps howl in chorus like the wolves, and it requires an expert to distinguish between the two.

About twenty-two years ago Flat Willow Creek, which runs south of the Judith Basin, Montana, into the Musselshell, was a pretty wild-looking country. We pitched camp there one winter's day in a very respectable and commodious-looking Sioux war house, built, tepee fashion, of dry poles and chinked fairly tight with broken slabs and sticks of cottonwood. We were after wolves, foxes and beaver.

In the afternoon I sallied out by myself to take a look at the country. Before me were the dark gulches of the Musselshell, topped by cedar-covered buttes that looked far away toward the Yellowstone. Crossing some little prairies and creeks, I came to a flat that had once been the home of a village of prairie dogs, and on a rise beyond it I saw a buffalo cow standing alone.

I maneuvered for some time to get close enough for a shot. When I looked again the cow had lain down. The point was rather difficult of approach, and I was crawling along low ground, when I saw two large wolves trot up to the cow in feint of attack, the cow getting up and lowering her head to repel them. It was then that I saw she was lame in one leg. The wolves sat down in the most impudent way and watched her. I presume these wolves had followed the cow some distance.

After a while they left the cow and trotted around to where I was partly concealed, and surveyed me with great curiosity from several points, coming within 15 yds. or nearer. I made no move for fear of disturbing the cow. I did not care about the wolves, although they were about as large as any I had seen. I have never heard of wolves attacking people in the Northwest. They soon left me and returned to the cow, and edging a little closer I pulled up my .44 Winchester and shot the cow back of the shoulder. She fell a short distance off, and approaching I saw, about 100 yds. away, some standing, some sitting, about twenty or more large wolves.

They formed a very pretty picture on the gray prairie, that was almost wind-swept of snow. They were not the dirty gray buffalo wolf, but seemed to be more of the timber species, with tawny markings, some approaching to creamy white. What surprised me was their utter unconcern as I came into view. They were lined up in a row, as if they had been bidden to a feast, and were not particular as to the manner in which it was served. I proceeded to satisfy them. Laying my gun and belt on the ground, I disemboweled the cow, cut and slashed the meat in the usual way, and loaded the carcass with about three-eighths of an ounce of strychnia. My audience took an unusual interest in the work of preparing this bait, but scarcely moved from their first position.

I surmised that this was not the first time they had posed as spectators of a meat-carving diversion, and that they had probably followed the Indians on a buffalo hunt. Though uninvited guests, I felt that their appreciation should not pass unrewarded. When I had finished cutting up the buffalo I gathered my gun and belt and retired from the scene as I came.

A day or two later as we rode that way their beautiful carcasses covered the prairie, and we secured twenty-two fine pelts.

WOLF COURSING
1893

 WOLF hunting was a time-honored sport in Europe. In the U.S., Theodore Roosevelt was among its adherents, and in "A Wolf Hunt in Oklahoma" (Scribner's Magazine, November 1905), he described some particulars, especially the dogs needed for such prey. Dogs had been bred to hunt wolves since ancient times, including the Irish and Russian wolfhounds, greyhounds, staghounds, and blood-hounds. The prey presented special challenges, so some dogs were needed for speed, some for strength, others for endurance, and still others for ferocity.

The complaints of sportsmen about wolves were very different from those of stockmen. For the sportsman, wolves were largely a nuisance: they stalked wounded game, robbed carcasses, invaded camps at night to eat lariats and other equipment, mauled the hounds, zig-zagged erratically across the prairies, and their incessant howling kept him awake all night. But that didn't stop Parker Gillmore from penning this homage to the wolf hunt in Gun, Rod, and Saddle: A Record of Personal Experiences *(London: W. H. Allen & Co. Ltd., 1893).*

❖❖❖

Few of us have not experienced the excitement of a gallop over a good grass country with the spotted beauties leading the way, getting over the ground at racing pace, while your mount is nearly hauling you out of the saddle with enthusiasm and inclination to make himself on still more famil-iar terms with the pack. By Jove, how reckless such excitement makes you feel! Fear is banished for the time being—all sense of danger is dispelled to the winds, and sooner than be thrown out you would ride at a canal, or charge any height of timber. You may be old—yet for the time feel young: you may be *blasé*—you feel as buoyant as when you made your *début*. But it is far from the grass counties, across three thousand miles of water and fifteen hundred of land—far beyond the giant Mississippi, to the illimitable prairies of the Far West I wish you to travel, in thought, at least. Imagine an unbounded expense of undulating land, covered with grass; here and there a sparse scat-tering of brush, with perhaps one or two lines of timber that mark the mar-gin of tributaries of some mighty river, and you have the landscape without entering into detail. What a place for a gallop! what a place for a buffalo run, or any other kind of run that will give your mettlesome nag an opportunity of showing his pluck and endurance. But take care, don't ride with a slack rein, keep your eyes open; all may look plain sailing from the distance, but on closer inspection you may come upon a densely populated prairie-dog town, or collection of cayotte earths, each hole of which is big enough to use a Newfoundland for a fox terrier.

Two varieties of wolves are found numerous all over this elysium; game is abundant, and the marauder is always on its track, looking out for the feeble or unfortunate. Skulking scoundrels are these members of the canine fraternity, and cunning withal; keen and successful hunters if necessary, but addicted to idleness; for if they can obtain their dinner at others' expense, they are always ready to sacrifice their principle and sponge upon the first acquaintance. If you go out for pleasure, or with the desire of replenishing your larder, you are certain to be attended; you cannot get away from camp without their watchful eyes detecting you. As you rise one knoll you may observe the escort topping the last, and intently keeping all your movements under their observation. Full well do they know that if elk or deer fall before your rifle, on the refuse that you reject, they will find a bounteous repast; or if your hands and eyes forget their cunning, and a wounded unfortunate goes off, then the chances are that the whole carcass will fall to their share, and an unstinted feast on titbits ensue, for master Lupus has wonderful scenting powers, and with the trail spiced with blood he grudges no amount of exertion.

Again, the wolf is always in disgrace; he steals your game if deserted for a few hours to procure assistance to transport it to camp; he eats your lariats, untying your animals, nibbles the flaps of your saddles, and keeps up an unearthly serenade through those hours that the tired sportsman is most disposed to rest. Is it any wonder that he is unpopular, that he has no friends, and that he is considered a vermin of the first magnitude? Although the American wolf is divided into many families, those we have to do with are the large grey species, and prairie variety, the former of which is a large ill-looking savage, the latter less repulsive, seldom over twenty-three inches at the shoulder, with more of the dog physiognomy and a good deal of the fox in his nature. In all shooting excursions you will have idle days, a lay off for the more serious duties of the morrow, when guns are cleaned, bullets cast, cartridge belts replenished, and wet and dirty clothes dried or washed. The forenoon having sufficed to perform these labours, a run with a wolf will be found not a bad appetiser for your evening meal, or remove of your little stiffnesses and ailments, in same way as a little exercise is necessary to the hunter the day after a long or hard run. To enjoy this pleasure to perfection you must be provided with dogs, and there are none so suitable as the strongest stamp of greyhounds; those that are addicted to grappling with the foe will get fearfully mauled, for the jaws of a wolf are almost as powerful as a hyena's, and consequently your limited establishment would be half the time on the sick list; with the greyhound it is different. As soon as you get a view of the quarry at him they go, and although the game is swift, still his adversaries are not long in ranging alongside, when a snap in the hams or loins immediately brings him to bay. Determined and numerous are his efforts to catch the nimble antagonists, who take precious good care to keep beyond reach. After a few moments of such skirmishing, the closer approach of the sportsman admonishes the wolf to be moving, and off he again starts, best foot foremost; but his persecutors are in attendance. A hundred or two yards may be traversed, and once more the game is brought up standing from a similar cause; thus the battle is played till the wolf is exhausted, and the sportsman gets sufficiently close to end the episode by a well-directed pistol bullet through the grizzly marauder's cranium.

Spearing the wolf on horseback is also capital sport; but it takes a great deal out of your nag, for the scoundrel while fresh will jink almost as sharply as a hare, and from his wonderful lasting powers take you over an immense distance, he invariably choosing the roughest ground. In this mode also you must constantly be on the *qui vive*, for if opportunity offers he will make either your horse or yourself acquainted with his grinders, and a snap from him will be a memento. In the neighbourhood of Fort Riley an accident of this kind almost occurred to me. A large grey wolf jumped up before me, and as my horse was fresh and the afternoon cool, I made up my mind for a run. Drawing my revolver, and taking my nag in hand, we were soon skimming the prairie at a slashing pace. After a mile of this work I ranged alongside, but on several occasions when about to press the trigger the wolf wheeled sharply to the right or left, once very nearly throwing my horse on his head. More determined to draw blood from the trick practised on me, I was soon again at his tail; but the foe tried a new and quite unexpected ruse, viz. suddenly slackening his pace, and as I overshot him, making a most wicked snap at my off foot, which fortunately was protected by a heavy cowhide boot; but the indentation showed that a lighter covering would have caused me to regret my prowess.

If ever you visit the far Western Prairies you will not regret the trouble of taking with you some good strong greyhounds; the rough Scotch dog I should prefer, for you will not only find them great promoters of your sport, wolf-hunting, but useful auxiliaries in pulling down wounded deer, as well as being most watchful and trustworthy camp guardians and companions.

BADLANDS BILLY
1905

 FEW names are more closely associated with wolves in the first half of this century than that of Ernest Thompson Seton, author of some of North America's best-loved wolf stories, including "Lobo: The King of Currumpaw," "The Winnepeg Wolf," and "Badlands Billy: The Wolf that Won." Although his stories have often been dismissed as anthropomorphic, their realism in depicting instinctive (rather than rational) behavior in animals created a new literary genre and renewed concern for wildlife conservation. Seton was also a superb wildlife artist whose most famous painting, "The Sleeping Wolf," earned him a first prize at the annual Paris Salon competition. In addition, he was a respected naturalist and scientist; his award-winning four-volume treatise Lives of Game Animals *devoted 100 pages to wolves.*

These two selections are from "Badlands Billy" in Animal Heroes *(New York: Charles Scribner's Sons, 1905). Among his other careers, Seton was for a while a "wolver" (or "wolfer"), engaged by ranchers and later the government to kill wolves in the West, primarily through trapping and poisoning. In this story, he joins forces with another wolver to end one wolf's stock killing in the Badlands of South Dakota. The first segment is part of Seton's fictional recreation of Badland Billy's early life, when he and his mother were known among the wolves as Duskymane and Yellow Wolf. The second segment takes place at the end of a long, intense hunt for Badlands Billy—a hunt that required the two wolvers, the Penroof ranch cowboys, and numerous hunting dogs.*

❖❖❖

THE LESSON ON TRAPS

A Calf had died in branding-time and now, two weeks later, was in its best state for perfect taste, not too fresh, not over-ripe—that is, in a Wolf's opinion—and the wind carried this information afar. The Yellow Wolf and Duskymane were out for supper, though not yet knowing where, when the tidings of veal arrived, and they trotted up the wind. The Calf was in an open place, and plain to be seen in the moonlight. A Dog would have trotted right up to the carcass, an old-time Wolf might have done so, but constant war had developed constant vigilance in the Yellow Wolf, and trusting nothing and no one but her nose, she slacked her speed to a walk. On coming in easy view she stopped, and for long swung her nose, submitting the wind to the closest possible chemical analysis. She tried it with her finest tests, blew all the membranes clean again and tried it once more; and this was the report of the trusty nostrils, yes, the unanimous report. First, rich and racy smell of Calf, seventy per cent.; smells of grass, bugs, wood, flowers, trees, sand, and other uninteresting negations, fifteen per cent.; smell of her Cub and herself, positive but ignorable, ten per cent.; smell of human tracks, two per cent.; smell of smoke, one per cent.; of sweaty leather smell, one per cent.; of human body-scent (not discernible in some samples), one-half per cent.; smell of iron, a trace.

The old Wolf crouched a little but sniffed hard with swinging nose; the young Wolf imitatively did the same. She backed off to a greater distance; the Cub stood. She gave a low whine; he followed unwillingly. She circled around the tempting carcass; a new smell was recorded—Coyote trail-scent, soon followed by Coyote body-scent. Yes, there they were sneaking along a near ridge, and now as she passed to one side the samples changed, the wind had lost nearly every trace of Calf; miscellaneous, commonplace, and uninteresting smells were there instead. The human track-scent was as before, the trace of leather was gone, but fully one-half per cent. of iron-odor, and body-smell of man raised to nearly two per cent.

Fully alarmed, she conveyed her fear to the Cub, by her rigid pose, her air intent, and her slightly bristling mane.

She continued her round. At one time on a high place the human body-scent was doubly strong, then as she dropped it faded. Then the wind brought the full calf-odor with several track-scents of Coyotes and sundry Birds. Her suspicions were lulling as in a smalling circle she neared the tempting feast from the windward side. She had even advanced straight toward it for a few steps when the sweaty leather sang loud and strong again, and smoke and iron mingled like two strands of a parti-colored yarn. Centring all her attention on this, she advanced within two leaps of the Calf. There on the ground was a scrap of leather, telling also of a human touch, close at hand the Calf, and now the iron and smoke on the full vast smell of Calf were like a snake trail across the trail of a whole Beef herd. It was so slight that the Cub, with the appetite and impatience of youth, pressed up against his mother's shoulder to go past and eat without delay. She seized him by the neck and flung him back. A stone struck by his feet rolled forward and stopped with a peculiar clink. The danger smell was greatly increased at this, and the Yellow Wolf backed slowly from the feast, the Cub unwillingly following.

As he looked wistfully he saw the Coyotes drawing nearer, mindful chiefly to avoid the Wolves. He watched their really cautious advance; it seemed like heedless rushing compared with his mother's approach. The Calf smell rolled forth in exquisite and overpowering excellence now, for they were tearing the meat, when a sharp clank was heard and a yelp from a Coyote. At the same time the quiet night was shocked with a roar and a flash of fire. Heavy shots spattered Calf and Coyotes, and yelping like beaten Dogs they scattered, excepting one that was killed and a second struggling in the trap set here by the ever-active wolvers. The air was charged with the hateful smells redoubled now, and horrid smells additional. The Yellow Wolf glided down a hollow and led her Cub away in flight, but, as they went, they saw a man rush from the bank near where the mother's nose had warned her of the human scent. They saw him kill the caught Coyote and set the traps for more.

❖❖❖

This second episode occurs a few years later, after Badlands Billy had become a cattle-killer that couldn't be caught. Seton joins the wolver King Ryder and the ranch hands in hunting him down with a pack of hounds.

WHEN BILLY WENT BACK TO HIS MOUNTAIN

We were back opposite to where the Wolf had plunged, but saw no sign. We rode at an easy gallop, on eastward, a mile, and still on, when King gasped out, "Look at that!" A dark spot was moving on the snow ahead. We put on speed. Another dark spot appeared, and another, but they were not going fast. In five minutes we were near them, to find—three of our own Greyhounds. They had lost sight of the game, and with that their interest waned. Now they were seeking us. We saw nothing there of the chase or of the other hunters. But hastening to the next ridge we stumbled on the trail we sought and followed as hard as though in view. Another cañon came in our path, and as we rode and looked for a place to cross, a wild din of Hounds came from its brushy depth. The clamor grew and passed up the middle.

We raced along the rim, hoping to see the game. The Dogs appeared near the farther side, not in a pack, but a long, straggling line. In five minutes more they rose to the edge, and ahead of them was the great Black Wolf. He was loping as before, head and tail low. Power was plain in every limb, and double power in his jaws and neck, but I thought his bounds were shorter now, and that they had lost their spring. The Dogs slowly reached the upper level, and sighting him they broke into a feeble cry; they, too, were nearly spent. The Greyhounds saw the chase, and leaving us they scrambled down the cañon and up the other side at impetuous speed that would surely break them down, while we rode, vainly seeking means of crossing.

How the wolver raved to see the pack lead off in the climax of the chase, and himself held up behind. But he rode and wrathed and still rode, up to where the cañon dwindled—rough land and a hard ride. As we neared the great flat mountain, the feeble cry of the pack was heard again from the south, then toward the high Butte's side, and just a trifle louder now. We reined in on a hillock and scanned the snow. A moving speck appeared, then others, not bunched, but in a straggling train, and at times there was a far faint cry. They were headed toward us, coming on, yes! coming, but so slowly, for not one was really running now. There was the grim old Cow-killer limping over the ground, and far behind a Greyhound, and another, and farther still, the other Dogs in order of their speed, slowly, gamely, dragging themselves on that pursuit. Many hours of hardest toil had done their work. The Wolf had vainly sought to fling them off. Now was his hour of doom, for he was spent; they still had some reserve. Straight to us for a time they came, skirting the base of the mountain, crawling.

We could not cross to join them, so held our breath and gazed with ravenous eyes. They were nearer now, the wind brought feeble notes from the Hounds. The big Wolf turned to the steep ascent, up a well-known trail, it seemed, for he made no slip. My heart went with him, for he had come back to rescue his friend, and a momentary thrill of pity came over us both, as we saw him glance around and drag himself up the sloping way, to die on his mountain. There was no escape for him, beset by fifteen Dogs with men to back them. He was not walking, but tottering upward; the Dogs behind in line, were now doing a little better, were nearing him. We could hear them gasping; we scarcely heard them bay—they had no breath for that; upward the grim procession went, circling a spur of the Butte and along a ledge that climbed and narrowed, then dropped for a few yards to a shelf that reared above the cañon. The foremost Dogs were closing, fearless of a foe so nearly spent.

Here in the narrowest place, where one wrong step meant death, the great

Wolf turned and faced them. With fore-feet braced, with head low and tail a little raised, his dusky mane a-bristling, his glittering tusks laid bare, but uttering no sound that we could hear, he faced the crew. His legs were weak with toil, but his neck, his jaws, and his heart were strong, and—now all you who love the Dogs had better close the book—on—up and down—fifteen to one, they came, the swiftest first, and how it was done, the eye could scarcely see, but even as a stream of water pours on a rock to be splashed in broken jets aside, that stream of Dogs came pouring down the path, in single file perforce, and Duskymane received them as they came. A feeble spring, a counter-lunge, a gash, and "Fango's down," has lost his foot-hold and is gone. Dander and Coalie close and try to clinch; a rush, a heave, and they are fallen from that narrow path. Blue-spot then, backed by mighty Oscar and fearless Tige—but the Wolf is next the rock and the flash of combat clears to show him there alone, the big Dogs gone; the rest close in, the hindmost force the foremost on—down—to their death. Slash, chop and heave, from the swiftest to the biggest, to the last, down—down—he sent them whirling from the ledge to the gaping gulch below, where rocks and snags of trunks were sharp to do their work.

In fifty seconds it was done. The rock had splashed the stream aside—the Penroof pack was all wiped out; and Badlands Billy stood there, alone again on his mountain.

A moment he waited to look for more to come. There were no more, the pack was dead; but waiting he got his breath, then raising his voice for the first time in that fatal scene, he feebly gave a long yell of triumph, and scaling the next low bank, was screened from view in a cañon of Sentinel Butte.

We stared like men of stone. The guns in our hands were forgotten. It was all so quick, so final. We made no move till the Wolf was gone. It was not far to the place: we went on foot to see if any had escaped. Not one was left alive. We could do nothing—we could say nothing.

THE HOME LIFE OF THE BIG WOLVES
1906

 THIS story is interesting not because of the carnage in it (in fact, no wolves are killed), but because it illustrates the institutionalization of "predator control." Biologist Vernon Bailey's visit to Big Piney, Wyoming, was the result of a "convergence of mutual interests" between the Forest Service, the Biological Survey—both quite new federal agencies in 1906—and ranchers in the West. He was there to study wolves in order to devise the best ways of killing them. This story appeared in the September 1940 issue of Natural History.

❖❖❖

My skis slid silently over the frosted crust of old snow still lying two feet deep over the upper Green River basin in early March of 1906. I was headed for the nearest badlands east of Big Piney, Wyoming. The temperature was near zero as I left the little log hotel half an hour before daylight, munching nut meats and candied ginger to keep me going for a three-hour run before breakfast.

Big wolves had been reported killing cattle in the Green River country, and the Forest Service, then new and generally opposed by local stockmen, was accused of breeding wolves on the national forests to eat up the cattle outside. The attitude of the ranchmen was understandable, for slaughter of their stock could mean economic disaster to them. Wolves are meat-eaters and so is man; and there was not enough meat to go around. It was inevitable that the wolves should be hunted down. They were entering their twilight in a country being converted from wilderness to pastureland. When an effort was made to check burning off the timber to make grassland, and a policy was suggested of charging a small fee for grazing cattle on the newly designated forests, friendship became very strained between cattlemen and a "tyrannical bureaucracy"; even the local papers clamored for removal of the latter.

BUTTES AND BADLANDS

The Forest Service had appealed to the Biological Survey for information and investigation, and that was why I was out on skis in the wolf country. I had been there before and knew where to look: I headed straight for the low line of buttes and badlands east of the creek valley in time to be in good wolf country by daybreak.

A dim winter light was breaking as I came in sight of the first round-topped butte. I was headed into the side gulch when, to my amazement, a gruff bark followed by a long, deep-throated howl came from close by. There on top of the butte in plain sight stood a big wolf watching me. I did not stop for fear of scaring him but, swinging spirally around the butte, drew nearer and nearer until close to the base. He gave another long howl and disappeared over the top. When I came close to the top so I could just peep over, I saw him standing facing me on the next summit only 150 yards distant. We watched each other for some time. I covered him with the sights of my .30-30 carbine, just to see how easily I could collect him for a specimen, but that was not what I was after. I wanted to learn something about wolves.

A Strange Game

After a few minutes he trotted down the other slope and reappeared on a ridge a quarter of a mile away and howled again. I followed. When I arrived he was out in the valley beyond, sitting down waiting for me. I howled and he answered, then trotted on out of sight over the next ridge. I was puzzled. For nine years I had been in wolf country every summer and had found these big fellows as shy and unapproachable as grizzly bears. But here was one coaxing me to follow him, deliberately risking his life to attract my attention. What could it mean?

I gave up following him and swung back on a wide circle through cattle pastures to watch for tracks. Moreover I wanted to get back in time for breakfast. Soon I struck a wolf track going to my right, then another close to it, and a little later two tracks going the other way. Farther on were others in pairs or single, all going toward or from a deep gulch off to my right. In summer, fall, and early winter wolves hunt in packs or family groups of generally ten or a dozen, led by the old male, the father of the family. But here were tracks in pairs or single. During midwinter, the mating season, a pair will desert the pack and keep close together until the young are born in early March. For the rest of the year they give their whole attention to the new family. It began to dawn on me that there must be a wolf den here, for the tracks radiating from the gulch located it as accurately as beelines to a bee tree. This big fellow was just leading me away from it.

Never before had I found a wolf den and here was a chance to learn something of wolf habits and wolf nature.

The rest of the day I skied over the valley and among the cattle browsing in the willow thickets to see how extensively they had suffered from wolves. A few had been killed and many had died of cold and starvation during the winter, but no fresh kills were found. All dead animals were frozen hard and would be good cold-storage beef for a month or more. Just now there seemed to be a truce of plenty while the pups were in the dens.

Next morning I was out at daylight again and found my old sentinel wolf on top of the same butte. In fact his beds showed that he had slept there part of each day and night for some time. As soon as I came in sight, he stood up, gave a few hoarse barks, then his long, deep howl as before, and waited till he was sure I was coming. He greeted me from the top of the next ridge and on as long as I wanted to follow. Knowing his game, I enjoyed it and we called back and forth with mutual interest.

For six mornings this old fellow led me over the same route away from the den where mother wolf and her puppies were well hidden, voluntarily risking his life every morning for their safety. More and more I grew to admire his courage and devotion as well as his wisdom. He was just about my size, about 135 pounds, but he knew from generations of experience that he was no match for man-made guns and traps and that the only safety of his family lay in well-planned strategy. It is just what Kipling puts in the laws of the jungle—"And seven times never kill man." The ranchmen in the valley might have had less tolerance if they had known that I was playing with their archenemy, but they were restricted to the few open roads and the wolves and I had the whole valley to ourselves.

On the seventh morning I went around and came into the den gulch from the other side. Far across I saw just a glimpse of my old wolf on his watch tower, but he said not a word and quickly disappeared. Then I saw mother wolf slip out of a low cave in the steep bank across the gulch and vanish around the point and up the next gulch. Neither came in sight again. In a few minutes, however, they were both calling from behind me, trying to lead me back and away from the den. But I had much to find out.

NINE PUPPIES

Heading rapidly to the little cave where all the tracks centered, I found an opening large enough to crawl into. Back some fifteen feet I found nine little black wolf puppies with blue eyes just opening, all cuddled in a nice warm bed of clean sand where mother wolf had left them. They were probably eight or nine days old as their eyes were not wide open, and they were almost coal-black except their brown heads. They were not afraid and were evidently obeying their mother in keeping still and cuddling close together in the warm nest hollow.

Outside on the clean snow were a dozen dead jack rabbits, the big white hares of the north country. Some were partly and some wholly eaten, and one freshly killed and untouched. Apparently a six or seven-pound rabbit was just a meal for mother wolf, and the hunter of the family had kept the larder well stocked while she was busy caring for her babies. Since there was no other visible food supply, father wolf had most likely eaten his rabbits where they were caught, or had dined on frozen beef. I could not find any freshly killed cattle for miles around, but he may have gone far beyond my range when he wanted a warm meal. In the next valley a pack of nine bachelor wolves was reported killing calves or colts every night.

Just beyond the entrance of the den a big plump cottontail jumped out of the sagebrush, and I saw him there several times later. He could easily have been picked up by either of the old wolves, but perhaps they were saving him close by for the puppies' first hunting lesson.

The old wolves did not return while I was there, but I knew they were just hoping that I would not find their home. It hurt me to break it up, but I had to take some of the young for further study and to prove that wolves were breeding in the valley right among the ranches and not in the high mountain forests. I left one little wolf for the mother, and before morning he was carried away to some distant den where he would be safe. I never saw him or either of the old wolves again.

Two of the young I gave to the ranch boy and his mother for taking care of the others until I was ready to ship them to Washington, where they lived long and safely in the National Zoological Park. When I returned from Wyoming six months later, I found the two puppies nearly full grown. Although they were playful and friendly and climbed all over me, I could not make myself believe that they remembered or were glad to see me. It was well that they did not know how I had broken up their devoted family and sent their parents away with only one young.

STERLING VIRTUES

Their behavior is one of many examples of the affection of a pair of wolves for each other and for their young. At one ranch I was told in touching reality of a female wolf shot in winter near the cattle pasture and how the lonesome calling of the male could be heard from the hilltops night after night for weeks. There are many such records.

Few animals are more devoted in their home life, braver, or more intelligent. Yes, they were cruel killers, but not half as cruel as we have been. The more we see of some wolves the less we think of some men. The big wolves are practically gone from the whole United States, though the coyotes are still with us. Occasionally a few wolves stray across the borders from Mexico or southern British Columbia but they do not last long among the ranchers, who are always on the watch for them. But even ranchmen will give them credit for their unusual intelligence among animals. Let us give them their just dues for the sterling virtues of affection and devotion. They are an enemy we can well admire.

THE WOLF TRACKER
1924

 ZANE Grey's western romances were enormously popular in the early part of the twentieth century, and his books have been issued in uncountable editions and languages and sold in millions of copies. Considered by many to be the father of the Western, Grey often depicted the power of the West's landscapes in shaping human character and history. This tale is a masterful inquiry into the motives that compel men to kill wolves. It appeared in the Ladies' Home Journal *in 1924.*

❖❖❖

The hard-riding cowmen of Adams' outfit returned to camp that last day of the fall round-up, weary and brush-torn, begrimed with dust and sweat, and loud in their acclaims against Old Gray, the "lofer" wolf, notorious from the Cibique across the black belt of rugged Arizona upland to Mount Wilson in New Mexico.

"Wal, reckon I allowed the Tonto had seen the last of Old Gray's big tracks," said Benson, the hawk-eyed foreman, as he slipped the bridle off his horse.

"An' for why?" queried Banty Smith, the little arguing rooster of the outfit. "Ain't Old Gray young yet—just in his prime? Didn't we find four carcasses of full-grown steers he'd pulled down last April over on Webber Creek? Shore he allus hit for high country in summer. What for did you think he'd not show up when the frost come?"

"Aw, Banty, cain't you savvy Ben?" drawled a long, lean rider. "He was jest voicin' his hopes."

"Yep; Ben is thet tender-hearted he'd weep over a locoed calf if it happened to wear his brand," remarked Tim Bender with a huge grin, as if he well knew he had acquitted himself wittily.

"Haw! Haw!" laughed another rider. "Old Gray has shore made some deppredashuns on Ben's stock of twenty head—most as much as one heifer."

"Wal, kid me all you like, boys," replied Benson good-naturedly. "Reckon I had no call to think Old Gray wouldn't come back. He's done thet for years. But it's not onnatural to live in hopes. An' it's hard luck we had to run acrost his tracks an' his work the last day of the round-up. Only last night the boss was sayin' he hadn't heard anythin' aboot Old Gray for months."

"Nobody heerd of anyone cashin' on thet five thousand dollars reward for Old Gray's scalp either," replied Banty with sarcasm.

Thus after the manner of the range the cowboys volleyed badinage while they performed the last tasks of the day.

Two streams met below the pine-shaded bench where the camp was situated; and some of the boys strode down with towels and soap to attend to ablutions that one wash pan for the outfit made a matter of waiting. It was still clear daylight, though the sun had gone down behind a high timbered hill to the west. A rude log cabin stood above the fork of the streams, and near by the cook busied himself between his chuck wagon and the camp fire. Both the cool pine-scented air and the red-gold patches of brush on the hillside told of the late October.

Adams, the boss of the outfit, had ridden over from his Tonto ranch at Spring Valley. He was a sturdy, well-preserved man of sixty, sharp of eye, bronze of face, with the stamp of a self-made and prosperous rancher upon him.

"Ben, the boss is inquirin' aboot you," called Banty from the bench above the stream.

Whereupon the foreman clambered up the rocky slope, vigorously rubbing his ruddy face with a towel, and made his way to where Adams sat beside the camp fire. In all respects, except regarding Old Gray, Benson's report was one he knew would be gratifying. This naturally he reserved until after Adams had expressed his satisfaction. Then he supplemented the news of the wolf.

"That lofer!" ejaculated Adams in dismay. "Why, only the other day I heard from my pardner Barrett, an' he said the government hunters were trackin' Old Gray up Mount Wilson."

"Wal, boss, thet may be true," responded the foreman. "But Old Gray killed a yearlin' last night on the red ridge above Doubtful Cañon. I know his tracks like I do my hoss'. We found four kills today an' I reckon all was the work of thet lofer. You don't need to see his tracks. He's shore a clean killer. An' sometimes he kills for the sake of killin'."

"I ain't sayin' I care about the money loss, though that old gray devil has cost me an' Barrett twenty-five hundred," replied Adams thoughtfully. "But he's such a bloody murderer, the most aggravatin' varmint I ever—"

"Huh! Who's the gazabo comin' down the trail?" interrupted Benson, pointing up the bench.

"Stranger to me," said Adams. "Anybody know him?"

One by one the cowboys disclaimed knowledge of the unusual figure approaching. At that distance he appeared to be a rather old man, slightly bowed. But a second glance showed his shoulders to be broad and his stride the wonderful one of a mountaineer.

He carried a pack on his back and a shiny carbine in his hand. His garb was ragged homespun, patched until it resembled a checkerboard.

"A stranger without a hoss!" exclaimed Banty, as if that was an amazingly singular thing.

The man approached the camp fire, and halted to lean the worn carbine against the woodpile. Then he unbuckled a strap round his breast, and lifted a rather heavy pack from his back, to deposit it on the ground. It appeared to be a pack rolled in a rubber-lined blanket, out of which protruded the ends of worn snowshoes. When he stepped to the camp fire he disclosed a strange physiognomy: the weather-beaten face of a matured man of the open, mapped to deep lines—strong, hard, a rugged mask, lighted by penetrating quiet eyes of gray.

"Howdy, stranger. Get down an' come in," welcomed Adams with the quaint, hearty greeting always resorted to by a Westerner.

"Hod do. I reckon I will," replied the man, extending big brown hands to the fire. "Are you Adams, the cattleman?"

"You've got me. But I can't just place you stranger."

"Reckon not. I'm new in these parts. My name's Brink. I'm a tracker."

"Glad to meet you, Brink," replied Adams curiously. "These are some of my boys. Set down an' rest. I reckon you're tired an' hungry. We'll have grub soon. Tracker, you said? Now, I just don't savvy what you mean."

"I've been prospector, trapper, hunter, most everythin'," replied Brink as he took the seat offered. "But I reckon my callin' is to find tracks. Tracker of men, hosses, cattle, wild animals, specially sheep-killin' silvertips an' stock-killin' wolves."

"Aha! You don't say!" ejaculated Adams, suddenly shifting from genial curiosity to keen interest. "An' you're after that five thousand dollars we cattlemen offered for Old' Gray's scalp?"

"Nope. I hadn't thought of the reward. I heard of it, up in Colorado, same time I heard of this wolf that's run amuck so long on these ranges. An' I've come down here to kill him."

Adams showed astonishment along with his interest, but his silence and expression did not approach the incredulity manifested by the men of his outfit. They were amiably nonplused as to the man's sanity. Nothing more than their response was needed to establish the reputation of Old Gray, the lofer wolf. But Brink did not see these indications; he was peering into the fire.

"So ho! You have?" exclaimed Adams, breaking the silence. "Wal, now, Brink, that's good of you. Would you mind tellin' us how you mean to set about killin' Old Gray?"

"Reckon I told you I was a tracker," rejoined Brink curtly.

"But, man, we've had every pack of hounds in two states on the track of that wolf."

"Is he on the range now?" queried Brink.

Adams motioned to his foreman to reply to this question. Benson made evident effort to be serious. "I seen his tracks less 'n two hours ago. He killed a yearlin' last night."

At these words Brink turned his gaze from the fire to the speaker. What a remarkable fleeting flash crossed his rugged face! It seemed one of passion. It changed, and only a gleam of eye attested to strange emotion under that seamed and lined mask of bronze. His gaze returned to the fire; and the big hands, that held palms open to the heat, now clasped each other, in strong and tense action. Only Adams took the man seriously, and his attitude restrained the merriment his riders certainly felt.

"Adams, would you mind tellin' me all you know about this wolf?" asked the stranger presently.

"Say, man," expostulated Adams, still with good nature, "it wouldn't be polite to keep you from eatin' an' sleepin'."

"Old Gray has a history then?" inquired Brink.

"Humph! Reckon I couldn't tell you all about him in a week," said the cattleman emphatically.

"It wouldn't matter to me how long you'd take," returned Brink thoughtfully.

At that Adams laughed outright; this queer individual had not in the least considered waste of time to a busy rancher. Manifestly he thought only of the notorious wolf. Adams eyed the man a long, speculative moment. Brink interested him. Brink's face and garb and pack were all extraordinarily different from what was usually met with on these ranges. He had arrived on foot, but he was not a tramp. Adams took keener note of the quiet face, the deep chest, the muscular hands, the wiry body and the powerful legs. No cowboy, for all his riding, ever had legs like these; the man was a walker.

These deductions, united with an amiability that was characteristic of Adams, persuaded him to satisfy the man's desire to hear about the wolf.

"All right, Brink, I'll tell you somethin' of Old Gray—leastways till the cook calls us to come an' get it. There used to be a good many lofers—timber wolves we called them—in this country. But they're gettin' scarce. Naturally there are lots of stories in circulation about this particular wolf. I can't vouch for his parentage, or whether he has mixed blood. Seven or eight, maybe ten years ago some trapper lost a husky—one of them regular Alaskan snow-sled dogs—over in the Mazatzals. Never found him.

"Some natives here claim Old Gray is a son of this husky, his mother bein' one of the range lofers. Another story is about a wolf escapin' from a circus over heah in a railroad wreck years ago. A young gray wolf got away. This escaped wolf might be Old Gray.

"The name Old Gray doesn't seem to fit this particular wolf, because it's misleadin'. He's gray—yes, almost white, but he's not old. Bill Everett, a range hand, saw this wolf first. Tellin' about it, he called him an old gray Jasper. The name stuck, though now you seldom hear the Jasper tacked on.

"From that time stories began to drift into camp an' town about the doin's of Old Gray. He was a killer. Cowboys an' hunters took to his trail with cow dogs an' bear hounds. But though they routed him out of his lairs an' chased him all over they never caught him. Trappers camped all the way from the Cibique to Mount Wilson tryin' to trap him. I never heard of Old Gray touchin' a trap.

"In summer Old Gray lit out for the mountains. In winter he took to the foothills an' ranges. I've heard cattlemen over in New Mexico say he had killed twenty-five thousand dollars' worth of stock. But that was years ago. It would be impossible now to estimate the loss to ranchers. Old Gray played at the game. He'd run through a bunch of stock, hamstringin' right an' left, until he had enough of his fun, then he'd pull down a yearlin', eat what he wanted an' travel on.

"He didn't always work alone. Sometimes he'd have several lofers with him. But Old Gray is a lone wolf. He didn't trust company. The government hunters have been tryin' to get him these several years. But so far as I know,

Old Gray has never been scratched. My personal opinion is this: He's a magnificent wild brute, smarter than any dog; an' you know how intelligent dogs can be. Well, Old Gray is too savage, too wild, too keen to be caught by the ordinary means employed so far. There, Brink, is the plain, blunt facts."

"Much obliged," replied Brink with a break in his rapt intensity. "Have you ever seen this lofer?"

"No, I never had the good luck," replied Adams. "Nor have many men. But Benson, here, has seen him."

"What's he look like?" queried Brink, turning eagerly to the foreman.

"Wal, Old Gray is aboot the purtiest wild varmint I ever clapped my eyes on," drawled Benson, slow and cool, as if to tantalize this wolf hunter. "He's big—a heap bigger 'n any lofer I ever saw before—an' he's gray all right, a light gray, with a black ring part round his neck, almost like a ruff. He's a bold cuss too. He stood watchin' me, knowin' darn well he was out of gunshot."

"Now what kind of a track does he make?"

"Wal, jest a wolf track bigger'n you ever seen before—almost as big as a hoss track. When you see it oncet you'll shore never forget."

"Where did you run across that track last?"

Benson squatted down before the fire, and with his hand smoothed a flat, clear place in the dust on which he began to trace lines. "Heah, foller up this creek till you come to a high falls. Climb up the slope on the right. You'll head out on a cedar an' piñon ridge. Halfway up this ridge from there you'll strike a trail. Foller it round under the bluff till you strike Old Gray's tracks; I seen them this mawnin', fresh as could be—sharp an' clean in the dust, makin' for the Rim."

Brink slowly rose from his scrutiny of the map. His penetrating gaze fixed on Adams. "I'll kill your old gray wolf," he said.

His tone, his manner seemed infinitely more than his simple words. They all combined to make an effect that seemed indefinable, except in the case of Banty, who grew red in the face. The little cowboy enjoyed considerable reputation as a hunter, a reputation which, to his humiliation, had not been lived up to by his futile hunts after Old Gray.

"Aw, now—so you'll kill thet lofer," he ejaculated in the most elaborate satire possible for a cowboy. "Wal, Mr. Brink, would you mind tellin' us jest when you'll perpetuate this execushun? We'll give a dance to celebrate. Say when you'll fetch his skin down—tomorrow around sunup, or mebbe next day, seein' you'll have to travel on Shanks' mare, or possiblee the day after."

Banty's drawling scorn might never have been spoken, for all the effect it had on the wolf hunter. Brink was beyond the levity of a cowboy. "Reckon I can't say just when I'll kill Old Gray," he replied with something sonorous in his voice. "It might be any day, accordin' to luck. But if he's the wolf you-all say he is, it'll take long."

"You don't say!" spoke up Banty. "Wal, by gosh, my walkin' gent, I figgered you had some Injun medicine thet you could put on Old Gray's tail."

The cowboys roared. Brink showed no sign of appreciating the ridicule. Thoughtfully he bent again to the fire, and did not hear the cook's lusty call to supper.

"Never mind the boys," said Adams kindly, putting a hand on the bowed shoulder. "Come an' eat with us."

II

The morning sun had not yet melted the hoar frost from the brush when Brink halted in the trail before huge wolf tracks in the red dust.

"Same as any wolf tracks, only big," he soliloquized. "Biggest I ever saw, even in Alaska."

He leaned his shiny carbine against a pine sapling and lifted his pack from his shoulders, all the time with gaze riveted on the trail. Then, with head bent, he walked slowly along until he came to a place where all four tracks of the wolf showed plainly. Here he got to his knees, scrutinizing the imprints, photographing them on his inward eye, taking intent and grave stock of them. For moments he remained motionless. Presently he relaxed, and seating himself beside the trail seemed to revel in a strange, tranquil joy.

Brink's state of mind was a composite of a lifetime's feelings. As a boy of three he had captured his first wild creature—a squirrel that he tamed and loved and at last freed. All his early boyhood he had been a haunter of the woods and hills. At sixteen he had run away from school and home; at fifty he knew the West from the cold borders of the Yukon to the desert-walled Yaqui. Caravans, mining camps, freighting posts, towns and settlements, ranchers and camps had known him, though never for any length of time.

The tracks showed sharply in the dust. Old Gray had passed along there yesterday. He was somewhere up or down those ragged slopes. Cunning as he was, he had to hold contact with earth and rock; he had to slay and eat; he must leave traces of his nature, his life, his habit and his action. To these Brink would address himself with all the sagacity of an old hunter, but with something infinitely more—a passion which he did not understand. "Wal, Old Gray, I'm on your track," and strapping the heavy pack on his broad shoulders, he took up the carbine and strode along the trail.

It pleased Brink to find that his first surmise was as correct as if he had cognizance of Old Gray's instincts. The wolf tracks soon sheered off the trail. Old Gray was not now a hunting or a prowling wolf. He was a traveling wolf, but he did not keep to the easy-going, direct trail.

Brink could not find tracks on gravel and boulders, so he crossed the wide bottom of the gorge, and after a while found Old Gray's trail on the opposite slope. Before he struck it he had believed the wolf was heading for high country. Brink tracked him over a forested ridge and down into an intersecting cañon, where on the rocks of a dry stream bed the trail failed.

At length he came to pools of water in rocky recesses, where the sand and gravel bars showed the tracks of cattle, bear and deer. But if Old Gray had passed on up that narrowing cañon, he had avoided the water holes. Patches of maple and thickets of oak covered the steep slopes, leading up to the base of cracked and seamed cliffs, and they in turn sheered up to where the level rim shone black-fringed against the blue. Here the stream bed was covered with the red and gold and purple of fallen autumn leaves.

The sun, now at the zenith, fell hot upon Brink's head. He labored on, to climb out a narrow defile that led to the level forest above. Here the wind blew cool. Brink rested a moment. Then he strode east along the precipice, carefully searching for the wolf trail he had set out upon. In a mile of slow travel, he did not discover a sign of Old Gray. Retracing his steps, he traveled west for a like distance, without success. Whereupon he returned to the head of the cañon out of which he had climbed, and there, divesting himself of his pack, he set about a more elaborate scrutiny of ground, grass, moss and rock.

He worked back from the Rim down into an aspen swale that deepened into a cañon, heading away from the Rim. He had no reason to believe Old Gray would travel this way, except that long experience had taught him where to search first for tracks. And quite abruptly he came upon the huge foot-print of the lofer, made in soft black mud beside elk tracks that led into a hole where water had recently stood.

"Hah!" ejaculated Brink. "You're interested in that yearlin' elk. Wal, Old Gray, I'll let this do for today."

The cold, raw dawn found Brink stirring. A blanket of cloud had pre-vented a white frost on the grass, but there glistened a film of ice on the brook. As the sun came up, it brightened a blue sky mostly clear. The drift of the thin clouds was from the southwest, and they were traveling fast.

Before the sun had warmed out the shade of the cañon Brink, pack on back and rifle in hand, had taken up Old Gray's trail. The wolf showed a preference for the open cañon, and in many places left plain imprints in the sand. The cañon, running away from the Rim, deepened and widened; and its disconnected pools of water at last became a running stream. Evidently the great wolf was not losing time to place distance between him and his last kill. Brink found no more sign of his evincing interest in any tracks.

About noon, by which time Brink had trailed the animal fully ten miles down the cañon, seldom losing the tracks for long, Old Gray took to an in-tersecting cañon, rough-walled and brushy, and soon he went up into the rocks. It took Brink all afternoon to find where the wolf had lain, but Brink would gladly have spent days for such a triumph.

"Aha, you old gray devil!" he soliloquized, as he bent his gaze on a snug retreat under shelving rocks, where showed the betraying impress of feet and body of the wolf. "So you have to sleep an' rest, huh? Wal, I reckon you can't get along without killin' an' eatin' too. Old Gray, you're bound to leave tracks, an' I'll find them."

At length Brink came to a beaver dam, and on the very edge of it, deep in the wet mud, showed the unmistakable tracks of the giant wolf. From that point Old Gray's tracks showed in the wet places up and down the banks of the narrow ponds of water. He had been vastly curious about these dams and mounds erected by the beaver. Everywhere he left tracks. But Brink could not find any sign of the wolf catching a beaver unawares. The beaver of this colony had been at work that night cutting the aspen trees and dragging boughs and sections of trunks under the water.

Sunset came before Brink had found a track of the wolf leading away from that park. Still he made camp satisfied with the day. Any day in which he found a single fresh track of this wolf was indeed time well spent. His hope was that he might keep the general direction Old Gray had taken until the snow began to fall.

Night settled down like a black blanket; the wind moaned louder than usual. Brink soliloquized that the wind was warning Old Gray to leave the country before the fatal snow fell. Contrary to his custom on preceding nights, he sat up a long time and, whether he had his face to the fire or his back, his palms were always spread to the comforting heat. Brink looked and listened with more than usual attention during this vigil beside the camp fire.

"Rain or snow sure," he muttered.

At length drowsiness made his eyelids heavy, and he sought his bed under the shelter of pine boughs. Sleep claimed him. He awakened with a feeling that only a moment had elapsed, but he could tell by the dead camp fire how misleading this was. Something had roused him.

Suddenly from the dark forest on the cold wind came the deep wild bay of a hunting wolf. With a start Brink sat up. No other wild sound in nature had such power over him. It seemed as if this bay came from a vague, dim past. Again it pealed out, but with a sharper note, not greatly different from that of a hunting hound.

"Lofers trailin' a deer," said Brink. "Two of them, mebbe more."

Again he heard the bays, growing farther away, and another time, quite indistinct. After that the weird moaning solitude of the forest remained undisturbed.

Brink lay back in his blanket, but not to sleep. He would lie awake now for a long while. He imagined he heard deep, low bays back in the forest. Always the wind made the sound for which the eager ears were attuned. Suddenly Brink again sat up. "Say, have I got a nightmare?"

He turned his ear away from the cold wind and, holding his breath, he listened. Did he hear a bay or a moan in the forest? Long he remained stiff, intent. Now he felt himself fooled, and then he was sure he heard something. His patience matched his imagination. Then came a slight lull in the wind, and into it rang a low, deep wolf-bay, wild and terrible in its suggestiveness. "Reckon that's a bigger, older wolf," observed Brink. "An' if he runs this way it means somethin'."

Not for a long time did the strange sound ring out, and then it was followed by another one, less hoarse and deep.

"Two more lofers, an' sure one of them is not what I heard before," said Brink.

Twice again he caught the lower, shorter sound, coming against the wind. Then ensued an interval fraught with listening suspense. Brink slowly sank back, almost convinced that his expectation was groundless. Close at hand then, across the pond in the forest, burst out a loud rolling, deep-throated bay like that of a great blood-hound, only infinitely wilder.

It thrilled Brink to the narrow of his bones. He jerked up with a burst of hot fire over him. "Old Gray! That's Old Gray!" he exclaimed exultantly. "No ordinary lofer could have a voice like that. He's fallen in with the bunch rangin' this forest. An' sure as I'm born they're relayin' a deer."

Far off in the woods the bay pealed out, clear on the wind now, remarkable in its appalling long-drawn note of savage nature. These bays came from the same direction as those that had awakened Brink. The wolves had resorted to a trick Brink new well. The pack had split into several parts, one of which relayed the deer for a time, driving it round while the others rested. In Brink's experience the trick was common for a pack that had a great leader.

III

A lowering gray dawn disclosed the forest mantled in a wet snow, deep enough to cover the ground and burden the trees. The wind had eased somewhat and was colder, which facts augured for clearing weather.

"Wal, reckon it's only a skift," remarked Brink. "But it's snow, an' right here my trackin' begins. If it melts, it'll leave the ground soft. If it doesn't, well an' good."

Brink was singularly happy. The Indian-summer days were past. The white banner of winter had been unrolled. Old Gray had passed in the night, ringing his wild and unearthly voice down the aisles of the forest. Somehow Brink had no doubt that the hoarse, hound-like bay belonged to the wolf he was stalking.

"I know his tracks," said Brink, "an' I've heard him yelp. Sooner or later I'll see him. Wal, now, that'll be a sight!"

His educated eyes sought the ground. He crossed the open glade to enter the forest. A blue jay screeched at him from an oak tree, and a red squirrel chattered angrily. Brink espied the wolf and buck tracks fully fifty yards ahead of him. Soon he stood over them. They had been made before the snow had ceased to fall, yet they were clear enough to be read by the hunter. The buck had been running. Two wolves had been chasing him, but neither was Old Gray.

Without a word Brink set off on the trail so plain in the snow. Through level, open forest, down ridge and over swale, into thickets of maple and aspen, across parks where bleached grass glistened out of the snow, he strode on with the swing of a mountaineer. He did not tire. His interest had mounted until the hours seemed moments.

The trail he was following swung in a ragged circle, keeping clear of rocks, cañons, and the windfalls where running would be difficult. Brink passed three relay stations where resting and running wolves had met; and at the last of these all five wolves took the trail of the doomed buck. They had chased him all night. Their baying had kept all of them within hearing of each other. The resting relay had cunningly cut in or across at times, thus to drive the buck out of a straightaway race.

Toward noon the sun came out, lighting up the forest. Everywhere snow was sliding, slipping, falling from the trees. On the snow lay leaves of yellow and red and brown, fallen since the storm. Pine needles were floating down from the lofty pines, and through the green-and-white canopy overhead showed rifts in the clouds and sky of deep blue.

Brink missed none of the beauty, though the grim task absorbed him. He arrived at last where the buck had reached the end of his tragic race, and by some strange paradox of nature the woodland scene was one of marvelous color and beauty. Over a low swale the pine monarchs towered and the silver spruces sent their exquisite spiral crests aloft. Underfoot, however, the beauty of this spot had been marred. Here the buck had been overtaken and torn to pieces.

As Brink had seen the beauty of the colorful forest, so now he viewed the record of the tragic balance of nature. The one to him was the same as the other. He did not hate Old Gray for being the leader in this butchery of a gentle forest creature.

"Wal, now, I wonder how long he'll trail with this pack of lofers," he soliloquized. "If I was guessin', I'd say not long."

How different from those running wolf tracks he had been following were these leisurely trotting paces that led up to the rough bluffs! Brink calculated they had been made just before dawn. The wolves had gorged. They were heavy and sluggish. At this moment they would be sleeping off the orgy.

Brink reached the foot of a very rugged butte, not so high as the adjoining one, Black Butte, which dominated the landscape, but of a nature which rendered it almost insurmountable for man. Obstacles, however, never daunted Brink. Laying aside pack and snow shoes, with rifle in hand he essayed the ascent. After an hour of prodigious labor he reached the base of a low, bulging wall of rock, marked by cracks and fissures. Bobcat, lynx, cougar, fox and coyote had climbed the bluff to their lairs. And then round on the windward side, Brink found the trail of the lofers. The difference between their sagacity and that of the other wild beasts was indicated by their selection of the windy side of the bluff. Brink tracked them toward the dark hole of a den. Upon reaching the aperture he was not in the least surprised to see Old Gray's tracks leading out. He had got a scent on the wind, perhaps even in his sleep, and had departed alone.

Brink took exceeding pleasure in the fact that the great wolf had been too cunning to be holed up by a hunter. This was just what Brink had anticipated. Old Gray was beginning to show the earmarks of a worthy antagonist. Brink knelt to study the tracks.

Old Gray kept to his straight course until halted by the trail he and his lofer allies and Brink and the buck had left in the snow. Here Old Gray had stood in his tracks. Brink imagined he could see the great gray brute awakening to the scent and trail of man in their relation to him. Old Gray had crossed and recrossed the trail, trotted forward and back, and then he had left it to continue the straight course at precisely the same gait.

This nonplused the hunter, who had calculated that the wolf would deliberately set out to find what was tracking him. But there seemed nothing sure here, except that the beast had tarried at this crossing to smell of the man tracks.

Brink took comfort in the assurance that the future trail would prove everything. He trudged on as before. A cold, drab twilight halted him in dense forest, mostly spruce. He selected one so thick of foliage that the snow had not even whitened the brown mat of needles and cones under it, and here he camped. Making fire, melting snow and roasting strips of deer meat occupied him till dark, and then he sought his fragrant bed under the spruce.

Next day it snowed intermittently, in some places half filling Old Gray's tracks. The wolf, soon after leaving the spot where he had crossed the old tracks, had taken to a running lope and had sheered to the east. The hunter had signalized this change by a grim "Ahuh!"

Brink was seven days in covering the hundred or so miles that Old Gray had run during the day and the night after he had left the den on the bluff. It beat any performance Brink could recall in his experience. The beast must have covered the distance in eighteen hours or less; and in his wolf mind, Brink was absolutely certain, he believed he had traveled far beyond pursuit. For then he had abandoned the straight running course for one of a prowling, meandering hunt. Three days more of travel for Brink brought him to the spot where Old Gray had pulled down a yearling.

"Nine days behind," soliloquized Brink. "But it has snowed some, an' I reckon I'm playin' on velvet."

What he was ready for now was to strike the trail Old Gray would break after a kill, when he was making for a high lair to rest and sleep during the day. Brink tracked himself back to the point where he had left the trail of the lofer, and here he camped. During the succeeding week he traveled perhaps fifty miles to and fro across country striking Old Gray's tracks several times, heading both ways. The morning came then, when as much by reason of Brink's good judgment as the luck that favored him, he fell upon a fresh trail, only a few hours old.

The snow lay six inches in depth. By the time Brink had climbed out of the cedars into the pines the snow was three times as deep. Old Gray had navigated it as easily as if it had been grass. Brink trudged slowly, but did not take recourse to his snowshoes.

The winter day was bright, cold and keen, though not biting, and the forest was a solemn, austere world of white and brown and green. Not a bird or a living creature crossed Brink's vision, and tracks of animals were few and far between. It so happened that there was no wind, an absolutely dead calm, something rather unusual for high altitudes at this season. This section of the country contained almost as much park area as forest. It was easy going, despite a gradual ascent.

Old Gray traveled at least eighteen miles up and down, mostly up, before he took to a rocky, brushy recess. Brink considered the distance at least that far because he had walked six hours since he struck the trail.

Taking the general direction of Old Gray's tracks, Brink left them, and making a wide detour he approached on the opposite side of this fastness. He encountered no tracks leading out on that side. The wolf was there, or had been there when Brink arrived. Naturally he wanted to see Old Gray, but not nearly so much as he wanted the wolf to see him. There was no sense in trying to surprise the lofer. After a careful survey of the thicketed ridge he chose the quickest way up and scaled it.

IV

Brink had long fortified himself to meet the grueling test of this chase— the most doubtful time; the weeks of cold tracking, the ever increasing distance between him and the great wolf. For when Old Gray espied him that morning, he took to real flight. Suspicious of this strange pursuer without horse or dog, he left the country.

Five weeks, six, seven—then Brink lost count of time. The days passed, and likewise the miles under his snowshoes. Spruce and cedar and piñon, thicket of pine and shelving ledge of rock, afforded him shelter at night. When the fresh snow covered Old Gray's tracks, Brink with unerring instinct eventually found them again. Old Gray could not spend the winter in a cave, as did the hibernating bears. The wolf had to eat; his nature demanded the kill.

Thus his very ferocity and tremendous activity doomed him in this contest for life with a man creature of a higher species.

His tracks led back to the Cibique, down into the Tonto Basin, across Hell Gate, and east clear to the Sierra Ancas, then up the bare, snow-patched ridges of the basin into the chaparral of juniper and manzanita and mescal, on up the rugged Mazatzal range; over and west to the Red Rock country, then across the pine-timbered upland to the San Francisco peaks, round them to the north and down the gray bleak reaches of the desert to the Little Colorado, and so back to the wild fastnesses where that winding river had its source in the White Mountains.

The king of the gray wolves became a hunted creature. He shunned the range lands, where the cattle nipped the bleached grass out of the thinning snow. At night, on the cedar slopes, he stalked deer, and his kills grew infrequent. At dawn he climbed to the deep snows of the uplands, and his periods of sleep waxed shorter.

Brink's snowshoes were as seven-league boots. The snow was nothing to him. But Old Gray labored through the drifts. The instinct of the wild animal prompts it to react to a perilous situation in a way that almost always is right. Safety for the intelligent wolf did lie away from the settlements, the ranches and the lowlands, far up in the snowy heights. Many a pack of hounds and band of horsemen Old Gray had eluded in the deep snows. In this case, however, he had something to reckon with beyond his ken.

Hunger at length drove Old Gray farther down the south slopes, where he stalked deer and failed to kill as often as he killed. Time passed, and the night came when the wolf missed twice on chances that, not long ago, would have been play for him. He never attempted to trail another deer. Instead he tracked turkeys to their roosts and skulked in the brush until at dawn they alighted. Not often was his cunning rewarded. Lower still he was forced to go, into the cañons, and on the edge of the lowlands where like any common coyote he chased rabbits. And then his kills became few and far between. Last and crowning proof of his hunger and desperation, he took to eating porcupines. How the mighty had fallen! Brink read this tragedy in the tracks in the snow.

For weeks Brink had expected to overtake Old Gray and drive him from his day's lair. This long-hoped for event at length took place at noon of a cold bright day, when Brink suddenly espied the wolf on the summit of a high ridge, silhouetted against the pale sky. Old Gray stood motionless, watching him. Brink burst out with his savage yell. The wolf might have been a statue for all the reaction he showed.

"Huh! Reckon my eyes are tired of this snow glare," muttered Brink, "but I ain't blind yet. That's sure Old Gray."

The black slash at the neck identified the notorious lofer; otherwise Brink could not have made certain. Old Gray appeared ragged and gaunt. The hunter shaded his eyes with his hand and looked long at his coveted quarry. Man and beast gazed at each other across the wide space. For Brink it was a moment of most extraordinary exultation. He drew a great breath; and expelled it in a yell that seemed to pierce the very rocks. Old Gray dropped his head and slunk down out of sight behind the ridge.

Brink plodded on wearily, every step a torture. Only the iron of his will, somehow projected into his worn muscles and bones, kept him nailed to that trail. His eyes had begun to trouble him. He feared snowblindness, that bane of the mountaineer. Upon rounding a thicket of spear-pointed spruce, Brink came to a level white bench, glistening like a wavy floor of diamonds in the sunlight.

Halfway across this barren mantle of snow a gray beast moved slowly. Old Gray! He was looking back over his shoulder, wild of aspect, sharp in outline. The distance was scarce three hundred yards, a short range for Brink's unerring aim. This time he did not yell. Up swept his rifle and froze to his shoulder. His keen eye caught the little circular sight and filled with gray.

But Brink could not pull the trigger. A tremendous shock passed over him. It left him unstrung. The rifle wavered out of alignment with the dragging wolf. Brink lowered the weapon.

"What's come—over me?" he rasped out, in strange amaze. The truth held aloof until Old Gray halted out there on the rim of the bench and gazed back at his human foe.

"I'll kill you with my bare hands!" yelled Brink in terrible earnestness.

Not until the ultimatum burst from his lips did the might of passion awake in him. Then for a moment he was as a man possessed with demons. He paid in emotion for the months of strain on body and mind. That spell passed. It left him rejuvenated. "It's man agin wolf!" he called grimly.

And he threw his rifle aside into the snow, where it sank out of sight.

Brink had to zigzag down snowy slopes, because it was awkward and sometimes hazardous to attempt abrupt descents on snowshoes. Again the lofer drew out of sight. Brink crossed and recrossed the descending tracks. Toward the middle of the afternoon the mountain slope merged into a level and more thickly timbered country. Yet the altitude was too great for dense forest. It was a wilderness of white and black, snowy ridges, valleys, swales and senecas interspersed among strips of forest, patches and thickets of spruce, deep belts of timber.

Brink did not see the wolf again that day, though he gained upon him. Night intervened.

In the cold gray dawn, when the ghostly spruces were but shadows, Brink strode out on the trail. There was now a difference in his stride. For months he had tramped along, reserving his strength, slowly, steadily, easily, without hurry or impatience. That restraint constituted part of his greatness as a tracker. But now he had the spring of a deer stalker in his step. The weariness and pang of muscle and bone had strangely fled.

Old Gray's tracks now told only one story. Flight! He did not seek to hunt meat. He never paused to scent at trail of deer or cat. His tracks seemed to tell of his wild yet sure hope of soon eluding his pursuer.

Before noon Brink again came in sight of the wolf. Old Gray passed the zone of snow crust. He walked and waded and wallowed through the deep white drifts. How significant that he gazed backward more than forward! Whenever he espied Brink, he forced a hard gait that kept the hunter from gaining.

The next morning was not half gone before Brink caught up with Old Gray. The wolf had not eaten or slept or rested, yet he had traveled scarcely ten miles. But he had lagged along. At sight of the hunter he exhibited the panic of a craven dog. The action of his accelerated pace was like the sinking of his body forward. Then he went on, and for long kept even with his pursuer.

The time came, however, when Brink began almost imperceptibly to gain. Brink's practiced eye saw it long before the wolf. But at length Old Gray looked back so often that he bumped into brush and trees. Then he seemed hurried into a frenzy which did not in the least augment his speed. He knew his pursuer was gaining, yet even that could not spur his jaded body to greater effort.

The hours wore on. The moon soared. The scene changed. A wind mourned out of the north. The spectral spruces swayed against the blue sky. A muffled roar of slipping avalanche rose from a long distance and died away. On the level reaches of snow that bright eye above could see the slow diminishing of space between man and wolf. Five hundred yards—four hundred—three hundred!

When daylight came, and Brink saw Old Gray dragging his gaunt body through the snow, now only a hundred paces distant, he awoke the cold, mocking echoes with his terrible yell. And the shock of it appeared to send the wolf staggering off his feet. When the sun the snow-rimmed mountain far above, to bathe the valley in morning glory, Brink was gaining inch by inch.

The end of the long chase was not far off. Old Gray's heart had broken. It showed in every step he made. Sagging and lame, he struggled through the snow, fell and got up to drive his worn-out body to yet another agony. Seldom he gazed back now. When he did turn, he showed to Brink a wolf face that seemed extraordinarily to express the unalterable untamableness of the wild. That spirit was fear. If in that instant Old Gray could have suddenly become endowed with all his former strength he would never have turned to kill his age-long enemy.

Brink's endurance was almost spent. Yet he knew he would last, and his stride did not materially lessen. Inch by inch he gained. But he stifled his strange exultation.

The battle must go to the strong, to prove the survival of the fittest. Nature had developed this wolf to the acme of perfection. But more merciless than Nature was life, for life had weakness. Man shared this weakness with all animals, but man possessed some strange, sustaining, unutterable, ineradicable power. Brink relied upon it. Old Gray was yielding to it.

The last hour grew appalling. Brink felt on the verge of collapse. Old Gray's movements were those of a dying creature. The hunter did not gain any more. Over white benches, through spruce thickets, under the windfalls man and beast remained only a few paces apart. Brink could have knocked the wolf over with a club. But he only stretched out a great clutching hand, as if the next moment he could close it round that black-slashed neck.

Under Brink's snowshoes the snow grew wet and soft. Soon he must take them off. But there would be drifts in the black belt of pine forest below. He smelled the tang of the pines, warm, sweet, woody. The irregular furrow which he trod out with his snowshoes led down over slope and bench to level forest. Under the stately spreading pines the snow swelled into wavy mounds.

Old Gray sank the length of his legs, fell on his side and lay still. Soon the wolf tracker stood over him, gazing down. "Ahuh! Old Gray, you're done!" he panted huskily.

All that appeared left of magnificence about this wolf was his beautiful gray coat of fur, slashed at the neck with a glossy mark of black. Old Gray was lean and thin. His wild head lay on the snow, with mouth open, tongue protruding. How white and sharp the glistening fangs!

It was nothing new for Brink to see the coward in a beaten wolf. The legend of the ferocity of a trapped wolf was something he knew to be untrue. This notorious lofer, so long a menace to the range, showed in his wonderful gray eyes his surrender to man. The broken heart, the broken spirit, the acceptance of death! Brink saw no fear now, only resignation. And for a moment it halted his propelling rush to violence.

Man and wolf, age-long hereditary foes, alone there in the wilderness! Man the conqueror, man obsessed with the idea that man was born in the image of God! No wolf, no beast had ever been or could ever be man's equal. Brink's life had been an unconscious expression of this religion. This last and supreme test to which he had so terribly addressed himself had been the climax of his passion to prove man's mastery over all the beasts of the field.

Yet, with brawny hand extended, Brink suffered a singular and dismaying transformation of thought. What else did he read in those wild gray eyes? It was beyond him, yet from it he received a chilling of his fevered blood, a sickening sense of futility even in possession of his travail-earned truth. Could he feel pity for Old Gray, blood drinker of the cattle ranges?

"Ahuh! Reckon if I held back longer—" he muttered darkly, wonderingly.

Then stepping out of his snowshoes, he knelt and laid hold of Old Gray's throat with that great clutching hand.

V

It was springtime down at Barrett's ranch. The cows were lowing and the calves were bawling. Birds and wet ground and budding orchard trees were proof of April, even if there had not been the sure sign of the rollicking cowboys preparing for the spring round-up.

"I'm a-rarin' to go. Oh, boy!" shouted Sandy McLean.

The shaggy, vicious mustangs cavorted in the corral, and whistled, squealed, snorted and kicked defiance at their masters.

"Reckon I gotta stop smokin'. I jest cain't see," complained Thad Hickenthorp.

"Aw, it ain't smokin', Hick," drawled the red-headed Matty Lane. "Yore eyes has plumb wore out on Sally Barrett."

"She's shore dazzlin', but thet's far enough for you to shoot off yore chin," replied Thad.

"Cheese it, you fellars. Hyear comes the boss," added another cowboy.

Barrett strode from the ranch house. Once he had been a cowboy as lithe and wild as any one of his outfit. But now he was a heavy, jovial, weather-beaten cattleman. "Boys, heah's word from my pardner, Adams," he said with satisfaction. "All fine an' dandy over on the Cibique. You got to rustle an' shake dust or that outfit will show us up. Best news of all is about Old Gray. They haven't seen hide nor hair nor track of that wolf for months. Neither have we. I wonder now— Wouldn't it be dod-blasted good luck if we was rid of that lofer?"

On the moment a man appeared turning into the lane, and his appearance was so unusual that it commanded silence on the part of Barrett and his cowboys. This visitor was on foot. He limped. He sagged under a pack on his shoulder. His head was bowed somewhat, so that the observers could not see his face. His motley garb was so tattered that it appeared to be about to fall from him in bits of rags.

He reached the group of men and, depositing his pack on the ground, he looked up to disclose a placid grizzled face, as seamed and brown as a mass of pine needles.

"Howdy, stranger. An' who might you be?" queried Barrett gruffly.

"My name's Brink. I'm new in these parts. Are you Barrett, pardner to Adams, over on the Cibique?" he replied.

"Yes, I'm Barrett. Do you want anythin' of me?"

"I've something to show you," returned Brink and, kneeling stiff legged, he laboriously began to untie his pack.

When Brink drew out a gray furry package and unfolded it to show the magnificent pelt of a great lofer wolf the cowboys burst into gasps and exclamations of amaze.

"Ever seen that hide?" demanded Brink, with something subtle and strong under his mild exterior.

"*Old Gray!*" boomed Barrett.

"I'm a locoed son of a gun if it ain't!" said Sandy McLean.

"Wal! I never seen Old Gray, but thet's him!" ejaculated Thad.

"It's shore the gray devil with the black ruff. Old Gray wot I seen alive more'n any man on the ranges!" added Matty Lane in an incredulity full of regret.

"Stranger, how'n thunder did you ketch this heah wolf?" demanded McLean.

Brink stood up. Something tame and deceiving fell away from the man. His face worked, his eye gleamed. "I walked him to death in the snow," he replied.

Barrett swore a lusty oath. It gave full expression to his acceptance of Brink's remarkable statement, yet held equal awe and admiration. "When? How long?" he queried hoarsely.

"Well, I started in early last October, an' I saw the end of his tracks yesterday."

"It's April tenth," exclaimed Barrett. "Tracked—walked Old Gray to death! By heaven, man, but you look it! An' you're come for the reward?"

"Reckon I'd forgot that," replied Brink simply. "I just wanted you to know the lofer was dead."

"Ah-hum! So that's why?" returned the rancher ponderingly, with a hand stroking his chin.

His keen blue eyes studied the wolf tracker gravely, curiously. His cowboys, likewise, appeared at the end of their wits. For once, their loquaciousness had sustained a check. One by one, silent as owls and as wide-eyed, they walked to and fro round Brink, staring from his sad lined face to the magnificent wolf pelt.

But least of all did their faces and actions express doubt. They were men of the open range. They saw at a glance the manifestations of tremendous toil, of endurance, privation, and time that had reduced this wolf tracker to a semblance of a scarecrow in the cornfield. Of all things these hardy cowboys respected indomitableness of spirit and endurance of body. They wondered at something queer about Brink, but they could not grasp it. Their meed of silent conviction, their reverent curiosity, proclaimed that to them he began to loom incomprehensibly great.

"Never felt so happy in my life," burst out Barrett. "Come in an' eat an' rest. I'll write you a check for that five thousand. An' fetch Old Gray's hide to show my womenfolks. I'll have that hide made into a rug."

Brink gave a slight start, and his serenity seemed to shade into a somber detachment. Without a glance at Barrett he knelt, and folded up the wolf skin and tied it in his pack.

But when he arose, lifting the pack to his shoulder, he said, "Keep your money. Old Gray is mine."

Then he strode away.

"Hey, what d'ye mean—rarin' off that way?" called Barrett, growing red in the face. It was as if his sincerity or generosity had been doubted. "Fetch the wolf hide back hyar an' take your money."

Brink appeared not to hear. His stride lengthened, showing now no trace of the limp which had characterized it upon his arrival.

The cattleman yelled angrily for him to stop. One of the cowboys let out a kindlier call.

But Brink, swinging into swifter stridge, remarkable even at that moment to his watchers, passed into the cedars out of site.

THE LAST STAND OF THE LOBOS
1925

 UNDER the weight of the relentless extermination program, the West's wolf population was reduced and fragmented until only a few isolated survivors remained. Like "Ghost Wolf of the Little Belts," "Badlands Billy," "Old Three Legs," and "Wolf Tracker," this story is yet another reminiscence about the tracking and killing of the last renegade wolf in a region. The two wolves in this tale were particularly famous because they were the parents of a movie star, a wolf named Lady Silver who played opposite the dog Strongheart in early 1920s silent films and who is the subject of "Winning a Wolf's Heart." The different attitudes toward wolves are especially striking here: on the silver screen, the daughter wolf may have been adored by millions, but her wild progenitors were still abhorred by the local ranching community.

This story, written by the wolfer himself, Donald Kenneth Stevens, appeared in Sunset Magazine *in January and February 1925. Very minor corrections in punctuation and spelling have been made.*

❖❖❖

The Little Belt range of Montana, sprawling northwestward, finally loses itself among low hills only to rise once more, a few miles farther on, in a sudden, isolated group of mountains that offer last resistance to the ever-broadening valley of the Missouri and the western sweep of the prairies.

Those are the Highwoods. Round their base a remnant of the old Montana cow range—of "the West that was east of the Rockies"—lingers yet.

And there two buffalo wolves, survivors of a pack, made their last stand against the creeping tide of civilization, even as did the cattlemen whose holdings bordered the foothills and among whose dwindling herds the two old wolves made yearly slaughter.

While this pair of desperate outlaws, both with paws long scarred by the steel of man—the steel alike of the trap, the plow and the barbed wire—while they fought their last savage, lonely fight there in the Highwoods, their silvery-furred wolf daughter, thousands of miles away, frolicked before the cameras of Hollywood for an audience of a hundred million.

Though Strongheart, the great dog, may boast of royal lineage, his pedigree contains no more illustrious names than those of Snowdrift and Lady

Snowdrift, the Highwood outlaws who were father and mother of Lady Silver, co-star of Strongheart. (Not the German shepherd dog, Lady Jule, but the remarkable wolf actress who did so much to make Strongheart's earlier pictures ring true.)

It was late in the winter of 1921. Nature betrayed her own when the tracks of Lady Snowdrift, the wild mother, led a man with a shovel to the hidden den and eight helpless puppies. Among them was a wabbly-legged, furry little female. Its life was spared by the hunter and it was destined to become the affectionate trailmate of a forest ranger and later the screen favorite known as Lady Silver.

But the father and mother, howling their grief over the loss of the puppies from the windswept ridges, fought on, matching wits with the riders of the foothills and each year leaving such a bloody trail among the dogie herds that it brought down heartier curses and heavier bounties upon their crafty heads.

The huge, peculiarly light-gray male or "dog" wolf and the mate whose fur was silver in the sunshine and as the snow in moonlight, had been known to the cowboys simply and aptly as "those two damned white killers." But after the name, given by another world to the illustrious daughter, drifted back to the Highwoods, the men of the mountains gave the old ones the names of "Snowdrift" and "Lady Snowdrift," partly in description of their unusually light color, partly in grudging admiration.

Bounties were posted not only for the capture of the old wolves, but especially for the yearly litter of pups. And twice more the Snowdrifts were robbed of their young. Yet, though the stockmen's "dead-or-alive" reward was high, offers for the young wolves alive were even higher. For the fame of the white strain was abroad.

Some of those young wolves are not in the movies. Some are in the tame pack of Dr. E. H. McCleery, of Kane, Pennsylvania. One is the pet of Lord Auckland. Another lives with Col. Henry W. Shoemaker, naturalist and historian of McElhattan, Pennsylvania. And Snowdrift had become, in 1923, the father of Lobo, the young wolf who was to be the mascot of Jack Dempsey in his training camp before the Shelby fight.

Since I have known wolves—since, years ago, I slid down a snowbank, took from beneath a granite ledge a coal black wolf cub with his eyes as yet unopened, carried him inside my shirt through a blizzard to camp, raised him on canned milk with a whisky flask as his nursing bottle, and then had to send him, friendly-tongued and waggy-tailed, to the far away Washington (D.C.) Zoological park and a cage-pacing existence—well, since I've known him and other wolves I sometimes wonder why I traveled clear across Montana to "get" the splendid two who were making their last stand in the Highwoods in the spring of 1923.

Of course it is because wolves kill cattle, coyotes kill sheep and mountain lions kill deer, that the United States Bureau of Biological Survey hires men, as it hired me, to destroy them, and stockmen vie with each other to get the "wolfer" to camp on the "home ranch."

But that isn't why the wolfer "wolfs."

And he doesn't wolf because he likes to kill. At least with me, after years in the wilderness from the Yukon to the Yellowstone, that urge had passed.

But those Snowdrift wolves—I simply couldn't resist their challenge. Never had they been completely outwitted. True, their big paw prints in snow or dust showed each had lost a toe in a steel trap. But that had only heightened their prestige in the range country and given the wolfer foemen worthy of his craft.

And, to me spur above all, an old partner of mine, formerly derisive of some of the trapping ruses of my earlier days in the game, had just spent ten months in the Highwoods with 180 steel traps, jar after jar of specially prepared poison, skis, snowshoes, horses, hounds and a pet long-range rifle—and come out without so much as a wolf toe!

When orders came in April, 1923, from R. E. Bateman, United States predatory animal inspector for Montana, to try my luck on the Snowdrifts, I was camped on the National Bison range on the Flathead Indian reservation, trapping and poisoning coyotes that preyed on the antelope of the reserve. I happened to have been so successful there with the new government poison that even "the stolid redmen" of the Flathead reined in their cayuses beside my cabin and grunted, "Huh! Heap coyote! How you catchum?" But I went up to the Highwoods determined not to poison, but to trap those wolves. For, somehow, as a professional wolfer my feeling about those two desperadoes of the Highwoods of whom I had heard and read in the newspapers for years, was different from that toward coyotes.

I arrived with my saddle, rifle, blankets and a few other personal effects at the Horsecollar-T ranch, on Highwood creek, on April tenth. Tales of how "Swede Peterson, the dude wolfer from Milk River," had all but wiped

out the Highwood pack eighteen years before; of how old Griffith, a government hunter—he died on the trap line in 1922 after his wife had snowshoed
twenty miles in an attempt to save him—had shot or trapped all the remaining wolves but Snowdrift and his mate; of how Stacey Eckert, the forest ranger,
had raised Lady Silver; of the recent depredations of the two outlaws; and
much advice to the effect that I could never trap them but must rely on a
chance shot, soon greeted me.

And now I learned, to my deep disappointment, that the day before I
arrived at the ranch, Ranger Eckert and Joe Brandel, a homesteader, had
dug seven wolf pups from a mountain den to which Lady Snowdrift had
been tracked, as in other years, through a tell-tale spring snow. My hope had
been to get there in time to manage the finding of the den so as to bag one or
both the old ones near it. But before I ever saw this den, man tracks had been
made in many directions from it and there was little hope of luring one of the
pair to a trap or into the nearby open for a daylight shot.

❖❖❖

Stevens quickly familiarized himself with the situation—the lay of the land,
the wolves' usual haunts and trails, the local ranchers—and set out to demonstrate
"the trapper's artistry." But shortly after his arrival, the two wolves stampeded a
herd of cattle and killed four steers in one night. All he caught in his traps, though,
was a bobcat, an eagle, and some coyotes. "And so passed the first weeks on the trail
of the Snowdrifts."

❖❖❖

One morning three weeks after my arrival in the Highwoods I left the
ranch aboard a rather snotty buckskin we had run in out of the hills the day
before. In the forenoon I visited the steers in Highwood gap. There had been
no disturbance. I rode on up a long gulch leading to the higher hills. Nearing
a scent-set close to the trail in which the big four-toed and three-toed tracks
had appeared ten days before, I noticed from afar that the scented cow chip
had been moved. Soon I could see an empty hole where the rock drag had
been buried. I spurred up to the spot.

A wolf paw print! And no other tracks near! Forgetting my mount had a
bad case of nerves, I nearly met disaster in swinging hurriedly to the ground.
But his jumps and snorts were uninteresting now.

The big wolf track showed a toe missing from a hind foot—Lady Snowdrift! The track was fresh—had been made just that morning. This was out

on a bare, rocky hillside, but across a big gulch lay a dark patch of timber. Over there—who knew?—

From occasional tracks I learned that the wolf had struggled on the dry open hillside for some time, trying to free a foot or a toe from the grip of the trap. Later she had headed down, over some rocky reefs. And then the rock drag, due to a flaw, had broken in the middle and left her with only the trap and chain. The Snowdrift luck had held.

After losing the rock she had raced down and across the gulch, leaving few tracks that I could find, and entered the heavy timber. I tied the buckskin in the gulch bottom, stripped away all useless weight of clothing—coat, chaps, spurs—tightened my belt and tried the action of the thirty-thirty. I remembered the time Bill Bennet and I had frozen our faces on the trail of a wolf with a trap, up on the Ruby river—I remembered other wolf chases—most of them undertaken in vain.

After tracing occasional scratches where the trap had struck the pine needles as the wolf hurried up through the timber, I found where the chain ring had caught in a bunch of underbrush and the hampered animal had struggled again to get rid of the trap. There was a little fresh blood and the willows were chewed considerably. There was long white hair on the brush and I scented wolf—strong.

BAFFLED AGAIN

From there on the ground was such that I couldn't follow the exact tracks fast enough. So I hiked on up through the timber in the general direction of her flight, hoping to catch sight or better track of her farther on.

Coming out of the timber at the top of the hill, I followed up the ridge toward the head of the creek, carefully watching for a track or scrape across a dusty horse-trail that led the same way.

An hour later I stood at the head of the gulch and its sidehill belt of timber and had not seen where the wolf had left the timber or crossed the ridge. Possibly she had lost the trap and a toe and leaped across the ridge trail in her flight without leaving a visible trace. Otherwise, she must have doubled back down through the woods and crossed out the other side of the gulch to the bare hillside again and over it, as she might not have been averse to doing had it been possible before daylight.

To find out if she had left the pine patch for the open hillside, I skirted the edge of the timber to the head of the little creek that flowed down the gulch. Carefully studying the soft creek banks, I was unable to find a fresh wolf track until I again reached my horse. And almost certainly, I considered, the fugitive would not have turned down the gulch toward the ranches. So as I drew alongside the horse, I was thrilled by realization that unless practised eyes had deceived me, the hunted one was at that moment within the circle I had made and was hiding somewhere in the big dark patch of timber at the lower corner of which I stood.

After thinking it over while resting, I decided not to track the wolf slowly from behind and risk having her sneak from the timber ahead and farther into the mountains. Accordingly, a half hour later, I had again reached the head of the creek by the shortest route, along the creek. Then, I started softly back through the middle of the forest on the hillside, watching and listening—even sniffing—for wolf.

A magpie, quacking excitedly from a pine top, fooled me into vain search of one part of the woods. A heavy blue-grouse, suddenly hurtling through the branches, startled the rifle half way to my shoulder and annoyed me by its possible betrayal of my movements. For I was all Indian now.

About a third of the way back to the horse I was halted by a scratch mark in the pine needles—a scratch that had not been made by a squirrel or rabbit. It was a faint mark of dragging. And here was the wolf paw print headed uphill. I must have passed near her in the pines above, if, indeed, she had not already slunk over the ridge since I had scanned the trail along it. The best scheme now seemed to be to follow the tracks.

I had worked out but a few yards of the trail when a glance uphill under the firs showed a weatherbeaten old mound of dirt. Probably it was a wolf den, like several others I had found in the past few weeks, that had been cleaned out early in the spring when the Snowdrifts were trying to decide where to hide their precious brood, or when instinct was furnishing them with emergency dens to which that brood might be moved on short notice. However, I would have a look at it. So I panted up alongside it.

Fresh wolf tracks led into the hole! Luck at last had swung against a Snowdrift and brought me on her trail that morning so soon after she had lost the rock-drag that she had feared to leave the timber, when she had seen me tracking her on the open hillside across the gulch, and she had taken refuge in the old den.

I knelt in the dirt and managed to see into the hole. For a minute there was nothing but darkness. Suddenly I made out a strand of bailing wire and the trap chain ring. I drew back quickly. As I looked again into the blackness, there were two green eyes, six feet from me.

As I grew accustomed to the faint light I was able to make out a great white head, a smooth muzzle, wolf ears—the whole quiet face of a wolf, watching me. Only her head was visible. The rest of her body was hidden behind a turn in the big burrow.

I sat down beside the mouth of the hole and took out my "brown papers." Well, I'd done it. Here she was. Lady Snowdrift, the famous white wolf. Mine. I could shoot her, now, whenever I got ready to.

I discovered, though, that I wasn't ready.

Sure, she was a merciless butcher, but—

Well, sometime after the cigarette had glowed too near my lips and been crushed slowly into the dirt with a bootheel, I lay down in position to get sight along the rifle barrel thrust ahead of me into the burrow.

The report of the shot underground was almost deafening. Drawing back from the powder fumes, I watched them slowly swirl and lift, in a silent blue veil, from the mouth of the den.

After a while I found a small dead lodgepole with a snap branch, got hold of the trap chain ring with the snag, and managed to pull the heavy, shaggy white body into the sunlight. The mother of Lady Silver had killed her last yearling.

After a fight with the buckskin, I arrived at the Horsecollar-T at dusk with Lady Snowdrift, as cowmen for years had hoped to see her, slung across the saddle. Many ranch telephones were busy that evening.

And all that night the lone, deep-moaning voice of Snowdrift haunted the Highwoods.

For several days I did not see another track of Snowdrift. He had vanished. Eventually I learned he had circled the whole range in search of the lost white queen. Yearling steers on both sides of the Highwoods bawled their last that week. But little of any of them was eaten.

My traps had finally come from headquarters. So by the time Snowdrift returned to the Dexter coulee-Highwood gap country, two freshly killed ponies and seventy-five traps waited on ridge and trail in scent, blind, bait and water sets galore. I had emptied almost my whole bag of tricks in his way. And he proceeded, for a time, to match them all.

I saw fewer and fewer tracks. And had I not happened, now and then, in the course of a week, to catch sight of a big paw print in some soft mole mound of the higher mountains, I might have been sure there wasn't a wolf in the country. He had stopped killing cattle and must have been living on woodchucks and other small animals that, having ended their hibernation, now repopulated the hills and in several ways added to my trapping problem.

Of course, all this time I caught coyotes occasionally, but not many, because my trap lines were higher in the mountains than coyotes, then raising pups in the foothills, often ranged.

Reports of cattle being killed by a wolf on the Merrimac ranch twenty miles away on the east side of the range took me on a two-day trip of exploration there. I decided to move some of my traps to that side of the range, as Snowdrift seemed to have quit the west side.

The day after I got back to the Horsecollar-T, I started round my Dexter coulee line to pick up some traps to take to the Merrimac's range. I caught two coyotes that day and experienced various delays. Along in the middle of the afternoon I placed my foot where a trap had been, to spring it. A recent wet snow followed by wind, had so smoothed the ground that, for a moment, I had not noticed that the trap was gone!

One big paw print was blurred in the mud where Snowdrift, with the trap on his foot, had leaped a creek and rushed for timber.

There were no other tracks. He had been caught two nights before. Snow, since melted, had covered the frozen ground. He had been gone forty-eight hours.

An hour of circling on foot brought me to a second-growth thicket where the evergreens had been chewed to a height of six feet and were covered with wisps of gray fur. The place still smelled slightly of wolf, though it had rained since he had been there, two nights before. He had been tangled several hours but, chewing down saplings, had cut a patch back to the open with trap, hook-drag and all.

Having turned my horse loose to graze with dragging reins, I slowly made out faint scratches, showing the wolf had soon re-entered the timber and carefully followed up a trail, the drag hardly turning a leaf. How he did this and other things will always be something of a mystery. For a while I even wondered if he had carried the drag in his mouth! I had never known any animal to go through such country and leave so few traces, even with only a trap, let alone a hook-drag.

I tracked him up the trail through heavy timber where the snow evidently had not lain deep and the dry pine needles had not been frozen, and out on to a bare, grassy ridge. There the trail ended.

After that I hunted in every direction. I went up and down trails. I followed ridge lines, scanning the wind-loosened dirt on their southern brows for tracks. I waded up and down little creeks through the thick brush, trying to find a track, and noting that of almost every coyote, cat, rabbit and porcupine that had crossed within the last two days. I found the clean-trotting track of the wolf, made as he had come down the mountains from Arrow peak the evening before the snow had commenced to fall. And that was all.

After walking for hours up and down hill in high-heeled riding boots, my feet were ablaze. I found my cayuse in the dusk, wearily slipped the rifle into the scabbard and rode to the ranch.

Tied the next noon at the edge of a natural clearing well up toward the head of Dexter coulee stood three drowsy cayuses. Once in a while they shifted weight from one hip to another, lazily switching tails at imaginary flies as though getting practise for the summer soon to come. The bay and the black carried stock saddles with empty rifle scabbards slung under the stirrup leathers. The buckskin was fitted with a pack saddle, from the crossed wooden forks of which hung two empty rawhide *alforjas* or pack bags. Steel traps lay scattered on the ground.

It had rained several times that morning. Little misty clouds still dragged against the snowdrifts and granite of the peaks not far away, or hung heavy in the heads of cañons. But most of the sky was blue. And in the southern center of it rode the sun.

Not yet dried since the showers of morning, the grass, fast greening up the southern slopes, sparkled in the light. A blur of sage was here and there on open hillsides, fresh gray and green. The baby leaves of willows—to some all trees not cottonwoods or pines are "willows"—looked green against the darker hues of pines, balsams, spruces, hemlocks, lodgepoles, piñons—they all were "pines". And the pines, like the sage, smelled of freedom.

At the edge of the clearing, new-leaved wild roses and buck brush clustered at the feet of thickets of awakening alders and poplars, of service-berry bushes and choke-cherry trees not yet in bloom. And in the open there were many buttercups, all wet.

Ranger Eckert and I had been hunting Snowdrift since dawn; and now we sat on a rotting fir log a little distance from our horses, eating cold meat and flapjacks.

THE LONG HUNT

While we talked we gazed, with careless, accustomed eyes, at miles of dim brown prairies that swept away from the foothills below. We saw the prairies and the far off river breaks. We saw the badlands, sun-painted butte by shadowed butte, quiet sentinels of distance. Beyond, from twisted cutbanked creek to lonely sandrocked draw and coulee, Montana sprawled away, brown bench on bench, gray plain beyond gray plain, and far hill rolled to farther hill, until all outlines, dimming, were lost in purple haze of other ranges and sinking skies.

"Well," Eckert drawled grimly, "we got to find him, that's all—him or that trap, one. If he's chewed out of that trap by now, the trap ought to be round here somewhere with his toes in it. It's got to be," he added, as though doubting himself. "Sure it can't fly any more 'n he can. But—walkin' rabbits!—after a man hunts for near two days and can't pick up a sign, he can believe most anything. Hell, this old Snowdrift always has had a charmed life. I missed him slick and clean at two hundred yards, standing broadside, last year, up on the North Fork."

He tossed down his cigarette and ground it very carefully into the dirt with a forest-protecting heel as he stood up, hitching his revolver holster into place. I picked up the thirty-thirty. The cayuses questioningly turned their heads to watch us as we crossed the clearing and entered the evergreens.

So again in the afternoon we followed creek and ridge lines. Again we crossed and recrossed each other's tracks as we hunted separately. Again we eagerly noted tiny scrapes, on mole mounds, that turned out to be but marks from the sudden kick-back of a rabbit, the dust-bathing of a grouse or the earth-cracking from the subterranean tunneling of a pocket gopher. Again we repeatedly met and compared notes, getting more discouraged after each circle, and at the same time more fanatically determined to solve the mystery. Perhaps, caught merely by a toe, the wolf had twisted free, leaving the trap in some unexplored thicket. Or was he, even then, tangled somewhere, and furtively watching us?

Weary of hunting alone, we took to tramping round together. We were tired, too.

It was when we were crossing the mouth of a rough little cañon, within a few feet of where we already had searched for sign, that I stopped to stare at a faint straight mark across the top of a mole mound. It had been rained upon, and was almost obliterated. But it was the drag mark.

"Hook 'em cow!" I exclaimed; and Eckert was beside me in a bound.

After a long pause he drawled: "Well, I guess nobody's going to back track to see how in hell he ever got here."

And he was right. We knew that up to the time he reached here the trap still had clung to his foot. He had been headed up the cañon.

Then we proceeded to make the old mistake of taking something for granted in regard to this wolf. With new vigor we hurried up the cañon. As hour later saw us stumbling back to unravel that trail inch by inch and, as Eckert expressed, "on our bellies with our noses in the dirt."

This time we managed, by the most painstaking care, to follow to a trail that turned up the right wall of the cañon toward a dense jungle of second growth and dead timber. He had held to the trail for some distance. We could see that one hook had dragged as it should, but that he had miraculously avoided the worst snags and been strong enough to break the rest when the hook caught them. At length we found where he had, indeed, been tangled for an hour or two. The sign from here on grew much fresher. We were on the tracks made that very—

A disturbance in the brush—a sudden crackle! Snap! Crackle! Pant, Pant, Pant!

We both got there first.

S-o-o-o-o-o-o-m-e wolf!

"Man—look at that head! Man—look at those teeth!"

For there stood Snowdrift at bay among the evergreens of his wilderness, while the sun, splashing down through the forest roof, glistened on his light gray fur.

As soon as we came near he quit struggling and sat on his tail to size us up, very coolly. Nothing coyote-like about this splendid animal, whose calm brown eyes held the intelligence and courage of the greatest of dogs.

The trap gripped him high on the famous three-toed right front foot. Perhaps that partly accounted for his adeptness in handling the trap and drag to avoid snags. Perhaps that other trap, that took the toe from this same foot years ago, had been dragged over hills for days after the chain, kinked in the frost of a winter midnight, had snapped to set him free.

And then we noticed the anchor-shaped drag. One prong of it, made of half-inch iron, had been pulled out straight! The heavy ring of the chain, too, was almost straightened. With all our previous respect for the old boy's endurance and craft, we were awed by this fresh evidence of sheer brute power.

But now the drag was caught between two trees. And perhaps it was well, for we noticed that in his occasional efforts he pulled in our direction more often than away from us. Yet, all in all, he was strangely calm and when I stroked his heavy gray muzzle with a stick, he didn't offer even to curl his lip. Yes, it was a long stick I used.

He was slightly darker and a good deal larger than his silvery mate, who had been no small wolf; and later we found that his hide, by actual measurement, with the massive head still in it, hung a length of seven feet eleven inches on a bunkhouse wall at the ranch—a trifle past a notch cut years before in a log of the same wall showed the hide of the biggest wolf on record in the Highwoods to have been. Snowdrift was a fit survivor of his race.

We debated taking him alive for a zoo. But, aside from the fact that it would have been a fine large job, we thought too much of him, perhaps, to put him in a cage—and, anyway, we knew the cowmen demanded the extreme penalty. So finally Eckert, loving step-dad of the old outlaw's famous daughter, Lady Silver, leveled his Colt's "forty-one" revolver.

Because we wanted to save the skull intact, the aim was for the heart. At the first shot, the big wolf merely snapped toward his breast as the impact of the heavy bullet slightly shook him. Then he surveyed us as coolly as ever, standing just as he had before.

Eckert shot that wolf five times through the breast, two of the bullets striking the heart, as we later found, and was just handing me the gun with the last bullet in it, and telling me, with a queer expression on his face, "Put it between his eyes," when the wolf, who had been standing there snapping at each bullet as it went home, suddenly put his nose in the air and dropped dead without a sound.

Such was the heart of Snowdrift, the outlaw.

GHOST WOLF OF THE LITTLE BELTS
1930

 THERE is an entire genre of literature that deals with the killing of the last wolf, or the last grizzly bear, or the last mountain lion, of a certain region. The stories focus on the losses of livestock, the cunning of the marauder, the near misses in the attempts to destroy him, and finally the one determined and skilled man who succeeds. They usually end with the satisfaction of having saved the livestock ("to say nothing of the deer and elk") and ironic admiration—even boasting—of the predator's endurance and intelligence. Stanley P. Young compiled an entire book of such wolf tales, The Last of the Loners *(1970).*

The "ghost wolf" of the Little Belt Mountains in central Montana was finally shot in 1930. This is local writer Elva Wineman's version of the event, originally entitled "White Wolf, Foe of Cattlemen, Is Dead," from Montana Wild Life, *May 1930. His fame lived on, however, as shown by this excerpt from the* Great Falls Tribune, *April 28, 1957:*

Residents of Stanford and surrounding areas in the Judith Basin boast perhaps the most wily wolf of all time— "the ghost-wolf of the Little Belts." But when the wolf was in its prime, curses rather than boasts followed him, for he was a killer . . . .

The finest authority today on the wolf and its antics is Elva Wineman, librarian at Stanford, who in the heyday of the wolf's activities, brought the animal to the attention of the nation with her pen. . . . [T]he finest obituary of the wolf was written by Elva, who like other citizens of Stanford, had grown to think of the wolf as a first citizen of the Judith Basin domain.

That younger generations know the exploits of the White Wolf, Mrs. Wineman is writing in book form an epic poem about its history. And such a poem will be certain to avoid mistakes some writers have made of confusing the White Wolf of the Little Belts with the two Snowdrift wolves of the Highwood Mountains. The latter two were of lesser capabilities and not white, but a light grey. One was killed in 1922, the other in 1923; the White Wolf did not meet his end until 1930. . . .

Elva quoted the man who killed the wolf in words that to this day convey a sentiment that the hunter can understand and appreciate: "And do you know," said Al Close, *"I almost didn't shoot. It was the hardest thing I think I ever did. There he was a perfect shot, the grandest old devil . . . I thought swiftly that these were hills over which he had hunted. I knew that it was the cruel nature of the wilderness, the fight for the survival of the fittest that had made him the ferocious hunter that he was. I thought of all the men who had hunted him, of how his fame had gone out all over the country, and I almost didn't shoot. Swiftly these things passed through my mind as I stood there with my rifle aimed, finger on the trigger, and luckily I came to in time and let the bullet fly fairly into the face of the old criminal. . . ."*

"He was a killer," admits Elva, *"but he was a gallant animal, one to make your blood pressure mount a little higher. He gave us food for speculation for 15 long years, as we bet on and against him. It's been awfully quiet in the Basin since he's been gone."*

❖❖❖

Never again will be heard from the hill-rim of the Little Rockies the soul-thrilling voice of the white wolf, monarch of the wilds. No more will the flying gray wraith strike terror and death into the heart of the frightened herd and feed like an epicure on the choicest animal of the lot. All that he ever wanted from life, he took, won by his own master strategy. But his agile spirit is quelled, his reprehensible career brought to a close, stubborn muscles refuse to respond. Deaf to the call of the wilderness over which he reigned supreme for many years, the shadowy trails will know him no more, for the lone white wolf is dead. As he lived, bold, courageous, arrogant, flaunting his contempt for man and beast alike—so he died, head up, facing the rifle, unflinching and fearless.

Ten, 15, perhaps 18 years, quite a span of life for a wolf under ordinary conditions it is said, and considering the manner in which he had been sought, the fact that every man's hand had been turned against him and he had been hunted from ridge to plain and back to mountain top with poisons, guns, traps, dogs and airplanes—that he lived as long as he did is nothing short of remarkable.

He was killed by A. E. Close, who was accompanied by Earl Neill and their two dogs, following a chase of several hours which began near the Close cabin. The dogs had caught up with the killer and attacked him, the outlaw turning ferociously upon the dogs and driving them back to the hunters whom he failed to see until within forty yards of them. Close fired from his position behind a tree, the shot taking effect in the front left cheek below the eye, "and that's all there was to it," he said modestly.

The men took the carcass to Stanford in the afternoon, accompanied by Gerald Hughes, secretary of the stockmen's association. While they were on the streets several hours the car was able to travel only by inches because of crowds which gathered rapidly as soon as the news of the killing went out.

Every one was trembling, including the hunters, but whether with cold or because of the excitement it is difficult to say. Cameras clicked madly. Every one wanted to see the man who did the shooting and personally ask him how it was done. Old stories of close calls and lucky escapes were brought out and refurbished, and the few persons who had been skeptical of the existence of such an animal were either silent or unusually garrulous in an effort to cover up their confusion and discomfiture.

By nature a cunning strategist, cruel and brutish, following the death of his mate in a trap a few years ago, the big white wolf became still more devilishly murderous, a killer and an outlaw, until his reputation had gone out far beyond the confines of the Jefferson Forest where he ranged.

Letters and wires have come in to Stanford, to stockmen, bankers, the postmaster, the sheriff and others, from hunters in all parts of the United States; from men who had been reading the accounts of the activities of the wolf and who were unable to resist the glamorous call of the wild, the subtle fascination of the mysterious gray-white essence of Satan, each man eager to join in the hunt. Men as far east as New Jersey were interested. Minnesota, Colorado, California and Wyoming sent queries, while fond grandmothers in Wisconsin and Iowa sent word to "keep those children near the house until somebody kills that terrible wolf."

Many sportsmen came to join the chase and after one first-hand view of the lone wolf's hunting ground, one good look at the million acres of lofty ridges and deep canyons, gave up the attempt. Some of them were clever hunters, too, western men, versed in the habits of the carnivore.

Some have almost doubted the evidence of their own eyes, so fleeting were the glimpses of the killer, but none could doubt the maimed and dead cattle left behind, ham-strung, tails bitten off, and often still living, though a meal had been taken from a hind quarter.

Four years ago Earl Neill shot the outlaw in the left hind leg, the wolf making all speed for a snowdrift where his protective coloring made him practically invisible against the snow. Neill has cherished the memory of that encounter, never quite sure that his story was believed. If there was any doubt about it it was settled here this week with the killing of the big wolf, when the left hind leg was found to bear a scar caused by a bullet wound.

R. C. Hardenbrooke tracked him all one day, giving up only when night fell. Many others had the same experience.

One of the most dramatic incidents in the career of the wolf occurred in February, when A. V. Cheney and his five Russian wolfhounds battled fiercely with him near the Cheney ranch for several hours. One of the dogs would do the tackling, grabbing the wolf by the tail and attempting to throw him around to the other dogs. The hound was bitten so many times as a result that he finally refused to fight longer.

Cheney, who had no rifle, then attempted to rope the wolf, but he escaped up a steep mountainside after tiring man, horse and dogs until they were unable to follow.

Alex Salminen and his brother almost succeeded in running him down with a car near Merino.

A train crew coming into Stanford late one afternoon saw him cross the tracks in front of the engine. Upon their arrival in town with the news, there was a general exodus of men and boys with rifles going to the scene, but they failed to get a glimpse of the clever animal. All they saw was an uneasy eagle soaring high above the entrails of a rabbit.

Another time he was seen to cross a field on the Oja ranch near Geyser. One of the Oja boys, who was ploughing near by, unhitched, mounted a horse and trailed the wolf until he was lost in the foothills of the Little Belts.

Skelton brothers of Geyser packed into the hills for a week's intensive hunting. They worked hard with saddle horses and hounds without getting a glimpse of the wolf, or seeing a track. Becoming disgusted, as there was no snow for tracking, they broke camp, loaded their stuff, and with the rifles lying in the wagon box they were about to start down out of the hills when they stopped, startled, while a flip of animated white fur tore across the trail ahead of them, vanishing into the brush beyond. They stared at each other in dismay as it dawned upon them that they had just seen the white wolf.

Early in March, M. G. Daniel, trapper in the employ of the Biological Survey, established a camp in the Little Belts, near Stanford, and for two months has worked on the trail of the wolf. He put out a line of 65 traps and in one isolated section spread poisoned meat. Another trapper joined him recently, bringing a pet wolf, which followed the men like a dog and it was hoped might be the means of attracting the attention of the outlaw, causing him to venture near enough for them to get a shot. But for the last several weeks no sign had been seen of the lone hunter and it was believed that he might have fallen a victim to the poisoned meat and crept off in some coulee to die.

Those who have seen the carcass of the killer say that he is as big as he has always been described: "As big as a full-grown calf," it was said. "He is almost snow-white," the stories went, and they were true. The carcass is six feet in length, including the beautiful brush, nearly 20 inches long. The head is massive, with a full set of teeth, the four sharp, long fangs not badly broken. Gaunt and lank of body, one would be prompted to believe that his hunting expeditions were not so successful of late. Too many interruptions, perhaps, with so many hunters hot on his trail. The pads of his feet are all intact, evidence that he has never been caught in a trap.

The value of cattle he has killed over a period of 10 or 12 years, to say nothing of deer and elk upon which he has fed, runs into thousands of dollars, the heaviest losers being Charles R. Taylor of Dry Wolf Canyon and W. I. Hughes, whose ranch is seven miles south of Stanford.

During a six weeks' period in January and February of this year, 10 kills were made, all registered stock. Stockmen now are relieved to know that they can put away the lanterns which burned in their corrals at night.

OLD THREE LEGS
1931

 AS the war of extermination took its toll until only a few isolated lone wolves remained, local communities developed a proprietary attitude toward "their" wolves. Such pride of ownership led to competing boasts about whose wolf had survived the longest, whose wolf was larger, or whiter, or blacker, or more courageous, or whose wolf had killed more livestock or outwitted more hunters. There was a begrudging respect, too, for the wolves themselves—once they were dead, of course. In fact, once they were dead, they had to be elevated to the status of "worthy foe."

That didn't diminish the intense and personal hatred, though, that burns through many stories about wolves. A 1941 Field and Stream *article, for instance, began, "The Northern caribou wolf rates a lot of superlatives. He is not only the largest, but also the smartest, orneriest, most vicious and blood-thirsty of his species. Further, he is the greatest single menace to the splendid big-game herds of Alaska, and probably the only predator native to the continent that habitually kills for the sheer lust of slaughter."*

Here is another classic tale of "an outlaw wolf that spread terror through the North Woods." The author is A. M. Thompson, and the article appeared in the April 1931 issue of Field and Stream.

❖❖❖

This is the true story of a merciless killer—a monster wolf that left a red trail of death and destruction in his wake. The phantom slayer destroyed thousands of dollars worth of live stock, caused the death of at least two humans and brought about an unprecedented reign of terror in four counties of northern Minnesota.

The life of this cunning beast out-rivals that of the famous lobos, or lone wolves, made popular by Curwood and Seton. Some of the shrewdest trappers and hunters in the country openly admitted that he was too much for them. His mother before him had an evil reputation in that section which was only exceeded by his own in years to come. The bold ferocity of the pair, coupled with their extreme cunning, set them apart from the common wolf and made it possible to get an accurate history of their bloody careers.

The mother was a freak wolf that never ran with a pack. Her head and forepart were those of a giant timber wolf, while her hindpart dwindled to the size of a brush wolf or coyote. She had often been reported as a hyena escaped from some circus, so much did she resemble one.

The earliest record of the killer wolf comes from Bill Foster, a woodsman living near Ponsford, Minnesota. In April 1917, he located the den of the mother wolf and watched it daily through glasses from a vantage point almost a mile away. He was waiting for the pups to be born so that he could realize an additional bounty of six dollars apiece, besides the rich reward hung up for the mother's head.

One day he saw the mother wolf come out of the den, followed by eight tiny specks. And then an unbelievable thing happened. The mother killed seven of the pups and, with the eighth tottering unsteadily after her, trotted off into the woods and never approached the den again.

Trappers and woodsmen who recognized the familiar tracks of the mother reported the amazing growth of the pup by the size of his footprints. Nursed with a bountiful supply of milk, he soon grew into a wolf of giant size.

As their depredations continued it soon became evident that the younger wolf was the bolder and more vicious one of the two. Like silent shadows of death, they would swoop down upon some unsuspecting barn-yard and slaughter every living thing there for the sheer love of killing. The despairing settlers were helpless before the super-cunning of the beasts.

When the young wolf was about two years old, his vicious nature was made manifest in a terrible manner. Theodore Gleesing, a homesteader, found the body of the mother wolf, cruelly torn by the fangs of the youngster. The viciousness she had implanted in his heart proved her undoing. Her body hung on display for two weeks in front of the Ponsford Mercantile Co. and was viewed by hundreds of townfolk and grateful farmers.

The first intimation that the wolf would attack a human came early one morning while Earl Ratcliffe, a teamster for the Duluth Log Co., was on his way to get his first load. The wolf had brought down a doe beside the logging road and was eating her remains when Earl approached. Ratcliffe was unarmed. The wily animal's keen scent must have detected that fact, for he made no move to slink away. He raised his head and drew back his bloody lips in a defiant snarl as he faced the oncoming team.

The horses, smelling the fresh blood and seeing this snarling, bristling, terrifying creature in their path, snorted and trembled in fear. When they were opposite the beast, he leaped. The horses bolted at the same time, and the collar of the off horse struck the wolf in mid-air, sending him rolling in a swirl of snow.

The wolf was up in an instant and leaped again, this time at the man. Ratcliffe, who had yanked a sled stake loose, swung it and knocked the wolf to the ground a second time.

The terrified horses fairly flew down the road, with the wolf in full pursuit. As the beast drew alongside, Ratcliffe hurled the heavy stake and struck the wolf in the side. This apparently discouraged him, for he gave up the chase. When Earl and some men from camp armed themselves and returned to the dead doe, the wolf had disappeared.

This incident was something unheard of before in that country. Wolves in a pack have, on rare occasions, been known to attack humans, but for a lone wolf to attempt such a thing was almost unbelievable.

Three weeks after this incident the killer visited the homestead of Grover Amundson and killed forty sheep, one cow and one heifer, all in one night. Mrs. Amundson was a frail, city-bred girl, unused to the harsh demands of this new country. The neighbors around there say the disappointment of this heavy loss was too much for her. At any rate, she died less than four months afterward.

Their two children were sent to relatives in Minneapolis, and Grover lived alone on the homestead. Constant brooding over his losses and the death of his wife must have upset him mentally. He became grim and silent, and some months later disposed of his livestock and took to the woods with traps and guns, determined to put an end to this wolf. Weeks and months passed by, but he kept doggedly to the trail. Nothing his friends could say would induce him to give up his mad quest. To get this killer became an insane passion with him.

Finally there came a day when it seemed that his persistence had won out. In avoiding one trap the cautious beast had planted his left forefoot directly into another. When Amundson got there in the morning, the trap, stake and all were gone. The bits of wood scattered about told of how the wolf had chewed on the stake until it had loosened. With the dragging trap and stake making a plain trail in the snow, the wolf had headed north.

Less than two hours after his discovery Grover headed a posse of nine men and six ferocious dogs, hot on the trail of the wolf. They all felt confident that at last the killer was doomed. But they reckoned not on the remarkable endurance of the beast. They followed the trail feverishly until nightfall, and put up with a farmer. At daybreak they took up the chase, and toward noon let the dogs loose. It was hoped that the dogs would hold the animal at bay until they could come up and kill him.

Late that afternoon they found three of the dogs at intervals of a mile or more apart, with their throats torn out. When they made camp that night, the remaining dogs came slinking back, whimpering and cowering in fear.

At ten o'clock in the morning of the third day they found the trap and stake. The entrapped foot had been neatly chewed off. They were in hopes the wolf would weaken from pain and loss of blood; so continued the chase. So far as they knew, it had eaten nothing since the chase began.

The third night was spent on the Clemmer farm. Early the next morning they were greeted with the disheartening information that the wolf had killed and eaten a good portion of a calf on the John Grammer farm during the night. They knew that, fortified with fresh food and freed of its impediment, the wolf was more than a match for them. All of the hunters except Amundson dropped out of the chase.

For the next month and a half Amundson would show up at intervals of a week apart, secure a fresh supply of food and slip back into the woods again. His face became gaunt and hollow, and his eyes took on a wild, staring look. He ignored his neighbors' pleas to give up the chase. There is no question but that the man was insane by this time.

There could be only one end to such madness. Old Oscar Nesbitt, a trapper, found Amundson's body, frozen stiff. He claimed that around the body he had found the tracks of the three-legged destroyer, which had come back to sniff—probably sneer—at this poor mortal who sought for so long to destroy him.

While Old Three Legs, as he was now called, was recuperating from his amputated foot he ranged in Itasca State Park. This is a state game preserve and consists of a vast area of virgin timber. The mighty Mississippi begins in this primeval forest and is so tiny that one can step across it here.

The large number of partially eaten does and fawns that littered the woods during Old Three Legs' sojourn there caused no little concern to the state wardens and foresters. They posted a reward of $200 for the head of this beast. The attractive bait drew grizzled veterans of the trap-lines from all over the North Country.

They caught lots of coyotes and other predatory animals, but not Old Three Legs. Most of them went away convinced that the animals could not be caught. It was here that some of the wildest and most fantastic stories of this wolf originated.

In northern Minnesota today one can meet any number of people who will solemnly swear that Old Three Legs was a phantom, a ghost wolf that traps could not hold nor bullets harm. They are sincere in their belief that he has never been caught, some even denying that the wolf mounted and on display at Detroit Lakes is Old Three Legs.

Others will tell you that they saw him with their own eyes as he put one foot into a trap, sprung it, then withdrew the foot unharmed and trotted to another trap to repeat the performance.

John Red Blanket and Jesse Mason, two renowned Indian hunters and trappers from the Red Lake Agency, were invited to try their luck against the beast. After two weeks of fruitless effort they came into Ponsford with the weirdest tale of all. According to them, the animal had appeared suddenly from nowhere and stood fifty feet in front of them, grinning over his shoulder. They both fired point-blank, but the wolf never budged. After they had emptied their guns, the wolf vanished before their eyes. They were extremely agitated and unnerved over their experience, and no amount of money could induce them to take up the hunt again. While some are inclined to blame bad prune whiskey for their impossible story, there's no denying that their simple minds were terribly upset over some unusual happening.

When Old Three Legs left the game preserve to roam the countryside again, he exacted a terrible toll from the none too affluent farmers for the loss of his foot. No one could foretell where he would strike next. Here one night, and often in the next county, forty miles away, the next night. Children were escorted to and from school by armed fathers. Every one was anxious to win the coveted reward and honor of slaying him; so every other man carried some sort of a weapon.

The harassed farmers were becoming desperate over their steady losses and appealed to the state for aid in ridding the country of this scourge. Their pleas met with no response. Huge drives consisting of hundreds of men were organized, and a number of times it was reported that Old Three Legs was surrounded. But always he managed to slip through the cordon of men closing in on him.

Finally a pool was collected, and Julius Skauge, a professional trapper from the West, was sent for. Mr. Skauge had an enviable record in destroying cougars, wolves and other predatory animals where other men had failed. Famous wolves that had cost ranchers of the West untold thousands of dollars have fallen before the cunning of this man. From Canada to Mexico and from the Mississippi westward, his reputation as a trapper is widespread.

But in Old Three Legs he found a foe worthy of his mettle. For three months he strung out his poison bait-lines and traplines, and in the end even resorted to an attempt to run the wolf down by using relays of tough Western ponies. And, like the rest who had tried, he finally admitted defeat.

Upon his recommendation Jack Holtan of Lammers, Minnesota, was sent for. Holtan had worked with Skauge in the Yellowstone and was considered a wizard with snares. It was believed that Old Three Legs had had no experience with snares.

Holtan arrived a day or so later with his cunningly contrived snares. He chose his locations carefully. When he had finished, he confidently announced that he would go out and bring in Old Three Legs the next day.

But old Jack Holtan was to learn a few things about this uncanny beast also. When he went over his line, he found he had snared three brush wolves, one bobcat, a young deer and a jack-rabbit. Old Three Legs was not yet ready to be taken.

In the fall of 1925 the inhabitants of that country noted with some apprehension the tracks of two smaller wolves beside the huge paw of the killer. If he had decided to mate, they saw the woods overrun with super-wolves, offsprings of this cunning beast. Up to now Old Three Legs had pursued a lone course, and any wolf, whether male or female, that chanced to cross his path was quickly torn to pieces.

But Old Three Legs hadn't mated. It was later discovered that his two companions were speedy little coyotes that would circle and chase the game close to the giant killer, where he made short work of them. His muscles and joints were probably beginning to stiffen with age, so that it was no longer easy for him to slip into that deceptive lope which would tire the swiftest deer. The killing power apparently remained just as strong in his muscular shoulders, neck and jaws.

It was fate which finally decreed that this bloody career should come to an end. Five deer hunters—Harry LaDue, Fred Darkow, Jack Robbins and

George McCarthy of Detroit Lakes, Minnesota, and Herb MacArthur of Ogema—started out one morning from Jerry Wettle's camp on Big Medicine Lake. McCarthy and Darkow took posts about a half mile apart, while the rest began a drive.

A few minutes later McCarthy was astonished to catch a fleeting glimpse of Old Three Legs as he disappeared over a knoll a few hundred feet away. He fired twice at the fleeing wolf, but was so excited that he missed both shots.

A doe, startled by the sound of the shots, started up right in the path of the killer. Straight toward Darkow ran the doe, with the old wolf hot on her trail. A strong west wind was blowing, and Darkow was down-wind from the doe and her pursuer. Notice how nicely fate maneuvered to bring about her ends.

First, McCarthy's shot. Next, the startled doe popping up right in front of the wolf. The chase, the wind blowing in the wrong direction. Last, the doe heading right toward Fred Darkow, one of the best shots in the country.

Darkow, alert and intent, heard a slight crackling in the brush to his right. Then he saw the frightened doe hurl herself from the woods into the clearing in front of him. His rifle flew to his shoulder. Just as his finger was tightening on the trigger the gray form of Old Three Legs, with his peculiar gait, loped into view.

Darkow claims that he almost succumbed to buck fever when he realized that here was the one chance in a million to get the killer wolf. He took a deep breath and gritted his teeth in an effort to steady his nerves. Slowly and with much deliberation he swung his gun until he had a dead bead on the old wolf's heart.

With the crash of the gun the wolf made a peculiar twist that almost saved its life. The eyes of the animal had caught the movement as Fred fired and, in the minute fraction of time which elapsed, had twisted so that the bullet intended for his heart penetrated his neck. The wolf leaped high in the air, and turned over and over in a swirl of snow. Fred pumped another bullet into the barrel and ran over to the dead wolf. He could scarcely believe his eyes.

The body was sent to Minneapolis to be mounted. Thousands of people who had read of Old Three Legs in the newspapers paused before the window of the taxidermist to gaze at the body of the notorious old fellow.

Old Three Legs is now mounted and stands on a huge pedestal in the lobby of the McCarthy Hotel at Detroit Lakes, Minnesota. Ranged around the foot of the pedestal are newspaper clippings covering the exploits of the beast. There is nothing in fiction to rival the accounts as related there.

As you stand before him and read of his bloody career you will shudder. When you look at those cruel fangs and think of the untold suffering they have caused, you feel that he deserved death if any living thing on this earth ever did.

But regardless of what your feelings are, you will find yourself unconsciously admiring the courage and uncanny intelligence which this dumb beast showed in outwitting the craftiest hunters who could be pitted against him. Even those who suffered most through his depredations regard his stuffed body with awe and respect and are heard to mutter: "Yes, sir! He was a smart wolf. He had us all licked, and if he'd a gotten an even break that last time he'd a still had us licked."

A CONTRARY POINT OF VIEW

JUST as the historical hatred of wolves had many components, so too does the more recent view of appreciation, even fascination with wolves, as shown in these ten stories from 1892 to 1944.

There is the somewhat anthropomorphic view that wolves and other animals may share emotions, personalities, and character traits with humans, as the "noble and heroic" wolf in "In Van Tassel's Corral," and may therefore deserve our respect. There is also the notion, still growing today, that they may deserve ethical consideration, as noted in "A Grave Mistake" and "The Price of Heredity." "The Wilds Without Firearms" suggests that wolves are a harmless part of the natural world: "Without a gun all objects, or my eyes, were so changed that I had only a dim recollection of having seen the place before." In "Winning a Wolf's Heart," a film director patiently appeals to the wolf's paramount sociability and intelligence and thus demonstrates that wolves are not monsters. And "The Polite Wolf" recounts the story of a pet wolf that was much loved by family and friends, but was eventually consigned to a zoo because his strength and high spirits exceeded his owner's ability to cope. The author of "The Wolf-Pack" takes another approach: he examines some of the charges against wolves and proves them to be absurdly, laughably impossible. "Departure for the Night Hunt" is an excerpt from the earliest scientific study of wolves, which provided a wealth of information about the behavior and ecology of the species that has since greatly enlarged the general public's knowledge and appreciation.

One more aspect of the contrary point of view of wolves has been their disappearance in this century from much of their original range. There was nostalgia for the loss of a creature that had for so long been a symbol of the mystery and power of wilderness, but there was also recognition that the loss had widespread consequences. The author of "Yellowstone Wolves" was thrilled to watch some of the last wolves ever seen in the park. Another author and his wife considered themselves very fortunate to have spent "Three Years in the Wolves' Wilderness," observing "those beautiful and most highly intelligent animals of the northern wilderness." Taken as a whole, these stories speak of humanity's genuine and abiding need for what is wild—including wolves.

A GRAVE MISTAKE
1892

 THIS poem by Emily Henrietta Hickey, originally entitled "A Wolf Story," was published in The Leisure Hour *in 1892. Ernest Thompson Seton was so impressed with the tale that he sent it to the widely read sports and outdoor magazine,* Forest and Stream, *which reprinted it on March 6, 1897, with Seton's comment that "It bears all the internal evidence of truth, and is, I think, about the best wolf story ever written." Thirty-five years later, Seton reprinted it again in a collection he edited,* Famous Animal Stories: Animal Myths, Fables, Fairy Tales, Stories of Real Animals.

❖❖❖

Instinct or reason, which, good sirs? Oh, instinct in brutes, you say!
And reason only in lordly man! Well, think of it as you may,
I'll tell you of something not unlike to reason I saw one day.
Is it only men that are makers of law? Perhaps! Yet hearken at bit;
I'll tell you a tale; say you if e'er you have heard a stranger than it.

It was many and many a league away from the place where now we are;
And many a year ago it happed, in the land of the Great White Czar.
It was morn; I remember how cold it felt, out under a low pale sky,
When we moored our boat on the river-bank, my companion Leigh and I;
And the plunge in the water unwarmed of the sun was less for desire than
    pluck,
And we hurried on our clothes again, and longed for our breakfast luck;
When, all of a sudden, he clutched my arm, and pointed across. And there
We stood side by side and watched, and as mute as the dead we were.

We saw the grey wolf's fateful spring, and we saw the death of the deer;
And the grey wolf left the body alone, and swift as the feet of fear
His feet sped over the brow of the hill, and we lost the sight of him,
Who had left the dead deer there on the ground, uneaten body or limb.

So, when he vanished out of our sight, we rowed our boat across,
And lifted the carcass, and rowed again to the other side. "The loss

For you, good Master Wolf, much more than the gain for us will be!
'Twere half a pity to spoil your sport except that we fain would see
The reason why, with hunger unstaunched, you have left your quarry be-
　　hind;
Red-toothed, red-mawed, forgone your meal! Sir Wolf, we'll know your
　　mind!"

Hungry and cold we watched and watched to see him return on his track;
At last we spied him a-top of the hill, the same grey wolf come back,
No longer alone, but a leader of wolves, the head of a gruesome pack.
He came right up to the very place where the dead deer's body had lain,
And he sniffed and looked for the prey of his claws, the beast that himself
　　had slain;
The beast at our feet, and the river between, and the searching all in vain!

He threw up his muzzle and slunk his tail, and whined so pitifully,
And the whole pack howled and fell on him,—we hardly could bear to see.
Breaker of civic law or pact, or however they deemed of him,
He knew his fate, and he met his fate, for they tore him limb from limb.

I tell you, we felt as we ne'er had felt since ever our days began;
Less like men that had cozened a brute than men that had murdered a man.

IN VAN TASSEL'S CORRAL
1901

 IN science, anthropomorphism—attributing human emotions, motivations, and thoughts to animals—is assiduously avoided because it is not an objective way of understanding what animals do and why they do it. But in folklore, animals have long had human qualities and symbolic meanings. They have even taken human form and speech to tell us about themselves, about ourselves, and about the world. These meanings derive from the cultures of the people and ultimately from observations of the animals in the ecological settings where they occur.

This story is a fictional account of what might be termed altruistic behavior by a wolf. The social nature of wolves as well as their intelligence, documented by many modern researchers, makes the story entirely plausible, even though the narrator's emotional involvement and anthropomorphism overstep the bounds of scientific description.

This tale by Western writer Franklin Welles Calkins appeared in Outing Magazine *in 1901.*

❖❖❖

In an old but refitted shack in Van Tassel's hay corral, and near its close-swung gate, I had comfortable division headquarters. By delay in construction, my section of the new railway line, cross-sectioned for the graders, was unoccupied for several months. There were thus a number of idle engineering forces along the line, and at our camp we spent the long, hot summer just lazing about. The hay corral, which served as a winter and wolf-tight pasture for colts, covered nearly two square miles of break and bottom, and was enclosed with a very formidable fence of eleven barbed wires, thickly studded with short cedar posts, and with ground-tight boards running the complete circuit at the bottom. Within this enclosure lay flat, low, hay lands; on either side [of] the Running Water a second bench of sage brush and cacti, inhabited by prairie dogs; then a series of chalky cliffs, topped with a narrow stretch of summit ridge as level as a barn floor. Along the crest of the hights grew scattering umbrella pine, wind-blown, thick-topped and rugged, affording grateful shelter from the fierce midday heat of a semi-arid region. To a certain aery upon these hights I carried my camp-made hammock of gunny sacks, and there, idling and reading, I spent many afternoons.

The only denizens of the corral were natives of the soil. There were numerous prairie dogs and jack rabbits, badgers, spermophiles or striped gophers [ground squirrels], pocket gophers, snakes, owls, and, on the bottoms, kangaroo mice. I soon discovered that a single prong-horn buck was imprisoned within this high enclosure; at first a saucy, whistling, stamping fellow; but presently he accepted me as a neighbor, and paid little attention to my comings and goings. A little later, when I had formed quite a habit of climbing to the umbrella pines and lolling there, I discovered another four-footed occupant of a larger breed, and also a curious intimacy which proves that the lion and the lamb may sometimes lie down in company. The day was hot and the prong-buck, to get the benefit of a slight breeze, and some immunity from the flies, lay upon the point of a ridge some hundred and fifty yards away and and a little below me. In that clear atmosphere the buck seemed even much nearer and, as I watched him lazily, he chewed contentedly at his cud, while cow birds hopped about him, pecking at the flies. Then, in a curiously indefinite way, I became aware of another living and moving form upon the ridge—a stealthy creeper whose coat of neutral gray blended with the tints of the sere buffalo grass and the lead color of the cacti among which it crawled.

A close inspection discovered in this intruder the outlines of a huge gray wolf, which was apparently stalking the prong-horn. Much interested and excited I rose cautiously in my hammock to watch the drama. The wolf seemed a monster of its species, its body scarcely less in size than that of the apparently unconscious buck. From a humane point of view I should, of course, have shouted to scare the stalker off, but the fascination of the game took strong hold of my imagination. Here was something worth while in wild life—to watch the great buffalo wolf, scarcely second to the cougar in size and strength, and quite its equal in ferocity, in a struggle with game worthy of its wiles and its fighting ability. I had actual knowledge that the prong-horn is a bold, vigorous and skilful fighter, and has ordinarily little to fear from any beast that attacks it—that it seldom runs from the mountain lion or wolf, and never from the coyote. Nearer and nearer crawled the gray beast, worming its way inch by inch, until so close that it seemed the buck must be blind of one eye. Suddenly the wolf leaped in a lithe bound, not upon the prong-horn but over him, snapping right and left at a bevy of cow birds which had been pecking about the animal's legs! Unconcernedly the prong-horn chewed at its cud, and the wolf walked away to a little distance, lay down, stretched its legs and lolled contentedly. And there this oddly assorted pair rested in perfect amity until the wolf, cocking an eye, caught sight of my lightly swaying hammock, and trotted leisurely away to cover of the rocks.

Much interested in this curious occurrence, I questioned the cow-men that evening at Van Tassel's. I was assured that the prong-buck and the wolf were considered excellent friends, and had often been seen together. Both these animals, said the punchers, had in their building the corral been closed in unwittingly, and they had lived together now three years. Both wolf and antelope had doubtless tried at first to jump the fence and had received such punishment from its stinging wires that they had since avoided its lines of cedar posts as men avoid a pestilence. It is a well-established fact that no wolf, deer or antelope, having once failed in an attempt to scale a wire fence, will ever again approach it nearer than a stone's throw. At first the foreman at Van Tassel's had intended to shoot or poison the wolf in the hay corral, but as time passed, and the animal did not disturb the colts in winter, it was allowed to live. The immunity of the young stock was due, beyond doubt, to the fact that marmots, jack rabbits, cotton tails, and other small creatures, free from inroads of pestiferous coyote packs, throve and multiplied exceedingly. I have never anywhere seen jack rabbits so plentiful.

In subsequent visits to my aery I often saw the wolf, which finally came, like the prong-horn, to regard me as an inoffensive creature. On a number of occasions I saw the two together—quite frequently enough to make apparent that a kind of comradeship existed. They never appeared to take note of each other, yet there was in their atmosphere a certain something—the feel of acquaintanceship and amity. In the narrow line of breaks which was their midday retreat they were simply at home together. My comings and goings came to be practically unnoted by them. Only when I jumped one or both in climbing or descending one of the narrow rocky draws was there any movement of uneasiness.

Then the animals simply threw up their heads in a brief survey, which came to have the feel of recognition, and loped leisurely away. I soon began to consider myself a biped member in an odd group of mammal friends. I came to know intimately the markings of my four-footed neighbors and could, I am very certain, have singled either of them out in a large company of its fellows. The prong-buck was rather slight in build, more gazelle-like in appearance than the average of its kind. Its markings of white were a little narrow and uneven, its horns an inch or two short and tilted uncommonly far forward. I have no doubt this last peculiarity added something to its fighting qualities. The canine was simply a king dog wolf, such an one as would, at large, have been acknowledged leader of a winter pack. His weight could not have been less than that of the prong-buck. In color he was of a light gray, almost white upon the throat and belly. He had, notwithstanding his uncommon size, the lithe, springy movement and the air of the young dog, and from these qualities I argued that he had been a mere pup, still haunting closely the home den, when the fence builders had shut him in. He was evidently well fed, for, early in July, he had shed his winter coat and presented a sleek, clean-limbed appearance.

It was not long before I saw him stalk and capture his favorite tid-bit, a fat marmot [prairie dog]. This was no easy task but one requiring infinite caution and a cat-like patience. It is only in sunshine that the prairie dog sits outside or wanders from the hole in its tiny mound, and then, despite its saucy chippering yelp, it is an exceedingly watchful and wary creature. So near you may come and no nearer, seems to be its watchword—a pert flip of the stubby tail, an expert dive and then silence and security. The big wolf, perfectly understanding this habit, stole toward a group of hillocks, from out the cover of a draw, and with more than an Indian's caution. He seemed scarcely to move, crawling flat upon his belly, and taking advantage of every small sage clump or spray of cactus which could cover, even partially, his advance. He often stopped stone still and lay for minutes without so much as wiggling an ear. He was a half hour going fifty yards, and when, at last, he had reached the nearer mounds I knew he had failed for every bobbing little speck upon the earth heaps suddenly disappeared. I thought he would return discouraged but no, he arose and looked about cautiously, then trotted to a sprawling cluster of sage bush and vanished as by magic. I watched until my eyes ached, and after a long time, the little gray figures reappeared, sitting bolt upright and peering with alert eyes until satisfied their coast was clear. For a still longer time the tiny fellows kept close to their mounds continually bobbing up to watch. Then an incautious one got within reach; there was a lightning-like pounce out from cover and the wolf snapped up the luckless one and lugged it away to his lair.

About the first of August the peace of the corral was rudely broken in upon by the coming of Alexander, our assistant chief engineer, a hardy, blustering and conceited Scot, who drove his grays in at the corral gate with his usual grand flourish and volley of orders. He was accompanied by six leaping, long-legged hounds as noisy and unwelcome as himself. Fortunately for the temper of my idle force, the man drove off early next morning for a hurried trip up the line, but, much to my disgust, he left his bellowing, nosing pack behind. As soon as he was out of sight I took ropes and stakes and picketed the dogs out safely at some distance from the shack. Yet, about four o'clock that afternoon, as I lay reading in my hammock, there broke out upon the flat a blatant yammering of hounds and I looked down to see the whole pack, in full cry, in chase of my prong-horn buck. One of the boys had sighted the antelope and thoughtlessly turned the dogs loose to see some fun. I was vexed enough but at first had no fear for the buck, for I had never known Alexander's dogs to lay tooth to any creature swifter than a molly cotton-tail.

As I watched the race, however, from my perfect point of vantage, I soon saw that inside the hay corral, big as it was, the dogs were running at tremendous advantage. Great as was the prong-buck's fear of the hounds, his fear of the deadly wires was greater. At first he ran straight at the western line of fence and, for a moment, I thought he would make an attempt to leap it and I watched with my heart in my mouth until, at fifty feet or less, he veered in a flash and ran alongside. He had gained upon the pack at every jump until the turn when they lined his course finely cutting its angle in a way to win a surveyor's admiration. The leader fell but a rod or two short of the buck's heels as they came on behind. Up the breaks they went, the prong-horn stretching away again in splendid leaps. At the northwest corner of the corral he was again turned and again the hounds cut the angle of his course and this time the pack's two leaders came in ahead. The buck's escape was narrow; a mighty jump carried him high over the head of the foremost hound but the second, springing at his neck, missed apparently by a hair's breadth. And now the chase came straight toward my perch. The buck passed within fifty feet sailing down the breaks like some great white and yellow bird. I ran in front of the hounds, shouting at them to come off and flourishing my walking stick but I would better have saved my breath. They tumbled past bellowing like mad things and the chase hurtled down the breaks and across the flat below.

As the buck lunged across a low ridge upon my left, a gray streak shot out from cover of rocks, across his heels. It was the big wolf going like the wind. He passed directly under the noses of the foremost hounds. He looked saucily over his shoulder as though daring the pack to come on. Its two leaders slowed up, hair on end, and the prong-horn dropped into a draw and out of sight. Then seeing only the great wolf, halting his pace temptingly upon the ridge, the hounds bowled after him in a fresh and savage outcry. I threw up my hat and cheered and ran to a nearer point of vantage. The wolf's plain dare could not be misinterpreted. He had been listening to those dogs and watching the chase and, when the opportunity came, he had run boldly in to draw off the pack. After the first lightning dash he purposely slackened his pace and as plainly watched, with critical eye, the advance of the bellowing dogs. He could easily have outstripped them but disdained to run. At the foot of the breaks some two hundred yards below me he allowed the foremost hound to overhaul him. And then I saw a sight!

The big wolf now plainly showed his hand, or rather his teeth. He sprang sidewise as the hound leaped at him and fastened his teeth behind the animal's ear with a snap of electric quickness. Then with mighty, backward wrenches he jerked that howling dog after him until his keen fangs had cut their way through skin and muscle and left a gaping wound. This effective and expeditious handling took the sand out of the pack's leader who stood back and yelped with pain as the other five bowled in, one after another, and flung themselves at the quarry. Numbers made them fearless and, had they been fresh, the issue could scarce have remained long in doubt. Not for an instant did the great *lupus* waver or shrink from their fierce attack. He leaped among and over the dogs in big, lithe bounds, cutting their skins with his keen teeth, snapping right and left with an energy which, as I ran closer in, made his white fangs seem to show on all sides at once.

Looking down upon the leaping canines, at the distance of a hundred yards, I could see distinctly every movement in this exciting fight, and I could hear plainly the click of the big wolf's teeth when he missed the skin of a dog. The wolf's activity was something tremendous, and yet he fought warily keeping outside every combined rush of the dogs. For fully five minutes the hounds rushed him, pluckily striving to fasten upon the lightning leaper and to bear him down. The fight swung, in a half circle, out upon the flat and then back upon the slope still nearer to my position. Plainly the hounds were tiring. All of them were cut and bloody. The wolf's jaws were literally red with gore. His activity never for an instant slackened, nor his wary watchfulness. And now, with rhythmic like precision, one after another of the hounds was snapped and, with a fierce muscular jerk, thrown rolling and sometimes end over end. Presently, when the hounds were fagging and seeking more to avoid his jaws than to fasten upon him, the wolf caught a big, woolly half-breed by the throat and sprang away, threshing the strangling brute upon the ground, and shaking the life out of it as I had seen him shake to death a tough but helpless marmot. This exhibition proved too much for their waning courage and joining helpless yelps with their leader the remainder of the pack, with tails drooping, fled away toward the shack.

With a final, fierce lunge the great wolf jammed his victim upon the ground and finished the kill. Then, with either forefoot, as if quite disdaining the taste of dog, he cleaned his jaws of hair, and loped away among the breaks. My cheers accelerated his pace, and I could not refrain. I shouted until I was hoarse. By his own instinct, and in his animal way, that bold gray wolf had done a noble and heroic thing. He had thrown himself into the breach to save his friend and he had fought as a brave man fights, with skill and judgment, and like a Trojan. In justice to Alexander I must add that when he returned an hour or two later, and had heard my story, he nursed his wounded hounds and did not let the sun go down upon his wrath.

THE PRICE OF HEREDITY
1908

 IN the study of both humans and animals, one of the oldest and most basic questions is whether behavior is innate or learned. Is behavior the "result of the genetic endowment of the individual" or is the primary determinant "the past experience of an individual"? Heredity or environment? Nature or nurture? Here is a brief musing on the question by John Franklin Lewis, originally entitled "The Price of Heredity: A Story of Ten Little Wolves," from Outing Magazine *(August 1908).*

❖❖❖

A scene recently witnessed at a court house in a small country town in Iowa would have made a good subject for a painting by a master.

A countryman living in a remote part of the county brought in ten young wolves which he had captured near his home. There is a price upon the heads of all wolves, old or young, and the man was after this bounty.

People crowded around to see the captives just as they have ever since the days of Caesar and Alexander. The little cubs were like young puppies, with soft fur and sharp, bright eyes that in blissful ignorance looked without fear or anger on their captors. Dimpled children and rosy-cheeked schoolgirls caressed the animals with their little hands with many exclamations of admiration and pity. How sweet! How pretty! The poor little things! Everybody seemed to shrink from the thought of slaughtering the little waifs of the wild.

The gruff old doctor who would cut up the living or the dead without the bat of an eye or the twinge of a nerve, said it would be more humane to send them to some park as "zoo specimens," and said he would pay the expense of forwarding them. The lawyer whose business is to fight for the conviction of erring women and miserable men, said he "hated" to see them killed. The judge, who for a score of years, has been sending human beings to the prison and the gallows, was moved to compassion and inclined to the side of mercy. He was anxious to commute the death penalty to one of life imprisonment, and gave the name of a man who had charge of a city park and directed the court reporter to call up the gentleman over the "long distance" and ascertain whether he wanted an addition to his menagerie.

All hoped for a respite and were greatly disappointed when an adverse reply was received. The old doctor who had saved many a life; the lawyer who had freed many a criminal, the judge whose edict was law, whose words could so often bind or unloose, liberate or punish, were all alike helpless, and unable to save the innocent victims of heredity and environment. The county attorney who was acting auditor, said he was no executioner—they would have to look up someone else to perform that office. Then they all turned to laugh at the expense of a man who had just been sent to state's prison for ten years and who expressed a desire to live the rest of his life to better purpose than the preceding part.

This incident is a striking illustration of the inexorable laws of fate, destiny and heredity, and is calculated to fill a thoughtful mind with feelings of awe and trembling.

Is there, after all, a preponderance of truth in the doctrine of predestination? We sometimes see human wolves who seem victims of destiny. We are compelled to hunt them down because they are wolves, and yet, they may have had no chance to be anything else. We see creatures wearing the human form who are "wise as serpents" and who prey upon their fellow creatures who are "harmless as doves." There are unfortunates whom nature turns out as wild beasts and society finishes up into galley slaves. "In vain," says Hugo, "we chisel as best we can the mysterious block of which our life is made; the black vein of destiny reappears continually."

THE WILDS WITHOUT FIREARMS
1909

 MILLIONS of Americans experience the outdoors these days without guns. But the very novelty of this notion in the early twentieth century shows that the conviction that nature was dangerous had been deeply ingrained. Early colonists and pioneers used guns not only to secure food, but also to fight fellow Europeans, subdue native people, and clear the land of "formidable and . . . dangerous animals," such as the wolf, which threatened their livestock and their peace of mind. But beyond this practical "need" for guns, a combination of unique circumstances in American history and society created a peculiar fondness for guns, according to a fascinating study entitled Gun and Society: The Social and Existential Roots of the American Attachment to Firearms *(1982) by William R. Tonso. Tonso explored the practical, recreational, and symbolic reasons for this phenomenon, which has led to such strong pro- and anti-gun advocacy today.*

This momentary encounter with wild wolves—without a gun in hand—led Enos A. Mills to experience the beauty, unity, and peacefulness of nature and to appeal to his readers to embrace "the gentle, kindly influence of Nature and hear her good tidings." This was a chapter in Mills' Wild Life on the Rockies *(Boston and New York: Houghton Mifflin Company, 1909).*

❖❖❖

Had I encountered the two gray wolves during my first unarmed camping-trip into the wilds, the experience would hardly have suggested to me that going without firearms is the best way to enjoy wild nature. But I had made many unarmed excursions beyond the trail before I had that adventure, and the habit of going without a gun was so firmly fixed and so satisfactory that even a perilous wolf encounter did not arouse any desire for firearms. The habit continued, and to-day the only way I can enjoy the wilds is to leave guns behind.

On that autumn afternoon I was walking along slowly, reflectively, in a deep forest. Not a breath of air moved, and even the aspen's golden leaves stood still in the sunlight. All was calm and peaceful around and within me, when I came to a little sunny frost-tanned grass-plot surrounded by tall, crowding pines. I felt drawn to its warmth and repose and stepped joyfully into it. Suddenly two gray wolves sprang from almost beneath my feet and faced me defiantly. At a few feet distance they made an impressive show of ferocity, standing ready apparently to hurl themselves upon me.

Now the gray wolf is a powerful, savage beast, and directing his strong jaws, tireless muscles, keen scent, and all-seeing eyes are exceedingly nimble wits. He is well equipped to make the severe struggle for existence which his present environment compels. In many Western localities, despite the high price offered for his scalp, he has managed not only to live, but to increase and multiply. I had seen gray wolves pull down big game. On one occasion I had seen a vigorous long-horned steer fall after a desperate struggle with two of these fearfully fanged animals. Many times I had come across scattered bones which told of their triumph; and altogether I was so impressed with their deadliness that a glimpse of one of them usually gave me over to a temporary dread.

The two wolves facing me seemed to have been asleep in the sun when I disturbed them. I realized the danger and was alarmed, of course, but my faculties were under control, were stimulated, indeed, to unusual alertness, and I kept a bold front and faced them without flinching. Their expression was one of mingled surprise and anger, together with the apparent determination to sell their lives as dearly as possible. I gave them all the attention which their appearance and their reputation demanded. Not once did I take my eyes off them. I held them at bay with my eyes. I still have a vivid picture of terribly gleaming teeth, bristling backs, and bulging muscles in savage readiness.

They made no move to attack. I was afraid to attack and I dared not run away. I remembered that some trees I could almost reach behind me had limbs that stretched out toward me, yet I felt that to wheel, spring for a limb, and swing up beyond their reach could not be done quickly enough to escape those fierce jaws.

Both sides were of the same mind, ready to fight, but not at all eager to do so. Under these conditions our nearness was embarrassing, and we faced each other for what seemed, to me at least, a long time. My mind working like lightning, I thought of several possible ways of escaping. I considered each at length, found it faulty, and dismissed it. Meanwhile, not a sound had been made. I had not moved, but something had to be done. Slowly I worked the small folding axe from its sheath, and with the slowest of movements placed it in my right coat-pocket with the handle up, ready for instant use. I did this with studied deliberation, lest a sudden movement should release the springs that held the wolves back. I kept on staring. Statues, almost, we must have appeared to the "camp-bird" whose call from a near-by limb told me we were observed, and whose nearness gave me courage. Then, looking the nearer of the two wolves squarely in the eye, I said to him, "Well, why don't you move?" as though we were playing checkers instead of the game of life. He made no reply, but the spell was broken. I believe that both sides had been bluffing. In attempting to use my kodak while continuing the bluff, I brought matters to a focus. "What a picture you fellows will make," I said aloud, as my right hand slowly worked the kodak out of the case which hung under my left arm. Still keeping up a steady fire of looks, I brought the kodak in front of me ready to focus, and then touched the spring that released the folding front. When the kodak mysteriously, suddenly opened before the wolves, they fled for their lives. In an instant they had cleared the grassy space and vanished into the woods. I did not get their picture.

With a gun, the wolf encounter could not have ended more happily. At any rate, I have not for a moment cared for a gun since I returned enthusiastic from my first delightful trip into the wilds without one. Out in the wilds with nature is one of the safest and most sanitary of places. Bears are not seeking to devour, and the death-list from lions, wolves, snakes, and all other bugbears combined does not equal the death-list from fire, automobiles, street-cars, or banquets. Being afraid of nature or a rainstorm is like being afraid of the dark.

The time of that first excursion was spent among scenes that I had visited before, but the discoveries I made and the deeper feelings it stirred within me, led me to think it more worth while than any previous trip among the same delightful scenes. The first day, especially, was excitingly crowded with new sights and sounds and fancies. I fear that during the earlier trips the rifle had obscured most of the scenes in which it could not figure, and as a result I missed fairyland and most of the sunsets.

When I arrived at the alpine lake by which I was to camp, evening's long rays and shadows were romantically robing the picturesque wild border of the lake. The crags, the temples, the flower-edged snowdrifts, and the grass-plots of this wild garden seemed half-unreal, as over them the long lights and torn shadows grouped and changed, lingered and vanished, in the last moments of the sun. The deep purple of evening was over all, and the ruined crag with the broken pine on the ridge-top was black against the evening's golden glow, when I hastened to make camp by a pine temple while the beautiful world of sunset's hour slowly faded into the night.

The camp-fire was a glory-burst in the darkness, and the small many-spired evergreen temple before me shone an illuminated cathedral in the night. All that evening I believed in fairies, and by watching the changing camp-fire kept my fancies frolicking in realms of mystery where all the world was young. I lay down without a gun, and while the fire changed and faded to black and gray the coyotes began to howl. But their voices did not seem as lonely or menacing as when I had had a rifle by my side. As I lay listening to them, I thought I detected merriment in their tones, and in a little while their shouts rang as merrily as though they were boys at play. Never before had I realized that coyotes too had enjoyments, and I listened to their shouts with pleasure. At last the illumination faded from the cathedral grove and its templed top stood in charcoal against the clear heavens as I fell asleep beneath the peaceful stars.

The next morning I loitered here and there, getting acquainted with the lake-shore, for without a gun all objects, or my eyes, were so changed that I had only a dim recollection of having seen the place before. From time to time, as I walked about, I stopped to try to win the confidence of the small folk in fur and feathers. I found some that trusted me, and at noon a chipmunk, a camp-bird, a chickadee, and myself were several times busy with the same bit of luncheon at once.

Some years ago mountain sheep often came in flocks to lick the salty soil in a ruined crater on Specimen Mountain. One day I climbed up and hid myself in the crags to watch them. More than a hundred of them came. After licking for a time, many lay down. Some of the rams posed themselves on the rocks in heroic attitudes and looked serenely and watchfully around. Young lambs ran about, and a few occasionally raced up and down smooth, rocky steeps, seemingly without the slightest regard for the laws of falling bodies. I was close to the flock, but luckily they did not suspect my presence. After enjoying their fine wild play for more than two hours, I slipped away and left them in their home among the crags.

One spring day I paused in a whirl of mist and wet snow to look for the trail. I could see only a few yards ahead. As I peered ahead, a bear emerged from the gloom, heading straight for me. Behind her were two cubs. I caught her impatient expression when she beheld me. She stopped, and then, with a growl of anger, she wheeled and boxed cubs right and left like an angry mother. The bears disappeared in the direction from which they had come, the cubs urged on with spanks from behind as all vanished in the falling snow.

The gray Douglas squirrel is one of the most active, audacious, and outspoken of animals. He enjoys seclusion and claims to be monarch of all he surveys, and no trespasser is too big to escape a scolding from him. Many times he has given me a terrible tongue-lashing with a desperate accompaniment of fierce facial expressions, bristling whiskers, and emphatic gestures. I love this brave fellow creature; but if he were only a few inches bigger, I should never risk my life in his woods without a gun.

This is a beautiful world, and all who go out under the open sky will feel the gentle, kindly influence of Nature and hear her good tidings. The forests of the earth are the flags of Nature. They appeal to all and awaken inspiring universal feelings. Enter the forest and the boundaries of nations are forgotten. It may be that some time an immortal pine will be the flag of a united and peaceful world.

THE POLITE WOLF
1914

 MUCH has been learned about wolf behavior by researchers who kept captive wolves. But unlike wolves' close cousins, our familiar and beloved dogs, wolves are wild animals that should never be kept as pets.

The characteristics that make a dog a good household pet have been acquired as a result of the deliberate manipulation of the gene pool by humans. The characteristics of the wolf, on the other hand, are the result of the influence of harsh environmental factors. Under natural conditions it is unlikely that many of the characteristics, such as obedience and subservience, that we consider desirable in dogs, would have much survival value to a wolf.

Kept as pets, wolves are likely to suffer from disease, parasites, and nutritional deficiencies, among other problems. Their strength and activity, unpredictability, and sociability are not accommodated by captivity. Nor do pet wolves contribute to the perpetuation of the species. Another deeper problem is reported by Barry Lopez in Of Wolves and Men *(1978): "Lois Crisler, who wrote about her life with wolves in Alaska in a book called* Arctic Wild, *killed the wolves she raised from pups because she couldn't stand what captivity had done to them. And her."*

Many of these problems surface in this story by Gilbert Coleridge, which first appeared in The Contemporary Review *(London, 1914), about a wolf taken as a pup in India and raised as a pet in Britain. Yet, here too are the social affinities, high spirits, and wildness that have led many people to a contrary point of view—appreciation and admiration of wolves.*

❖❖❖

It was a fluffy little grey ball which was brought into camp at the edge of the Bikkaneer Desert in the early morning by a native coolie, and shown to the army officer in charge. It was about nine inches long, its mother had been killed, and the native desired to do business. The officer, impelled by curiosity, took it in his hands, and gravely considered what he would do. A refusal would have ended the matter there and then, and the young life would have bubbled out in a water bucket, or been cut short by some means equally expeditious. The animal was helpless, and had a piece of old and frayed string tied round its neck, which gave it a kind of forlorn appearance as it snuggled against the arm of the officer's coat. To order the slaughter of an innocent is always repulsive, and the trouble of its nurture did not appear pressing at the time. Besides, there is really no great difference between the whelp of a wolf and that of a dog, and you do not recognise the future strength and fierceness in the downy, soft, wet-nosed puppy. Officers in India are rather addicted to the keeping of strange pets, and it occurred to this one that it would be rather a sporting thing to keep a tame wolf, and if he proved intractable of course there was a gun on the rack. There was also the chance that, when the little beast came into his own strength, he would turn and rend someone, which would be awkward. In that case the doctrine of "first bite" would never be allowed to apply to a wolf in a regiment of soldiers. At any rate there was always that gun, and as the wee thing continued to nestle trustfully in his arms, the officer resolved to take the chance. After a preliminary haggle, the parties met at a price of one rupee, but when the grasping Oriental demanded two annas for the piece of string, he was bundled out of the presence with scant ceremony. So the word went forth that the puppy was to be spared, and he was delivered over to the care of the syce.

His first journey was taken to the nearest railway station, in the friendly company of two fox terrier puppies, on the lap of a servant who rode a camel. Then he was put into an old cartridge box to sleep the night in the waiting room, whereat he lifted up his voice and wept bitterly; but at his journey's end he was consoled by having a place assigned to him in his master's quarters.

He was named Rania, after the Highland custom, from the district whence he originally sprang, and he settled down to the liberal education usually meted out to the domestic dog, in the hope that he might forget his father and mother and live like a gentleman. But parental influence is not easy to eradicate from the brute creation, and, as he grew in strength and stature, the education had to be somewhat liberal as regards the rod, for, do what he would, the instincts of his savage ancestors kept cropping up in unexpected places, and impelling him to do wild and uncouth things.

On one occasion he went for a swim in the river, and, finding himself still wet on his return, sought refuge in the Colonel's bed, and went fast asleep. The gallant Colonel could storm a fort, or defend a position, without turning a hair; but to make a wolf leave his bed was another matter. To be bitten under these circumstances would be somewhat inglorious for a commanding officer, so the invader's master was sent for, and the beast unceremoniously ejected.

Although well fed, the appetite of Rania was prodigious, and he was for ever eating as though face to face with immediate starvation. The policy of a wolf's constitution is to eat as much as you can, while you can, in view of contingencies, no matter whether it is good for you, or whether the substance is one which comes under the usual head of food. One day it happened to be a set of harness, and this caused a grave commotion in his interior. On another occasion he spied a cat eating its dinner, and it struck him that the cat might not mind giving him a share; but she stood on her dignity, and snubbed him so severely that for one brief impulsive moment he lost his temper, and killed her, which unjustly enabled him to increase his dinner by another course. Another time it was a native's parrot which he proceeded to consume, feathers and all. Perhaps the gay plumage attracted him like a coloured sweetmeat. For this offence he had to be beaten severely, to satisfy the feelings of the native, and also those of his master for having to pay for the parrot. He received sometimes from his cousin the dog that correction which is so good for precocious and spoiled pets, for, meeting one day with a mongrel spaniel with whom he wished to play, the latter, taking his advances in the wrong spirit, ran at him, knocked him down, and sat heavily on him. It is good for the young to be well sat upon. But he suffered all these early vicissitudes, the life of restraint, the early hours, and the chain, without any sourness in the temper, in short, with the philosophy which befits a gentleman of clean descent.

As a fact, the wolf is nearer to the dog in temperament than the wild cat is to our domestic puss on the hearthrug—indeed the latter is said to be descended, not from our European wild cat, but from the Egyptian species— and the affinity between man and the dog tribe is of very old standing. The vulpine nurture of Romulus and Remus was never held to be a disgrace. In ancient times man lived much closer to Nature. Queer fauns and forest gods peeped at him through the brushwood, every cluster of reeds was the potential hiding place of Pan or Syrinx, every rustle of the wind in the trees suggested the wood-notes of the Dryad; and when the imaginary relation of man with Nature and beasts suggested such forms as the Sphinx and the Centaur, the wolf was nearer to man than he has ever been since. The difference between the dog and the wolf was never so great as that which now exists between the wolf and the hyena. The latter is still difficult to tame, and cannot be handled with safety.

Unfortunately, modern writers seem to have conspired together to give the wolf a bad name and hang him. He cannot hold up his head in modern fiction. The legend of Red Ridinghood has been too much for him, and, remembering well the struggle for supremacy that we had with him in past times, we cannot forgive him. It must be admitted there was ample ground for this dislike when he was still the scourge of Europe and master of the wild, and when a price was set on his head. The innate fear of him is illustrated by that keen observer and collector of ancient lore, Sir Thomas Browne, when he speaks of the belief that "a man becomes hoarse or dumb if a wolf have the advantage 'first to eye him.'" The intent stare of that fierce eye before the fatal spring would doubtless produce a choke of terror in the throat. It was a bitter war with mankind, in which the beast often won the victory. And this strife has made an indelible mark upon his nature. That he still retains an instinctive memory of it was proved by an experiment made by the late C. J. Cornish at the Zoo. The snap or twang of a string caused instant signs of fear among the caged wolves. From what distant ages must this little scrap of caution have been handed down in the wolf tribe, and fossilised as it is in their nature!

Neither do we forget, it seems, this ancient hostility. For instance, Mr. Jack London, in his *White Fang*, appears to take a delight in dwelling on the dramatic possibilities of a lone settler in the backwoods in the presence of a pack. The agony is artistically prolonged, and the cruelty of the wolf held up to odium, as through the killing of quarry for food was something exceptional. You don't expect mercy from a wild animal when hungry. When Dr. Nansen and Sir Ernest Shackleton take tame animals with them on their gallant expeditions, and, after working them to the last gasp, kill them at length for food, it is only an unfortunate necessity. After all, hunger and love are the two great passions which sway the animal kingdom, including man, and it makes no great difference whether the food is killed singly or in packs. Have we not heard of starving men deliberately eating one another, as in the "Mignonette" case? A cat with a mouse, or a spider with a fly, will give an exhibition of apparent cruelty compared with which the conduct of the wolf is kindness. And if we consult Colonel J. H. Patterson concerning his experiences with lions in East Africa, we shall find that the king of beasts, so far from exhibiting those copy-book virtues so dear to those who watch him lazily yawning and stretching himself in a cage, wages an unceasing war against mankind in the regions of Tsavo, and satisfies his hunger with the same stealth, cruelty, and cowardice as are attributed to the wild wolf.

The late Phil Robinson, usually a most impartial and sympathetic observer of animals, piles epithet on epithet against him in that charming and too-little-read book, "Noah's Ark." "Bandit," "assassin," "implacable brute," are some of the choice terms employed to decorate some doubtless true tales of the wolf's manner of getting a meal. Even when in captivity at the Zoo, "he would far rather eat the children themselves than the buns which they give him"—a sad indictment against the amount of provender provided by the Society. And as for his eyes, there is "a sinister proximity about them, and a fierce tiger eloquence." Could prejudice go further? Why, in the depths of those yellow-grey questioning eyes, which look at you straight and unashamed, there may be, and very often is, a world of trust, affection, and fun. In the yellow eyes of the cat tribe you find the first two, but not the latter; for life to them is a very solemn thing, and not to be trifled away to the detriment of personal dignity; but your full-grown wolf will sometimes play like a puppy when the spirit moves him. *Homo sapiens*, unfortunately, possesses eyes of two shades only—blue and brown—but I believe I could embrace a man with yellow eyes if I chanced to meet him, and I am certain that he would not bite—after dinner. Ruskin puts the point with a lucidity all his own. "There is in every animal's eye a dim image, a gleam of humanity, a flash of strange light through which their life looks out and up to our great mystery of command over them, and claims the fellowship of the creature, if not of the soul."

The best about a wolf is that, like a horse, you always know when he is going to bit: the chine of his back rises, the shoulder blades stiffen, and the ears fly back; his whole expression is a gentlemanly warning to look out for squalls. Contrast this with the benevolent, ungainly advance, affectionate in its awkwardness, with which a parrot will march up to your finger, survey it like an art critic with head on one side, choose the spot, and then bury his beak in it. Not a feather ruffled, and nothing but a stony stare from his beady eye.

Time came, and the Fates decreed, that Rania should accompany his master to England. When I first saw him he was chained to the banisters of a London staircase, where he was being restrained by the white arms round his neck of two ladies in evening dress, in order that the maid, who was nervous, should pass by with the luggage. For a short period his exercise consisted in dragging his master, a strong man, round about the town at the end of a heavy chain cable. It was hard work for both, as his strength and activity were prodigious. His fearsome play terrified even large dogs in Kensington Gardens, and it became evident that London was scarcely a suitable place for a wolf in his salad days. Consequently, for his next experience of life fitter surroundings were chosen, viz., a deer forest in the far north. There he could range at will without his chain. Did he ever break loose from control, and chase the deer from the high ground, or even worry the sheep on the lower level? Not a bit of it. Once, and once only, did he swerve from the path of virtue, and then he went on a solitary night excursion. We all thought the old Adam would be sure to show itself, and grim fears pervaded the household of torn sheep, stags hunted from the sanctuary, a deserted ground, and no stalking for days. A plaintive whimpering at the gun-room door denoted the return of the strayed reveller. There was no guilty droop about his tail, but a fierce flourish of joy at being admitted. Careful enquiries showed that the deer were undisturbed, and that no sheep or living thing was missing. He had only wandered about and taken the air. One wonders what would have occurred had he taken a collie for company, and whether, as sometimes happens, the evil communications of the civilised would have corrupted the wild.

As he grew in years the gentler he became. His great delight was to play with the cadet of the house, and roll down the slope of the lawn in affectionate embrace till you could scarce tell boy from beast. So fond was the lad of his friend that on one occasion he sulked all day because he thought his brother had been too hard on the wolf in his discipline. One form of exercise which the wolf took was somewhat inconvenient. Whenever the laird rode along the road on his bicycle the wolf would watch his opportunity, race after him, and dance in front of the machine, or make playful snaps at his ankles, to his great discomfiture. Such exuberance of spirits, combined with tremendous activity and strength, became tiresome even in the wilds of the Highlands; you could not find it in your heart to shoot him, and to be perpetually superintending the gambols of an adult wolf was rapidly reducing life to the level of that of a circus trainer. Could anyone else be induced to take on the business? There were no bids.

In the result he was offered to, and accepted by, the Zoological Gardens.

Alas! poor Rania! The rest of his life was spent in tedious captivity for no fault of his own, save natural strength and high spirits. For some months most of us paid periodic visits to Regent's Park to cheer the prisoner in his captivity. In defiance of rules we went inside the barrier, coats were doffed, shirt sleeves rolled up, and bare arms inserted through the bars to play with our old pet, and sometimes a sympathetic keeper gave admission to the cage itself, separating him from his table companion, a huge Afghan wolf called "Joseph."

But the satisfaction of our visits paled before the delirious joy shown when his master went to see him. He would leap and squeak in the wildest delight, and when his master crouched down on the floor of the cage he would spring on his back, execute a *pas seul*, and make playful snaps at this ears. And when his master's artistic sister, who paid many visits to him in order to paint his portrait, went round to the back of the cage to enter it, the moment she was out of sight, he would follow round the wall with his nose pointing in her direction till she appeared at the door. Then the joyful greeting began. You wanted old clothes for an interview with Rania. He never licked his friends like a dog; his mark of affection was to draw back his lips and press his closed teeth against your cheek, or to gently chaw your fist.

He had a power of discrimination in his likes and dislikes, for though I would never accuse poor Rania of snobbery, yet it is a fact that he knew a gentleman when he saw him. In spite of their advances, he always showed an antipathy to the Scottish keepers and outside servants in the Highlands, and if a red-coated soldier approached his cage at the Zoo it was impossible to do anything with him. Memories of regimental teasing would make him stand stiff, with back erect and teeth shown, and gaze with hostile eyes at the soldier till he had passed out of sight. He was never known to snap or growl at a woman, and strange ladies would often play with him under the impression that he was a very active and frolicsome collie. The tent of a female skirt often afforded a harbour of refuge to him when he was chased, and this sometimes caused consternation to the owner thereof when he proceeded to bite her ankles in play.

His messmate, Joseph, had a bad temper, and bullied Rania unmercifully: he seized the lion's share of the food, and treated his companion with the contempt with which the mature regard striplings. But a day of reckoning was at hand, and he was soon to "hear the younger generation knocking at the door," as Ibsen says. A time came when Rania felt strong enough to fight for his rights, whereupon a pitched battle ensued, which might have ended fatally for the curmudgeonly Joseph, had not the keeper, in whose composition fear of animals was omitted, entered the cage and separated the combatants single-handed; not without injury, however, for, in the midst of the struggle, he fell and cut his face against the water-trough. But for the sticking-plaster on his face, and my enquiry as to its cause, I should never have heard of this Homeric fight, unless indeed I had been quick enough to perceive a kind of subdued air about Joseph.

This keeper was a remarkable man, and had an extraordinary way with his charges, for they respected his pluck and loved him all the same. As he is no longer there it is no breach of confidence to record that in the early morning when no one was about, in order to give the young wolves and himself healthy exercise, he would harness a pair of them to a go-cart, an improvised structure of old sugar boxes, and drive them lustily round the Gardens. This performance, however, was not without risk, for one morning they gave him a bad spill against the iron railings of the goat cage, which necessitated the wearing of more sticking-plaster. Another time, while harnessing his team, one of them broke loose, and then a chase began round the Zoo which he told me he hoped never to repeat. As for the wolf, he had never had such a game with his keeper before, and never will again, for the man soon found this early morning exercise too strenuous for even his buoyant constitution.

Imitation is the sincerest flattery, and it was not long before nearly all the wolves paid Rania such a compliment as each individual nature would permit. On seeing him petted, having his ears and tail pulled, pretending to bite our bare arms thrust through the bars, licking and gently gnawing our fists, being swung by his master by the legs, a thing which few dogs will allow, one by one they came whining at their bars, and asking for a like favour with wagging tails. Very soon, two magnificent young Canadian wolves next door, named "Lobo" and "Juno," became almost as tractable as Rania. Crusty old Joseph, too, would sit with his back pressed against the bars to be scratched, and that we did constantly to please the old gentleman, but never would he trust himself to eye us face to face, lest his nature should assert itself, for he could not resist, as often happened, giving an ugly snap. Normally he was a great consumer of umbrellas.

One summer evening it was closing time, and we had been more than common familiar with the pack; after a last salutation through the bars from

Rania, we turned away wiping from face and hands the marks of affection. Down he sat on his haunches, and, lifting his nose in the air, howled forth a heart-breaking note. Instantly the rest followed suit, and a row of uplifted heads poured out in chorus an evensong of sad farewell. We are told that the poignant note strikes terror into the heart of the lonely settler and denotes ferocity and hunger, but it may also be expressive of the keenest affection and regret.

Was he happy during the eight or nine years of his monotonous captivity? I think so, for he had abundance of food and a kindly keeper. In the fulness of time, before old age and decrepitude had set in, a disease of the throat carried him off in spite of the efforts of his keeper and the "vet."

Farewell, good Rania, thou leavest behind a wild and sweet memory!

If in a future state an all merciful Providence has ordained a Paradise for animals, and, unless the Divine care for sparrows in this life, spoken of in the Gospel, implies no care or other existence beyond the grave, if the gates of Heaven are not entirely closed to the animal kingdom, then we may imagine our friend with shining ruff and white breast, his yellows eyes dancing with fun, leaping around with wayward joy, and playing with the tips of angel's wings. Is this an extravagant idea? If it is, the wish is parent to the thought.

WINNING A WOLF'S HEART
1927

 THIS is the story of the arrival in Hollywood of Lady Silver, the "remarkable wolf actress who did so much to make Strongheart's earlier pictures ring true"—Strongheart being a famous dog actor. This according to the author of "The Last Stand of the Lobos," who makes much of the fact that the wolves he was hunting in Montana were Lady Silver's parents. Lady Silver and Strongheart starred together in such silent films as The Silent Call *(1921),* Brawn of the North *(1922), and* White Fang *(1925).*

Although "taming" a wild wolf may seem reckless, researcher L. David Mech asserted that "probably the creature's strongest personality trait is its capacity for making emotional attachments to other individuals." Still, to tap this innate tendency toward sociability, film director Lawrence Trimble needed considerable patience, intelligence, and trust to overcome the wolf's fear and shyness. Trimble's tale, which originally appeared in The American Boy, *was excerpted for* The Literary Digest, *January 29, 1927, from which this version comes.*

❖❖❖

"Eighty pounds of wolf landed on my back, and through the opening of the cage we rolled together!" But the apparently luckless gentleman wasn't torn to pieces at all. Instead, Lady Bobs, the furry hurricane, had a boisterous romp with him, and ended by licking his hand. Lawrence Trimble, who writes in *The American Boy* of training wolves to act for the movies, was the recipient of Lady Bobs's favors, altho he had gone to the Denver Zoo that September to make friends with Lady Silver, whom he describes as the most savage wolf he had ever known—and the most beautiful. He first saw her gazing at her mountain home through the bars of her cage. Like all her upland kin, she was very proud, and incidentally so bad-tempered she would have nothing at all to do with the other wolves. "I tried in every way to attract her interest, " says Mr. Trimble, " but she glanced my way only once." In fact—

So complete was her disdain that I felt snubbed and, I confess, embarrassed in the presence of the sarcastically grinning headkeeper. I had assured him I got on with wolves and had been knowing them pretty well all my life. However, I managed to save my face with him by making a hit with another wolf—Lady Bobs, who had replied to the funny throat sounds I made in addressing Lady Silver.

When I left, Lady Bobs and I called back and forth to each other until I was beyond earshot—but Lady Silver was not aware of anything this side of her mountains. It was not hard to part with Lady Bobs—but I could not help leaving something that was a part of me in the cage with the far-eyed Lady Silver.

Bobs had been born in a flat land's gully, beside a muddy river. When her newly opened eyes had first met the sun, she had seen it from under the shading thumb of a gentle-handed engineer. I did not have to win her friendship. It was simply a matter of getting acquainted. But then she had never run freely wild, nor leaned against the wind over a mile-high chasm and seen a lazy, winding river far below, looking like a strip of sky, carelessly dropt and left there, forgotten. Yes, I could say "Good-by" to Bobs—but I could not say anything to my Silver Lady. As far as she cared, I had not even been there.

Through the influence of my old friend, Hal Felker, a popular Denver lawyer, it was arranged with the city park commission that a telegram from me would start Lady Bobs, by express, direct to whatever location I might choose for the filming of a Northern picture I planned to do the following winter.

During the next several months I visited many zoos, both in the States and in Canada, looking for a dozen or so individuals to make up a wolf pack. And I chased down many false rumors of splendid wolves, privately owned. But in all this time the picture of Lady Silver, with her cold eyes, did not grow dim. I simply could not forget that I wanted to know her—to own her. But I knew I must be practical; I could not, I thought, spare the time from my work to win her friendship, much less educate her to act before a camera.

Late March found Mr. Trimble and a production crew on location in the Sierras at Boca, California, and the animal actors, huskies and wolves, arriving by every train. "The dogs were fretful and quarrelsome, but the wolves were altogether a bad-tempered lot. The train journey had left some of them raging and others sulkily waiting a good opportunity to vent their spleen." None of Mr. Trimble's assistants had worked with wild animals before. However, two of them, Bill Sproat, a former trapper, and Johnnie Burch, an electrician, proved to be friends in need. The latter was especially fascinated by the wolves, so much so that Mr. Trimble relates:

> He wanted to stay on and work with them when his job was done, but I did not believe I needed him, until a little while before his train time.
>
> Just as I had succeeded in getting the whole pack into the big exercise pen without a fight starting, and was drawing my first easy breath, I noticed Johnnie leaning interestedly against the outside of the fence.
>
> "You'll miss your train, " I warned him.
>
> "Hope I do!" and he grinned, ruefully, as the train whistled signaling the station. It also signaled the start of a fight that made Johnnie lose his train and win the job he wanted.
>
> Mormon, a raw-boned wolf from Utah, who had acted like a coward up to that minute, jumped Bad Boy, from Montana. Before I could swing the broom I happened to have in my hand, the whole lot were busy trying literally to tear each other to pieces. Johnnie, seeing me pile into the mêlée with the old reliable housewife's weapon, rushed around, found another broom, scaled the wire fence, and shoulder to shoulder with me, helped sweep the fight right out of those madly whirling, would-be murderers. While a broom can not hurt more than a wolf's feelings, it certainly makes him feel foolish. Moreover, Johnnie laughed right heartily at their absurd scrambles to avoid the flailing brooms. His laughter helped to restore peace, too. For, like dogs, wolves simply wilt and lose their conceit before the ridicule of man.
>
> So in short order we swept them into their separate kennels. Then, taking one at a time, we examined them for hurts and drest their cuts, which were not serious—the fight was too brief.

After a bitterly cold and trying night, spent in attempting to separate a raging she-wolf from her new-born litter, which she was in danger of destroying, the writer was unable to go to the station to meet Lady Bobs. We read on:

> Presently one of the boys rushed in. "Come quick!" he yelled. "That

Denver wolf is chewing out of her crate—and she is worse than a red-hot buzz-saw!"

As I neared the station, I heard a fiendishly raucous snarl. Then a wolf's head lunged through the wrecked side of the crate, and it was not Bobs—it was my beautiful Silver Lady. A stout chain drawn tight about her neck was the reason she had not made for the near-by mountains. Looking closer, I saw that a link of the chain was wedged into a crack in the floor of the crate; otherwise it was not fastened. She was tied thus so short that she could not stand fully erect. How she hated that chain! She fought it and feared it like a trap. Apparently she had not forgotten the one that had cost her the freedom of her native mountains.

I was annoyed because all that Hal Felker had said in his wire was:

"Shipped lady wolf to-day sorry for delay stop have written explaining."

I was bothered, too. I had scenes to shoot in which I must have a gentle wolf, because there must be a human baby in them as well as his movie mother (Irene Rich). But secretly I felt more pleased than anything.

I knew it was now or never that my Silver Lady must be won.

It required just a few minutes to carry the crate and its outraged occupant into the special home intended for Lady Bobs. But it took two very full hours of tact and persistence to loose the chain from the crack in the crate's bottom. I had to talk my Silver Lady into enough confidence in me so that she would allow me to put my hand into the crate and slowly work at the jammed chain link. She simply would not permit my touching her neck where her lovely coat had become matted and twisted into the chain. I would get the link almost free—then suddenly back she would strain and lunge at my face, her gorgeous teeth clicking and chattering wickedly. Then I would have to wait a bit, and talk her wild panic down, and all over again begin the tedious business of reaching my hand in between her forefeet—moving at the rate of about six heartbeats to the inch; and when success seemed sure, her eyes would begin burning with greenish flame, shot with red, and again her nerves would give way. A vibrant growl that seemed to come from underground would warn me that another frantic seizure of rage and terror was due. The rumbling growl would change to a snarl and end in a hoarse, metallic scream—as she pulled at the chain and alternately tried to destroy it and me. Then I could only sit and wait for her to blow off the edge of her pent-up fury.

All the while Johnnie Burch and several of the boys sat on bales of straw and just watched. And with them was my friend Talbot Mundy, author of those African hunt stories. He did not speak either, but I knew by his groans that he wanted to warn me a couple of times.

Gradually, Silver Lady responded again to my repeated, monotonous sing-song assurances: "It's all right, Lady—it's all right—easy now—easy—easy."

Softly, unconsciously, Johnnie began whistling an old tune. Silver listened and, lowering her head to see him better, gave me plenty of slack chain with which to work freely, and stood rigid with suspicion long enough for the troublesome link to be eased out of the crack.

Silver did not sense, at once, that she was no longer tied. And I continued to sit quiet, repeating over and over in the same monotonous song: "It's all right—it's all right—easy, Lady—easy, Lady—"

Then for the spectators' ears, I droned: "Leave quietly—quietly—don't sneak—just go to lunch as tho we weren't here—go now—you can talk—better talk—as you go—"

And they did talk and Silver listened till their voices were lost in the distance. But as they went, Bill Sproat remarked, "He'll never tame that baby!"

"What will you bet—I can't put—my hand on her—by the time—you've finished lunch?" I chanted at him.

Bill shook his head, dead sure I'd be a loser.

"When we were quite alone," continues Mr. Trimble, "Silver discovered that the chain no longer restrained her, but the tormenting thing still hung about her neck." However—

She made no move to leave the crate; so I slowly hitched over until I was sitting in the middle of the pen. She watched my every move, but pretended to look far beyond me. I deliberately turned my back on her, and apparently ignored her as completely as she had ignored me that day at Denver.

Leisurely I lighted a cigaret, and smoked and hummed a tune. For a long time, or it may only have seemed long, she was still. The chain began to chink—chink, then to rustle in the straw on the pen floor. Very slowly, and with frequent, sniffing pauses, she went around the wire fence, and keeping close to it and as far as possible from me, she circled the enclosure. When passing directly in front of me she bristled and growled. But I did not attempt to touch her—not even with my eyes. I, too, could look miles beyond anybody and still see all I needed to. Her second complete journey encircling the pen, which was roughly fifteen feet across and free from sharp corners, did not take long, and the third journey took even less time. She was watching me now, frankly puzzled, as I saw in a one-wink look. Another time or two she gingerly dragged the hateful clinging chain around the path she was making in the straw. But I smoked and hummed and concentrated strictly on my own affairs—I simply was not interested in her.

I moved a little toward the side of the enclosure opposite to where she had paused for a moment. And when she got around again to the same place, I moved some more in the same direction as before.

After a while there was just enough room between me and the fence for her to pass comfortably without touching me.

When she crossed behind me she would halt, each time coming a shade nearer, until I could feel her warm breath on my neck as she sniffed curiously.

She seemed to realize that she was being snubbed, and it troubled the lady. Suddenly, I got a thrill and a surprize. She would have been just as surprized, too, had she been aware of her wholly unconscious action: she gave voice to those low, pleading, staccato whines common to all canines when they ardently desire attention, but do not want to ask right out for it.

And just at the critical moment, Johnnie Burch's muffled voice cried "Atta girl!" He had been peeping through a knothole instead of going to lunch. Whereupon, relates the much-tried wolf-director:

Silver coughed a hot growl into my ear, and snarling as she went, passed between me and the wire. And tho she brushed against my shoulder, she did not shrink at the touch.

"Whistle Johnnie Burch—and keep it up, and keep it up—" I begged mumblingly as I continued to hum, "Just a Song at Twilight."

After a while, Silver appeared to forget Johnnie, but I did not. His whistling gave me a chance to concentrate on the lighting of a fresh cigaret—I was getting pretty tired of doing a lullaby.

After a while, Silver came close behind me again, and sniffed and sniffed, and repeated the little pleading sounds, which steadily grew more insistent. But I sat indifferent, relaxed and still, something not so easy to do when she so far forgot herself as to jab her nose into my right ear. Then she came in front of me and pranced stiffly, as dogs do when inviting one to romp with them. But still I did not let her see I cared a hang what she did—tho I had to do some real acting to keep the show going.

She appeared to give up the idea of my being worth so much trouble, and flopped down disgustedly in the rounded corner directly in front of me.

Apparently, she had forgotten my existence as she yawned and rolled completely over and braced her feet against the wire netting, and began pushing herself toward me, and digging up the straw with her snout with each shove.

Every time she moved, I slid a bit nearer the fence. When her head came to rest on my knee, she simply lay and waited with half-closed eyes. And as my hand, moving ever so slowly, touched her foreleg and continued in a caressing advancing and retreating motion, her lip quivered, showing her fangs—but her eyes did not open. It took a long time to get the chain loosened from her neck, tho I worked with both hands. I was afraid that Johnnie's whistle, which was getting dry, would play out, or that somebody might come. It was tense business, and I scarcely breathed until as the chain came away and slid noiselessly into the straw, I was forced into taking a quick, deep breath.

Up and away Silver flung herself—but it was a joyous wolf that darted wildly about her new home. She burrowed and wallowed in the deep straw, and fairly exploded herself into the air. Once she came down plump into my arms—and there she lay, her eyes big with surprize and lurking fear. I had to lean forward to keep my balance. Her face came slowly up to meet mine; out flamed a red tongue; she kissed me on the chin. She could not seem to get close enough to suit her. In a frenzy of joy she trampled and rolled me down in to the straw, kissing my face and hands as a long-lost dog might do on suddenly realizing his old master had turned up to take him home. Laughing with, not at her, I struggled to my feet. And still she tried leaping into my arms. She would rub around my knees, tail wagging violently, body twisting and turning, all the time giving voice to the most eloquently joyous sounds, which tingled with glad emotion. Then she would crouch and pretend she was going to fly at my throat—but instead she would aim a kiss at my face, springing and giving me a staggering punch as her nose bumped mine.

I was relieved when Bill Sproat's voice froze her with: "By the great white-whiskered Old Hughie!"

The boys had returned from lunch and neither Silver nor I heard them.

I invited them to "Come on in," but only Johnnie Burch and Freddie MacBan responded. She accepted Johnnie's presence with dignified approval, and ignored Freddie—but then, Johnnie had whistled while she danced.

THE WOLF-PACK
1927

 DAVID Mech defined the pack as "the basic unit of wolf society," "a group of individual wolves traveling, hunting, feeding, and resting together in a loose association, with bonds of attachment among all animals." Packs generally number between two and eight animals and are regulated in size largely by social factors. Until modern times, however, the size, the definition, and even the very existence of wolf packs were questioned.

Early in this century, scientist and Arctic explorer Vilhjalmur Stefansson tried to determine whether the enormous, man-killing wolf packs of Russian and Arctic folklore really existed. In Adventures in Error *(1936), he reported that he had talked to every American and Canadian expert about the rumors. He also investigated Old World accounts, such as a 1927 Swiss newspaper article entitled "Caucasus Wolves Bombed from Airplane; Hungry Packs Invade Towns, Killing Peasants." Stefansson startled some people by wondering if this dispatch "could possibly have been some sort of a cipher message on behalf of almost any sort of secret organization"; that is, "wolves" might be a code word for, say, "an anti-Bolsheviki outfit."*

Although Stefansson was convinced "that wolf-packs which come up to motion picture and folklore standards do not exist," he admitted there would always be believers. "Finally," he concluded, "there will be no wolves left, except in zoos. The belief in packs will have survived the means of refuting it. It will have become a truth."

This account by Stefansson appeared in 1927 in The American Mercury. *Incidentally, modern research also has refuted Stefansson's claim that wolves hunt by pursuing their prey "from several hours to several days."*

❖❖❖

Everyone knows that wolves run in packs. One of the standard definitions of the word pack is: "A large number of wolves banded together for the purpose of hunting their prey."

That used to be an undisputed statement of the case. But now there is an argument about whether any wolf-pack ever really existed, with the scientists nearly all on one side, the general public nearly all on the other, and the sportsmen divided about half and half.

On the affirmative side we have the undoubted fact that "everybody knows," especially in Russia, that wolves do run in packs. If you want to refresh your mind as to what Russian wolf-packs are believed to be like, you can do so easily and pleasantly by turning to Willa Cather's "My Antonia," page 63. The people Miss Cather is going to feed to her wolves are the very diet to which Russian wolves are most accustomed—a wedding party. There are six sleighs drawn by three horses each and carrying from six to twelve passengers. There is starlight on the snow and the road is through a forest. The first distant wolf howl does not drown the tinkle of the sleigh-bells or the laughter of the wedding guests. But the rallying cry is answered from many sides, the leaders of the pack draw nearer, and fear grips every heart. The bride sobs on the groom's bosom and the drivers lash their horses to breakneck speed. The rear sleigh upsets, the passengers sprawl out over the snow and the wolves are on top of them in a moment. The screams of horses being eaten alive are more dreadful than the shrieks of people whose entrails are being torn out. The cries of terror from the remaining sleighs are as loud as the cries of pain from the dying. The wolves are silent now—they have other work to do.

And so the story goes on for sleigh after sleigh in Miss Cather's story, and in all the typical stories, until only the bridal sleigh is left. About forty or fifty people have now been eaten, and fifteen horses, but the wolves are still hungry and going strong. There are hundreds of them, you see, and wolves have proverbially good appetites. Nothing will save the last sleigh but throwing the bride to the wolves. This Miss Cather accordingly does, and so do half the other authors of tales. But it seldom happens that quite everybody is eaten. Somebody has to be saved, to give the narrator a chance to portray the survivor's life of shame and remorse through many effective pages that lead to a distant and friendless grave.

Such tales as Miss Cather's we usually consider to be "true in spirit" only, since they occur in novels, but we take them for sober fact when we see them in books of travel or in newspapers. The press stories excel the books in verisimilitude, for they tell us what is said to have happened yesterday or last week. They give the names of places that are on every map, they frequently mention the widow and orphaned children, they sometimes tell that the funeral of the fragments left by the wolves was conducted by the local chapter of Masons. There is every detail to prove that what you see in the *Sun* (or the *Bee* or the *American*) is really so.

If you look in the invaluable semi-annual index to the news published by the New York *Times*, you will discover scores of authentic-looking wolf-pack stories. I have the space to reproduce here only a sample:

WOLVES DEVOUR 3 MEN IN NORTHERN ONTARIO
An Elderly White Trapper and Two Indians Fall Victims
to a Horde of Hungry Beasts

Port Arthur, Ont., Dec. 27—A great roving bank of hungry timber wolves has devoured three men . . . Last Saturday an elderly trapper left his cabin in the woods seventy miles north of Ignace to mush down to the settlement for his Christmas mail. . . . There was no mail, however, and the old man said he would come back Christmas morning. At noon he had not arrived. The postmaster sent two Indians to follow the trail. . . .

About two miles from the settlement the Indians found a spot pounded down in the snow. There was blood. Bits of dog harness torn to shreds were scattered about. In the midst of them the Indians found human bones. They hastened back to report their discovery. The lure of the bounty on wolves, however, urged the Indians to take the trail again, with extra ammunition. They sped behind the dog team into the woods as the villagers waved good-bye. They did not return.

Yesterday a new searching party departed. They found another patch trodden in the snow, with much more blood, about two miles from the first. The two guns the Indians had carried were lying in the crimsoned snow. Scattered about were bones, bits of clothing and empty shells.

The carcasses of sixteen dead wolves—some half eaten—lay stretched in a circle about the remains of the two Indian hunters.

I quote from the *Times* of December 28, 1922. The story, from what is justly considered one of the world's greatest and most reliable newspapers, gives proof of the cunning no less than of the ferocity of the American wolf. Judging from the evidence, the pack must still have been hungry when they got through eating the trapper (perhaps he was small and skinny), so they laid in wait to finish their meal on the search party, which they evidently knew was coming. Then, still hungry, and fearing the size and prowess of the second search party, they reluctantly ate a few of each other for dessert before retreating into the shadows of the forest. That was discretion and admirable generalship. They fought when there was a chance to win, and then withdrew before superior numbers.

There are plenty of such wolf stories in the papers, and now and then others even more impressive. Six months ago, for instance, packs of wolves held Italy under a reign of terror in the pages of the New York *Sun*; a bit later villages in Siberia were barricaded against wolves in the New York *Times*. Two million cattle and many people were killed. Thus stands the evidence for the affirmative—wolves *do* run in packs. They devour wedding parties in Russia and they eat trappers and Indians in Canada. They terrorize Italy and lay siege to towns in Siberia—in the papers, at least.

But there are skeptics who do not believe all they see in the papers or read in books of travel. These iconoclasts tell you that every story of a wolf-pack that you ever read or heard is fib, fiction, or folklore, and that there never has been a pack of wolves in Russia, America, or anywhere except in people's imagination. That seems a hard position to defend, but they go at it valiantly. Their defense lies in both logic and fact. They ask you to consider, for instance, the caribou-hunting wolf.

Their argument begins with the generally accepted fact that there are more than ten million wild caribou in Northern Alaska, Northern Canada, Northern Siberia and the Arctic islands. From these at least two million caribou are born every year; two million must, therefore, die, or the numbers would increase. Certainly less than 10% of these are killed by human hunters. None die of old age and very few of accident or disease, for if a caribou is old or sick it moves slowly and is soon devoured. This means that wolves kill every year a good deal more than a million and a half caribou.

In Summer, when their puppies are being brought up, the northern wolves live largely on eggs, fledgling or moulting birds, and rodents. But in Winter the birds have flown south, the rodents are safe asleep in their frozen burrows, and almost the only thing a wolf can find to eat is caribou. I know how wolves kill caribou, and I can offer some personal testimony on wolves in general, for I was born on Lake Winnipeg in a great wolf country; I was brought up among wolves and coyotes in Dakota before it became "civilized" and was split up into North and South Dakota; I lived for some eleven years in the Arctic, supporting myself most of the time by hunting. I have shot wolves with a rifle and have seen hundreds of them either trotting quietly along or loping steadily in pursuit of caribou. I have seen the tracks of thousands following game, and have found traces of hundreds of tragedies where they had killed some bird or beast. I have asked dozens of Arctic Indians (Slaveys, Dogribs, Loucheux) and hundreds of Eskimos about how the wolf hunts, and there has been no divergence between what they have told me and what I have seen.

A wolf cannot run nearly as fast as a caribou, and he must, therefore, secure it by tiring it out. That is the essence of all I have seen and all I have been told. It means that, before it is killed, each caribou has to be pursued by the wolves from several hours to several days—nobody knows exactly how long. All hunters agree that (except for newborn calves) the youngest caribou are the swiftest and staunchest runners. The ones killed by wolves are therefore chiefly the old bulls and old cows. A cow may weigh two or three hundred pounds, and a bull three or four hundred, live-weight. Nearly half of that is waste. The wolves are, then, pursuing anything from 100 to 200 pounds of food. For, no matter how large the caribou herd may be when the pursuit begins, they eventually scatter, and the pack, if there is a pack, finds itself following the single slowest animal.

Suppose, now, there are 200 or 300 wolves, as in Miss Cather's heartrending story. She provided hers with six sleigh loads of Russians, six to twelve in a sleigh, and three presumably fat horses hitched to each. That would make a square meal for even 300 wolves. But not so if the 300 followed a single 300-pound caribou for three days, or even one day. They would be so hungry that there would be nothing for it but to resort to another well-known habit of the fiction wolf and use their whetted appetites on each other—eating, let us say, a dozen to correspond to the soup course, a dozen for the fish, and two dozen for the roast, with at least another dozen of the youngest and tenderest for dessert. But the continued practice of dining on each other like that would soon reduce a wolf-pack below fiction and movie standards. In fact, you might as well do without a pack altogether; for it is scarcely worth the bother to build one up laboriously to the required size, just to have it disappear again in a few weeks by the members of the troupe swallowing one another.

Those who are trying to prove that the wolf-pack really exists will perhaps admit that the abstract logic of pack hunting seems a little faulty, but will insist, and quite rightly, that logic does not amount to a hill of beans when contradicted by facts. The pack stories, they will tell us, are simple truth. Newspapers may exaggerate, but the better ones never invent. Besides, nearly everybody has an uncle or an aunt who had a grandmother or grandfather that was eaten or nearly eaten by a pack of wolves.

That brings us to the evidence—are the wolf-pack stories true? To save time, we shall take at once the testimony of a group of scientists and practical hunters who ought to know because they make the study of wolves their profession—studying also the testimony of everyone they ever heard of who claimed to have seen a pack of wolves. They are Americans, too, and within your reach, so you can write postcards to them tomorrow and see what they really think. Don't be diffident about asking. You are probably a taxpayer. In that case, they are your servants, for they work for the government that taxes you.

The branch of the government that studies wolves as a part of its business is the Bureau of Biological Survey at Washington, and the head of it is Dr. E. W. Nelson, a lifetime student of wild animals. He was four years among Arctic wolves in Alaska (1877-81) and has himself studied wolves in Mexico and all over the United States. Furthermore, he has under him other men who have studied wolves, among them Edward A. Preble, who has spent much time in the sub-Arctic and Arctic forests and prairies of Canada. But more significant still, there is under Dr. Nelson's direction the wolf-killing service of the United States Government. This is a body of men who hold themselves in readiness to respond to telegraphic appeals from stockmen, usually in the West, who find their animals being destroyed by wolves. They come and exterminate the wolves "scientifically," and the flocks and herds are safe again.

In gathering material for a book I am writing about wolves, I consulted Dr. Nelson. We agree, first, that the accepted meaning of the word pack, when applied to wolves is a *large number of wolves that have come together to help each other in hunting.* In other words, one mother with her puppies would not constitute a pack. Dr. Nelson felt so positive about the nature of wolves in North America, from Mexico to the Arctic, that he thought I would be safe in denying flatly in my book that any wolf-pack ever existed on our continent. But, just to make sure that no different opinion was held among people of authority corresponding to his own, we formulated a letter which he addressed to certain scientific students of wolves, and to all his wolf-killers.

As to how many wolves had been seen together, the various replies naturally gave different answers, for experiences varied somewhat. But they ranged only from two to five. They were unanimous in reporting that if several wolves were seen together then these were always the mother with her puppies, or conceivably the father and mother. with their puppies, and never a pack in any usual sense of that word.

Then what about the story of the wolves that killed the elderly trapper and the two Indians on the front page of the *Times*? Surely that was no family of puppies—sixteen dead wolves, killed by the Indians; a few, presumably, killed by the old trapper, and enough left over to eat up one white man, two Indians and part of sixteen dead wolves. To the inquiry into the truth of the story official and more authoritative than if I were doing it myself, I suggested to Dr. Nelson that he write to Ignace, Ontario. For checking up, I wrote also to Mr. J. B. Harkin, Commissioner of National Parks, Ottawa, who was at that time (1922) in charge of the administration of the game laws of Canada, and therefore in a position to set in motion official machinery to find out about this wolf story. Thus I received the same replies from two directions, one through Dr. Nelson and the other through Mr. Harkin. They were, in substance, that no such man as the old trapper ever existed and that no white man had been killed by wolves. No such Indians as described existed there and none had been killed by wolves, whether in packs or otherwise, either in the vicinity of Ignace, or anywhere in the world, as far as anyone living in the vicinity of Ignace knew.

Hundreds of other tales about wolf-packs, published in newspapers or books, have been traced by the United States Biological Survey and by various students, including myself. In no case was evidence found to support them. Just try it yourself on the next American despatch you read. In spite of all the pretended details—the sorrowing family, the Masonic funeral—it will be reasonable odds to bet dollars to doughnuts that the story will turn out pure fiction, or at best will rest on testimony no court of law would accept as proof. In brief, the case seems to be definitely settled against the wolf-pack in North America. But there still remains Russia. Well, why not let Russia remain? No one seems to have checked wolf-pack stories in Russia for everyone is so sure they are true. And perhaps they are. Besides, it is a distant country, and the fancy must somewhere have play.

YELLOWSTONE WOLVES
1937

 WOLVES suffered massive slaughter throughout Yellowstone National Park in the 1870s, according to Paul Schullery and Lee Whittlesey in The Documentary Record of Wolves and Related Wildlife Species in the Yellowstone National Park Area Prior to 1882 *(1992). Because they were considered "a decided menace to the herds of elk, deer, mountain sheep, and antelope" (as per a 1915 government report), wolves were killed "in numbers that now seem nearly fabulous," but the authors point out that this was true throughout the West at that time. They suggest that a second, later extermination program, "the notorious wolf-killing era of 1914 to 1926, which shocks the sensibilities of many modern people, was not much more than a mopping-up operation of a job almost finished by 1880."*

The wolves seen by the author of this story in 1934 were either survivors of the later control program or animals that moved in afterward, according to John Weaver (The Wolves of Yellowstone, *1978). There has not been a viable population of wolves in Yellowstone until the species was reintroduced to the park in early 1995. Marguerite L. Arnold published the story of her thrilling observation in* Nature Magazine *(August 1937).*

❖❖❖

For more than ten years the big timber wolf and the mountain lion have been more or less of a myth in Yellowstone Park. True, each year someone sees, hears, or observes the tracks of what was *undoubtedly* a wolf or a lion. Some of these reports are, without question, authentic, although one is inclined to question the lad who, sleeping out not more than half a mile from Park headquarters, "heard a mountain lion scream in the night." That there used to be many more wolves is shown by old wildlife reports, some of which state "they are much too common," "they destroy many elk" and so on. Vernon Bailey in his *Animal Life of Yellowstone National Park*, says, "During the summers of 1914-1915 they were especially destructive in the park and were following the elk herds to their high pastures of Mirror Plateau, returning with them in winter to the valleys along the Lamar and Yellowstone Rivers." It is well known that wolves and mountain lions are the most destructive of predators, yet they have become so scarce in this section of the country that for a number of years both have been protected in our greatest National Park, and during the past two years the coyote has joined the ranks of the protected.

In former years, during the winter months, Yellowstone rangers spent a lot of their time hunting the wily coyote, which, if allowed to multiply unmolested, takes a heavy toll of deer and antelope. Often a winter-killed elk lured coyotes to repeated feasts, and rangers with their rifles took advantage of this fact. My husband returned late one evening from a patrol on skis to the head of Tower Creek, and I sensed immediately, before he said anything, that something unusual had happened. Ben made a practice of telling the baby and me all about the taking of each "dog" as he brought him home. Most of the stories were thrilling too. This particular night I rushed to the door to see the quarry he had brought, but found nothing. Finally he said, "Guess what?"—and then a long pause during which I became more curious and impatient. "I just saw four wolves!" "Oh, not wolves!" I said, foolishly, knowing very well there was no mistake this time. We had observed what we were satisfied were wolf tracks, but had said little or nothing about them because we knew of the "undoubtedly" reports. We knew wolves to be more or less migratory in habit and thought the tracks had been made by one or a pair of them traveling through the district.

So Ben told me how, on the way up, he had found the carcass of an old winter-killed cow elk that coyotes were beginning to work on. On the way back, just before looking over the top of a little knoll that hid him from the carcass, he had heard the sound of teeth crunching bones, so he was especially careful, knowing "dogs" were there eating. As he peered cautiously over the top he said he refused to believe his eyes. His first thought was that bears had come out of hibernation, although it was mid-winter, but there, tearing and gulping at the tempting food, were four great, dark, hulking wolves. In the background three coyotes stayed at respectful distances, hungrily watching the feast. The wolves appeared three times larger than the slim, gray coyotes, and nearly black by comparison. As Ben crouched the gun lay forgotten at his side in the snow. The wolves literally lunged into the carcass, pulled back with a huge bite, "wolfed" it down and were right back for more. Finally a slight shift in the wind or the uncanny danger sense of the coyotes prevailed, and one by one they slipped away into the fast-gathering dusk. Soon the wolves, gorged, left also, trotting off unhurriedly along the trail.

The next day was one of the red letter days of my life in Yellowstone. It has always been my highest ambition to observe and study all the animals here in their natural setting. Lying prone in the marsh grass all of one afternoon I watched a family of six otters at play, and I have pried closely into the intimate family life of bear, buffalo, elk, deer, antelope and many others. When lions and wolves were plentiful I was too young to be anything but frightened by the prospect of getting near one. All unexpected, here was my golden opportunity. So, when the next dusk started to gather, I pulled on my snowshoes and started out, leaving my generous husband at home with the wee one, so mother could have her adventure. Climbing the long steep hill, I about decided it was to be fruitless effort—that it was most unlikely that the wolves would return to the same spot. But I used every precaution in stalking the spot, nevertheless. For the last two hundred yards the trail was nearly straight up, and, between the exertion and the excitement, I was certain any animal within half a mile would be frightened away by the pounding of my heart and my gasps for breath. But I kept on, and finally, near the very summit, I lay flat for a few seconds to regain some of my composure. While I waited there, not more than seventy-five yards now from the elk, I could distinctly hear a crunching of bones—my trip had not been entirely in vain!

It is a treat for a housewife to be able to observe just one lone coyote at his meal, and now I knew I would see at least that. Finally my curiosity got the better of me and before I was much rested I raised my eyes slowly, slowly, up behind a small sagebrush and over the crest of the hill. There I saw not one, but four coyotes at their evening feast of elk. I felt a slight disappointment at first that none of the wolves were there, but was soon absorbed in the antics of the "little wolves." After that evening I can readily understand why it is so difficult to sneak up on a coyote. They gnaw on a bone for a while or dig around inside the carcass and then up goes a head to test the wind and at the same time to make a visual and sound survey. Fortunately the wind stayed in my favor and, with just my eyes over the top of the hill and a grove of dark firs back of me, they failed to see me at all. Once or twice one looked right at me and I "froze" to escape the notice I felt was imminent. By this time it was really growing dark, and I was just about to attempt an exit, when something caught my eye down one of the animal trails. It couldn't be! It was! There was no doubt at all even though I had never in my life seen such an animal before; no, not even in a zoo. Not just one of them, but two huge black fellows loping easily along the trail, noses down as though following a scent. They had a peculiar jack-knife gait like that of a greyhound, utterly different from the gliding, noiseless gait of the coyote. On they came, straight toward me and the carcass, and my heart did something 'way up in my throat. They didn't look up at all but loped straight into the choicest part of the elk and commenced tearing out meat and bones, gouging, springing in, pulling back, gulping down huge bites. The coyotes did not leave the scene but discreetly withdrew from striking distance and sat, or walked slowly about, intently watching their big cousins. They appeared to be of an entirely different family from the great dark wolves—so much smaller, more slender and much lighter in color. The heavy shoulders and forequarters of the wolves were especially impressive. I remember blinking and straining my eyes to see every single detail in the fast-thickening dusk, and just after that the climax of the whole episode occurred. One of the wolves decided to look about and see that all was well and started off at an angle that brought him to the edge of the hill not more than forty feet from where I was hiding. He was so close that I could see the black line that runs from the corner of the eye back across the face. As he stood, broadside, I could see perfectly how proportionately more powerful he was than any coyote. I certainly held my breath then, for he turned and looked straight at me! I was in plain view, but I remained perfectly motionless as he looked at me with an uncomprehending stare for part of a minute—it seemed ten! Finally he turned silently and, without a sound, disappeared into the night. The others were, even then, not warned, for their activities continued undisturbed. But I could no longer contain myself—childishly I "had to see what they would do if they saw me." I stood up. Simply that and as quietly as I could, but the remaining wolf and the four coyotes scattered without a sound in as many directions. I don't know how I got back to the cabin, I was so excited and so brimming over with my story. I guess I was a little bit frightened too, as I realized what great hulking beasts those wolves were!

It will be many a day ere an adventure comes to me that will eclipse this twilight meeting with the big wolves.

THREE YEARS IN THE WOLVES' WILDERNESS
1937-41

 IT has been the dream of many to get away to a quiet, private, and beautiful place, to live a simple life, to rediscover what is most important. Henry David Thoreau's sojourn at Walden Pond in the 1840s was one eloquent articulation of this perennial American dream: "I went to the woods because I wished to live deliberately, to front only the essential facts of life, and see if I could not learn what it had to teach, and not, when I came to die, discover that I had not lived."

Here is the story of a couple who sought their utopia in an isolated valley in British Columbia in the 1930s. One of the particular appeals of this place for them was timber wolves, animals that epitomized "the spirit of the wilderness itself." Theirs is truly a new attitude toward wolves: there is no trace of fear, conquest, greed, or even scientific pursuit, but only curiosity, patience, respect, delight. Like Thoreau, and like many of the other authors in this section who saw wolves through new eyes, they seem to have understood the importance of the wild.

This account by John F. Stanwell-Fletcher appeared in Natural History *in March 1942.*

❖❖❖

On a rainy August morning in 1937 my wife and I set off into the mountains from Hazelton, British Columbia. We were in search of a spot somewhere in the 800 square miles of the wild, uninhabited Driftwood Valley where we could build a cabin home and live a peaceful, simple life, in natural surroundings; where we might find an existence which would lead to a greater mental and physical health than that which was lived by most of our friends in towns and cities. We were not on a big game hunting or scientific expedition. We wanted to study the wildlife in natural conditions throughout all the seasons, especially during the long months of a northern winter. Our collections and observations were to be made on behalf of the British Columbia Provincial Museum at Victoria. For the greater part of three years we studied the wildlife and we worked to live, a none too simple business in a northern wilderness.

After traveling almost 200 miles from Hazelton we found for our home a lovely little lake surrounded by great mountains and spruce forests. It was an isolated spot, 200 miles from the nearest auto road, electric light, and telephone. The nearest settlement, composed of a Hudson's Bay Company trading post, a few white families and prospectors, and some Indians, was 75 miles to the south, at Takla Landing. A few Indian families lived 30 miles to the north, at Bear Lake. We were cut off from all communication with the outside world for months at a time. We had no radio for the first two years, and we were entirely alone. Our contacts with humans came chiefly during the winter when we infrequently saw the few Indians whose trap lines were in the Driftwood Valley region.

We hiked and climbed over mountains and valleys, easy going and hard going. Our snowshoe trails radiated from the cabin over many miles of territory, and by the end of the first winter dozens of tall trees had sheltered the beds of spruce and balsam boughs where we had slept, sometimes in temperatures of 50 degrees below zero and with eight to ten feet of snow. Often we reached places where no white man had ever been before. This immense forested mountainous land, which we had for so long wanted to see, was very beautiful at all seasons and especially in winter. It was kind to us sometimes, and sometimes it was harsh and inhospitable and bitter, but we loved our life there and were very content.

Our cabin is situated at the northern end of a small spring-fed lake which drains into the Driftwood River by a short channel. The surrounding country supports mixed forests of spruce, balsam, pine, and poplar. Numerous lakes, beaver ponds, sphagnum bogs, and mountain streams thread the entire district. The Driftwood River, with its gravel bars and log jams and marvelous Dolly Varden and rainbow trout, winds its erratic way through the center of the valley, between the Driftwood Mountains on the west and the Omineca Mountains on the east. To the north of the valley lies Bear Lake, while Takla Lake, 50 miles away, bounds the southern end. Most of the country west of the Driftwood River is cut by high mountain ranges and long ice fields. It has not yet been explored or surveyed, and only a small portion of the valley is known to the white man. In winter the valley is particularly isolated, and the wildlife probably approximates a natural state.

The most common mammals were moose, wolves, black and grizzly bears, beaver, otter, marten, fisher, mink, varying hares, weasels, red and flying squirrels, chipmunks, and a variety of mice and shrews. On the mountain ranges, mountain goat, marmots, porcupine, and some caribou were to be found. With the exception of some of the smaller mammals these animals were inaccessible and very difficult to observe. The bird life of this region was fairly abundant; we noted a total of 134 species.

Of all the wild animals around us we were perhaps most interested in the timber wolves, those beautiful and most highly intelligent animals of the northern wilderness. The writer was fortunate enough to observe wolves at distances of fifteen to 75 feet on at least 20 occasions during 1941; and it is from these personal observations, together with reports from local Indians and notes made during fourteen years spent in those parts of Canada where wolves are found, that opinions have been formed.

As the snow deepened in December, we noted more wolf tracks than the occasional single or double track that had previously been seen. Two wolves ordinarily originated a trail, then other wolves would follow it, each stepping in the other's tracks. The trails usually led through the forests to a moose-yard or its vicinity, where the moose fed on tall grasses below thick spruce trees. But there was little snow under these trees, and the moose was seldom attacked, for its hoofs are sharp and deadly when it has firm footing.

By the first of January, Indian trappers began to report small and large packs of wolves. All of these were seen traveling along the edges of lakes. They were in groups of from four to 31, moving slowly and in single file. By the end of January, with six to eight feet of snow, the wolves began to hunt moose in earnest. Deeper snow beneath erstwhile sheltering trees forced the moose to travel farther for food, and in deep snow they were easy prey for the wolves. Within an area of five square miles just north of us, seven moose were killed by wolves during the winter of 1938-39. Although all of these were not eaten at once, the wolves returned and cleaned up the carcasses later.

At this time of year, the weather obliges the wolf to subsist chiefly on moose flesh, fresh or ancient. In the deep snow the lightweight snowshoe rabbit can easily avoid the heavier wolf; and grouse and ptarmigan cannot easily be stalked by an animal that sinks to the belly or lower with each step. Only the moose, whose great weight forces him to travel with bent forelegs used as snowshoes, can be hunted successfully. That the wolf's food is not easily obtained even then, is evident when one follows a trail in the snow. We have the skull and skin of a large black dog wolf which was found alive with broken ribs and leg bones, underneath a tree. Surrounded by moose tracks, blood patches and moose hair, the wolf had been crippled in a great battle. Similar cases were frequently reported by Indians and apparently usually occurred when the wolf had attacked the moose alone.

The power and endurance of wolves is astonishing. We have two large dogs, one of which weighs a little over 100 pounds. He is remarkably powerful—capable of carrying a 50-pound pack for eight hours and then romping playfully after the pack is removed at camp. Without the aid of a snowshoe trail these two dogs were physically incapable of traveling more than five miles in one day through the six-foot soft snow of the forest. They sank almost out of sight and were forced to make progress by great leaps which quickly exhausted them. Even when following a trail made by two pairs of snowshoes, the two dogs, hardy as they were, soon tired. And yet the wolves, many of them weighing 130 pounds and over, with no broken trail to follow, travel incredible distances.

In one instance, during the first week of February, 1941, I followed two wolves, presumably mates, for 27 miles. The larger tracks were partly obscured by the smaller ones over the first fourteen miles. Then the larger wolf moved to one side, with no perceptible change in pace, and dropped behind the smaller one. The snow was approximately six feet deep and very soft. The track made by these wolves resembled a shallow trench one foot deep and sixteen inches wide, with foot and leg tracks going deeper. The leading wolf simply pushed its way through the snow. After the change in leadership there was one pause—not a rest—where both wolves sprinkled a dead stump. Then they continued on their way. Two days later I followed these same tracks eight miles in the opposite direction, and there was no change in leadership—no sign of rest being taken, just the same deep furrow in the snow, made by a powerful chest. The dog wolf had apparently led for a total distance of 22 miles, breaking the trail without rest. I lost the trail when heavy snow came.

Toward the end of February, after being noticeably silent, the wolves began to give voice. Often on still days or nights the Driftwood Valley echoed with their love song, which is the most beautiful of wild music—markedly different from the hunting cry, which is a prolonged series of high notes, persistent and savage. The movement of packs could be followed by the echo of their voices as they went along the valley. Longer days and ever-increasing sunshine, with cold nights, brought a crust on the snow, and snowshoe rabbits became once more a part of the wolf diet.

It is in February and March that one can find evidence that the big wolves apparently appreciate the beauties of their surroundings. I am aware that this statement may be considered fanciful. But after fourteen years in parts of Canada where wolves are found, and with many opportunities of observing them and their signs, I believe that the timber wolf, in common with many other wild animals, enjoys lovely surroundings.

Within a few minutes' snowshoeing from our cabin in the Driftwood Valley, a hill rising abruptly above a small lake gave a magnificent view of six separate mountain ranges, snow-covered peaks, glaciers, mixed forests, and frozen lakes. In late winter we visited this enchanting hilltop, particularly when the moon's brightness lit up the snow-covered valley and mountains clearly. At the top of "Wolf Hill," as we called it, we invariably found wolf tracks. On the western rim, where there were many open vantage points, we would find the impression of a wolf that must have sat for a long time, facing the best of views. The imprint of the hind quarters was hard and ice-encrusted, such as is left by a dog that has slept in snow all night. Little or no food was to be gotten on this hilltop, for deep snow covered the few mouse holes. Varying hare and squirrel tracks were rarely noted there. Dense forest hid any sign of moving game in the valley below. The wolf tracks always led directly from one vantage point to another. Spots favored by the wolves were precisely the ones where we delighted to linger ourselves because of the view. We were always careful to avoid unnecessary trampling of the snow and left the wolves a clear way to each spot.

Once at midnight on Wolf Hill, while we silently drank in the beauty of a cold February night, with a brilliant moon lighting the entire valley for miles, a wolf immediately below us sent out a call to his mate; a low, musical note, deep and vibrant, more like a movement than a sound. Then he gave a rising, ringing call which faded gradually and ended in two distinct and incredibly low notes. Twice the call went out, and from far away there came an answer, faint but clear. Three more calls and answers rang out before the two wolves apparently came together. Then silence, and we were left with the view.

From our first arrival in the country we made every effort to preserve a sanctuary around the cabin and the lake by which it was built. After two years we were rewarded by an increasing number of observations on birds and mammals. The wolves, perhaps the most cautious and wise of all creatures, began to use our snowshoe trails.

On numerous occasions one or both of us were followed by as many as six wolves, particularly when we traveled at night. Once, as we were returning by moonlight from a long day's trip, I went ahead to start the cabin fire, leaving my wife to travel more slowly a mile or so behind. She was an expert on snowshoes, was always armed, and often traveled alone in this country. With that peculiar sixth sense one acquires alone in the wilderness, she felt she was being followed, though she could hear and see nothing. This fact was confirmed the next day by two Indians traveling an hour or so behind us. They had seen the tracks of six wolves closely following the snowshoe trail of my wife. At other times we frequently found fresh wolf tracks made over our snowshoe prints of the day before. We often noted spots where wolves had apparently watched from behind undergrowth as we went by, and their voices were sometimes heard within 100 yards of the cabin. In summer the loud cowbells on our two pack horses seemed not to disturb the wolves, nor did the barking of our big dogs at play.

THE WOLF AND MAN

Toward the end of our stay I became convinced, by actually watching wolves, who in turn watched me, that they were unafraid and quite familiar with my habits. Possibly they realized that because they were never hunted or trapped by us there was nothing to fear. At the same time, I felt no fear of the wolves—only a tremendous respect and admiration.

There are many stories of European wolves hunting and attacking man, but we have not been able to discover any authentic case of a person being attacked by the timber wolf of North America. It is my belief that there are no authentic cases. Indian hunters, from the Hudson Bay to Alaska confirm this belief. A wolf in a trap will fight and bite, naturally. Wolves do not hunt man; they hunt for food, and man flesh is apparently distasteful to them. The bodies of men who have died in the wilderness remain undisturbed, except by birds and flies, until they rot and are moulded into the ground. Cleaned skeletons are the result of maggots, not wolves. The timber wolf apparently prefers the meat which he kills himself; occasionally he touches kills made by man, but he shows remarkable intelligence in avoiding man-made traps, no matter how cleverly disguised.

In the Driftwood Valley district the wolves are apparently most vociferous in March and August. In late February and March, the love song, so clearly different from the hunting song, is such that once heard it is never forgotten. A pair of wolves begin the chorus, usually in the late evening. Others near and far take up the song in low and high pitch without a discord, and the whole valley resounds with melody. There is something vital and soul-stirring in it, which makes the listener feel that these wolves have a great soul as well as love of life. It is a wild song—everything about the wolf is wild, in the true sense of the word. Wolves, perhaps more than any other creatures, seemed to us to be the spirit of the wilderness itself. Everything that we learned of them pointed to the fact that they are strong, fearless, peace-loving, faithful to each other. With their great intelligence they seem determined to live on in spite of man's attempt to destroy them, in spite of his unreasonable and selfish desire to dominate the universe and subdue all other living creatures.

When the young are born, usually about the first week of April, the wolves are heard only rarely. Occasionally there was the cry of what we believed to be a solitary wolf, whose lonely call was a throbbing succession of low notes, rising slightly in pitch as they faded away. Once or twice a single voice was heard in the valley, which might have come from a dog whose mate was with her offspring. On these occasions there were the usual low notes, but instead of loneliness, a joy and awareness of life sounded so clearly that it made the listener smile in sympathy. In late May and early June, when the young were growing rapidly, the wolves were heard more frequently. In the early morning, soft yaps and yelps from young wolves could be easily distinguished, while the older ones gave short cries and lazy howls as though they were just waking.

In the summer months food is more easily obtained and one wolf no longer needs to join forces with others in hunting. Then we saw individual wolves, in many types of country, from valley streams and river beds to snow-covered mountain peaks. On the mountaintops wolves hunt young goats wherever they can separate them from their elders. One night I remained on a mountaintop in bitter cold at 8500 feet altitude. Early in the morning I was rewarded by the sight of seventeen goats who, fleeing from two wolves, ran and leapt where there appeared to be no possible foothold. Eventually they climbed to safety on a jagged, precipitous face of rock.

THE SUMMER FISH FEAST

Early in August the clear water of the Driftwood River is turned to red-gold by spawning Kokanee salmon, a small, red, subspecies of the sockeye.

For ten days or longer, countless numbers of this fish fight their way up the river, to spawn and then die, fouling the water with their decaying bodies as they are washed downstream. Thousands of dead fish are left on the banks and gravel bars, and for a few days a great stench pervades the country, calling all wildlife to the river. Birds, bears, wolves and lesser animals then enjoy a fish banquet. Soon the gravel bars and river shores are clean once more and the stench is gone. For a few more days the wolves move slowly along the banks, fishing for the last of the kokanee. Wading and swimming across still pools, fording shallow rapids, they eat and sleep and sometimes gather together for a song. I was present at one of these song-fests, an unforgettable experience and a privilege which is perhaps seldom granted to man.

For three years we had hoped and tried in vain to get pictures of wolves, particularly in 1941. We had visited and revisited many moose kills, and we had traveled considerable distances during winter and spring to regions where the Indians thought wolves most numerous. We had various harrowing adventures as we blazed our trails over that tough unexplored country. On one trip when loose rocks gave way beneath him, our fine old pack horse "Baldy" fell hundreds of feet down a mountainside. Overbalanced by his pack, he rolled and crashed down the mountain, out of sight. He stopped, feet in air, against a huge dead log, less than ten feet from a sheer drop onto solid rock. A minor scratch and a badly bent frying pan were the only results other than the fright we received!

Toward midsummer we had almost given up hope of ever getting sufficiently close to photograph even one wolf. Sometimes as we lay in our sleeping bags under the trees, we heard wolves calling. As we climbed the mountains or forded streams we saw wolf tracks. From camps on high alpine meadows where wolf food was abundant, we hiked and climbed over many, many miles, in hot blazing sun or ice-cold snow and hailstorms. When we returned to our cabin we had given up all hope of pictures. The thing seemed to be an impossible job, but we would make just one more trip.

We were almost ready to depart when we were startled by a sudden outburst from wolves by the river, a quarter of a mile from our cabin. Thick undergrowth, willows, and dry ground made a silent approach to the spot impossible, even though I wore moccasins. As I neared the river all became abruptly silent. For an hour I remained as still as possible, but saw and heard nothing until I returned to the cabin. Then the singing began again from the same place as before.

Still hoping to get pictures, I hurried across the lake in our small, home-made skiff, and, coming to the river, poled my way up as quietly as possible against the rapid current. When I reached the spot from which the singing had come there was nothing but silence. Dozens of wolf tracks had just been made along the shore and sand bars.

After an hour or more of waiting under a bank overhung with willows a black bear and cub came from the bushes on the opposite shore, 40 feet away. For a few minutes they caught kokanees in the shallow water, taking them up in their mouths. While I was watching them in the late afternoon light, I suddenly saw a large gray-black male wolf standing in the middle of the river. Wolf and bears looked at each other for some moments and then turned away to hunt for fish. The wolf eventually saw my skiff, 30 feet away and, after a moment of statue-like stillness, he loped slowly and gracefully off, across the river into the willows, where he apparently stopped. The bears moved quickly away, and the next hour or so passed quietly.

As daylight faded, I saw willow branches moving in three places, as though shaken by a moving body. No sound was heard, and I seemed to have all of that still and darkening country to myself. Then, without any stirring or preamble, wolves began to sing in the willows opposite. The river at that point was shallow and quiet. There were probably ten or twelve wolves, judging from the noise and different voices. They did not move about, just sat still and sang. Each outburst was started by the same wolf, whose voice was the lowest and most dirge-like of any I had ever heard. The volume of sound, its wildness, and the nearness of it all held me spellbound. Seldom is the wilderness so kind to man as to allow him to be present at such a moment.

GRIZZLY AND CUB

Inadvertently I had parked my skiff directly below an opening in the willows which marked the end of a game trail. Suddenly there was a crash, and I turned to find a grizzly bear with its cub. They had not seen the boat and were starting to climb down just above me. My .348 game rifle flashed flame a foot over their heads. A few more steps and the bears would not have been able to turn round. However, the blinding flash from the gun fright-ened them properly, and they departed in a hurry. I swallowed and tried to regain composure, feeling greatly annoyed at what I supposed was surely a termination of the singing. But almost at once it began again, from the same place across the river. The wolves were determined to sing; even the loud report of a rifle, so near by, could not deter them.

At this time, my wife was doing home chores around the cabin a mile away; cooking supper, watering, the horses, and tying them up for the night. She heard the rifle shot and thought that undoubtedly I had been obliged to shoot a grizzly bear in self-defense, for there was almost no other reason why I would shoot at that hour of the night. Then she heard the wolves howling again. It was phenomenal for them not to have been silenced by the rifle shot, and although she was usually fearless and had a remarkable sympathy with the wilderness creatures, she was badly frightened. The one dirge-like note of the wolf I have already mentioned, different from all wolf notes with which she was familiar, sounded so like a human voice in pain that she was about to start off into the dark to find me. Luckily I was on my way home by that time, and she heard me paddling up the lake. The wolves were still singing at intervals.

I found that ten or more wolves were in the habit of traveling along the river slowly, up one side and down the other. At one large gravel bar they appeared to spend some time in catching Kokanee salmon; so I went there every morning before three o'clock for the next three weeks.

COLD WORK

Facing the gravel bar was a pool or backwater from the river, which afforded an excellent hiding place. Sometimes I simply sat in the skiff; sometimes I stood in the water in my waders. It seemed to be entirely a matter of keeping absolutely still and waiting indefinitely. Every day, from three in the morning until noon or later, sometimes in the late afternoon and evening, I waited and watched. During that time I saw sixteen wolves, all within fifteen to 75 feet of my skiff. It was the coldest job I have ever known, and the most exciting.

The first wolf I saw was a gray fellow, standing in the water with a flapping kokanee in his mouth. The skiff was moving at the moment, and the wolf saw it at once. For a second he stood still, then lowered his head eight inches, while the hairs on his shoulders rose stiffly. A moment later he loped away. On the fourth morning, after I had sat quietly and shivered in the raw air for two hours, a large yellowish wolf appeared. It moved to the water's edge without the slightest sound, gliding along with the wolf's stiff-legged yet lithe, almost cat-like gait. It pounced on a kokanee, then at the sound of the movie camera stopped dead still. Again the head lowered and the ruff stood stiff. The camera stopped, and what was to become a frequent game began: the single movement of a cramped finger would send the wolf away.

Three more wolves were seen, but in such bad light that pictures could not be taken. They all appeared silently, and were well out into the open before I was aware of their presence. They vanished as soundlessly, stepping over the small stones of the gravel bar as though they walked on broken glass.

As possible bait for wolves I had brought from the mountains the fatty lining of some mountain goat stomachs. No part of the bait had been handled except with clean gloves. As I drifted by in the boat one day I dropped three pieces of it on the gravel bar. The first wolf to appear stood stiff-legged, head low and moving slowly from side to side, inspecting the bar. It was 4:15 in the morning. A minute later the wolf backed carefully away to the willows and vanished. Some time afterwards a low howl came from the willows behind the boat, and I had the feeling that I was being watched. Crows took the bait when the sun came up.

A LONELY FEMALE

At six o'clock the following morning, with the temperature twelve degrees below freezing and a cold, clammy mist lying over the river, a large coal-black bitch wolf appeared. She was thin and very hungry. Her belly was drawn in, and I had the impression that she was old, without young. Moving leisurely up the gravel bar, she stopped once or twice to catch struggling salmon in the shallows. Then she came to a piece of bait, seeing it without apparently getting the scent first. Without any hesitation she ate the bait. Then she went to the river and caught three more kokanees in rapid succession. A few minutes later she vanished, but she returned in fifteen minutes or so, examined the place where the bait had been and once more entered the river. At that moment a number of wolves, probably a family gathering, began a song near by. The voices of young puppies were plainly distinguishable, their high quavery notes straining to compete with the louder, more mellow ones of the elders. On hearing this the black wolf waded across the rapid current to within 20 feet of the skiff. Then she leapt up the bank, three feet high at that point, and sat down in the tall grass, showing only a vague outline of her body. She began to sing.

In a low, vibrating dirge she seemed to bewail her loneliness. Not loud, but soft and mournful came the lament, and it was easy to imagine that this wolf had lost her mate and was alone in the world, with only memories of a happy past and of litters of frisky young pups at her side. For perhaps an hour she sat there, then she returned to the water and, approaching the boat to within fifteen feet, buried her head to the shoulders to catch a fish.

It was a moment later that she saw me or heard the camera, and for a long time we watched each other. Her beautiful golden eyes widened. The only other touches of color in the coal black body were her white and gray whiskers and muzzle. Long minutes passed, then she turned slowly, forded the river, stood where the bait had been, and once more looked at me.

With teeth chattering, and belly shivering from the cold, I tried to expose as much film as possible, rewinding the camera with stiff fingers at the moments when the wolf was turned away or had her head in the water. It was with the greatest effort that I could hold the camera even reasonably still. Most of the resulting pictures are shaky.

By August 20th there were few kokanees left in the river. The dead fish had all been picked up, and only one or two struggled in the shallow waters. Almost a week passed with no sight of wolves, although we heard some. Bears crashed around in search of berries; an otter was seen once, and two coyotes. A large number of muskrats appeared every morning.

HIDE-AND-SEEK

Then I saw more wolves. The third one was a young male, well fed and strong. His belly bulged uncomfortably, and he moved slowly, though with an air of abandon. Approaching to within 30 feet of the camera, he saw the boat and stopped, leapt back a dozen yards, and then sat down to watch. After a few minutes he came on again, head lowered, ears pricked forward. Once more he sat down and for a few minutes peered this way and that, with head low, then high, staring at the boat with great interest. Then I said "Hello!" The young wolf bounded into the air. For a while he played hide-and-seek with me, in and out of the willows, once interrupting the game for a good long scratch. Then he vanished into the bushes and began to circle the boat. Three times his head showed out of the willows at different places. Later, I thought I saw the same pup twice. On the last occasion I was almost chagrined at his complete disregard of my presence. The young fellow fished and amused himself happily until a call, which must have been from home, came from far away, and off he ran into the forest.

I believe that most of the wolves seen at close quarters were aware of my presence. Since no wolf was shot or harmed in any way by us or others in this area, it seemed probable that they realized there was no danger. Had one of them been harmed, the others would doubtless never have allowed themselves to be seen and watched. I do not believe that wolves are afraid of man; there is nothing even remotely cowardly about their actions. The wolf is a truly wild creature and a very valuable factor in controlling overpopulation of one district by any other race of animal. It is my opinion that bounties on wolves are now, in most districts, unnecessary and unjust. If the wolf is exterminated we shall have lost one of the most virile, wise and beautiful of all wild creatures.

DEPARTURE FOR THE NIGHT HUNT
1944

 WOLF researcher L. David Mech dedicated his 1970 book, The Wolf: The Ecology and Behavior of an Endangered Species, *to "Adolph Murie, who in the early 1940's became the first biologist to conduct an intensive and objective ecological study of the wolf." Murie's pioneering research was done in Alaska while he was a biologist with the U.S. Fish and Wildlife Service. His extensive, detailed observations of wolves resulted in a monograph called* The Wolves of Mount McKinley *(1944), from which this excerpt is taken. This scientific study not only looked at the ecology and behavior of wolves—physical characteristics, breeding, home life, hunting, food habits, etc.—but also examined their prey (Dall sheep, caribou, and moose) and competitors (grizzlies, red foxes, and golden eagles). Murie considered it his good fortune to conduct this study to answer the questions "What is the ecological picture centering about the wolf of Mount McKinley National Park?" and "Is it feasible to permit moderate representation of the wolf in the fauna of Mount McKinley National Park?"*

In this excerpt, Murie describes in detail the behavior of the wolves of the East Fork River den as they prepare for their nightly hunts.

❖❖❖

There was considerable variation in the time of departure for the night hunt. On a few occasions the wolves left as early as 4 p.m., and again they had not left at 9 or 9:30 p.m. They were seen departing for the hunt 11 times. Five of these times they left between 4 p.m. and 5:45 p.m., and six times they left between 7 p.m. and 9:30 p.m. Usually the hunting group consisted of the three males, but sometimes one of the females was in the group. The wolves hunted in a variety of combinations—singly, in pairs, or all together. In the fall the adults and young traveled together much of the time, forming a pack of seven adults and five pups.

Usually the wolves returned to the den each morning, but three wolves which left the den at 4 p.m. on May 26 had not returned to the den the following day by 8 p.m. when I left the lookout, after watching all night and all day. They wolves had probably spent the day near the scene of their hunt. These wolves were again at the den on May 28.

Considerable ceremony often precedes the departure for the hunt.

Usually there is a general get-together and much tail wagging. On May 31 I left the lookout at 8:30 p.m. since the wolves seemed, after some indications of departure, to have settled down again. But as I looked back from the river bar on my way to camp I saw the two blacks and the two gray males assembled on the skyline, wagging their tails and frisking together. There they all howled, and while they howled the gray female galloped up from the den 100 yards and joined them. She was greeted with energetic tail wagging and general good feeling. Then the vigorous actions came to an end, and five muzzles pointed skyward. Their howling floated softly across the tundra. Then abruptly the assemblage broke up. The mother returned to the den to assume her vigil and four wolves trotted eastward into the dusk.

On June 2 some restlessness was evident among the wolves at 3:50 p.m. The two gray males and the black male approached the den where the black female and some pups were lying. Then the black male lay down near the den; the mantled male walked down on the flat 100 yards away and lay down, and Grandpa, following him, continued along the bar another 150 yards before he lay down. At 6:45 p.m. the mantled male sat on his haunches and howled three times, and in a few minutes he sent forth two more long mournful howls. Grandpa stood up and with the mantled male trotted a few steps toward five passing caribou. Then the mantled male howled six or seven times, twice while lying down. The gray female trotted to the gray males, and the three of them stood together wagging their tails in the most friendly fashion. The mantled one howled and they started up the slope. But before going more than 200 yards they lay down again. A few minutes later, at 7:15 p.m., the mantled male howled a few times and walked to the den followed by Grandpa. The latter seemed ready to go whenever anyone decided to be on the move. At the den the black female squirmed and crouched before the mantled male, placing both her paws around his neck as she crouched in front of him. This hugging with the front paws is not an uncommon action.

Later the two gray males and both black wolves were in a huddle near the den entrance, vigorously wagging their tails and pressing against each other. They gray female joined them from up the slope and the tail wagging became more vigorous and there was a renewed activity of friendliness. At 7:30 p.m. the mantled male descended the slope to the bar and started to trot away. He was shortly followed by the black male and Grandpa. The black female followed the departing males to the bar, then returned to the gray female at the den. Both females remained at the den this time.

On June 8 at 7:15 p.m. Grandpa approached the mantled male, wagging his tail. The mantled male stood stiffly erect and wagged his tail slowly, with a show of dignity. The two walked over to one of the blacks and lay down. The mantled male turned twice around like a dog, before lying down, then rose and turned around again before settling down.

There was no movement until 9 p.m., when Grandpa rose, shook himself, and walked over to the mantled male. They wagged tails and were joined in the ceremony by the black female. The mantled male sniffed at the black male who was still resting. He rose and the tail wagging began again. The gray female hurried down the slope to the others and the tail wagging became increasingly vigorous. The friendly display lasted 7 or 8 minutes and, led by Grandpa, who seemed specially spry this evening, they started eastward. The black female followed a short distance, then stopped and watched them move away. A quarter of a mile farther on the four wolves commenced to play on the green flat. The black female trotted rapidly to them and joined in the play. After a few minutes of pushing and hugging the four again started off, this time abreast, spaced about 50 to 75 yards apart. The black female followed for a short distance and lay down. She appeared anxious to follow. After 15 minutes she returned to the den, and two or three pups came out to join her.

The gray female at first led the wolves up the long slope toward Sable Pass, but later the two gray males were in front, running parallel about 200 yards apart. They trotted most of the time, but galloped up some of the steeper slopes. On a snow field they stopped for a time to frolic. The black female remained at the den all night. The hunters returned at 9:15 the following morning. The gray female hurried unhesitatingly to the burrow, like a mother who has been absent from her child for a few hours. The black male flopped over on his side a short distance from the den and lay perfectly still and relaxed. About 1 mile north of the den the mantled male was stretched out on his side on a high point. The wolves had been away on the hunt about 12 hours.

At 4 p.m. on June 16 the two gray males, the black male, and the gray female left the den, led by the mantled male. Soon the female took the lead and she headed for a spot where some eagles were feeding. She nearly captured one of the eagles by jumping high in the air after it as it took off. These wolves went directly to Teklanika River some 7 or 8 miles from the den.

It was evident that by evening the wolves were rested and anxious to be off for the night hunting. The time of their departure for the hunt no doubt varied from day to day depending somewhat upon how soon they came in from the previous night's expedition. Theirs is not a lazy life for the nature of their food demands that they travel long distances and work hard for it, but they seem to enjoy their nightly excursions.

EPILOGUE
The Voice of Wilderness

TWO aspects of wolves mentioned by many early travelers were their ubiquity—"The bisons are yet numerous, and the white wolves also abundant" and "In our excursions we everywhere met with wolves, foxes, hares, weasles, and mice" and "the wolves are in great numbers . . . loling about in the plains"—and their howling, which unloosed surprising rhapsodies from adventurers in the West. When one wolf raises his voice in song, others will respond and join in. The howl of the wolf draws the same ineluctable response from us: we answer in song and story, myth and poem, diary and dream. These several selections about wolf howls—as well as all the stories in this book—are some of our very human responses to a creature that has called out to us for thousands of years, to "the beast," says Cormac McCarthy, "who dreams of man."

❖❖❖

I had scarcely viewed the delightful scene around me, when those sleepless sentinels of the deserts raised their midnight howl. It rung along the chambers of the mountains, was, at intervals, taken up by kennel after kennel, till, in the deep and distant vales, it yielded again to the all-pervading silence of night. This is one of the habits that instinct has taught their race. As soon as the first light of morning appears in the east, they raise a *reveille* howl in the prairies of the Western States which, keeping company with the hours, swells along the vast plains from Texas to the sources of the Mississippi, and from Missouri to the depths of the Rocky Mountains. All day they lurk in silence. At midnight, another howl awakens the sleeping wilderness—more horrible and prolonged; and it is remarkable with what exactness they hit the hour.

Thomas J. Farnham, *Travels in the Great Western Prairies, the Anahuac and Rocky Mountains, and in the Oregon Territory, May 21-October 16, 1839* (1843).

❖❖❖

I was awakened by a confused noise, which, in the fear of the moment, I mistook for impending danger. I imagined, in my first terror, that the Pawnees, conspiring to dispute with us the passage over their lands, had assembled around our camp, and that these lugubrious cries were their signal of attack.— "Where are we," said I, abruptly, to my guide. "Hark ye!—Rest easy," he replied, laying down again in his bed; "we have nothing to fear; it is the wolves that are howling with joy, after their long winter's hunger: they are making a great meal to-night on the carcasses of the buffalos, which our huntsmen have left after them on the plain."

Father Pierre Jean de Smet, *Letters and Sketches: with a Narrative of a Year's Residence among the Indian Tribes of the Rocky Mountains* (1841-42).

❖❖❖

And then the wolves! There seemed to be thousands and thousands of the great shaggy fellows. By day and by night their long-drawn, melancholy howls echoed and re-echoed through the valley and along the beetling cliffs. There was something indescribably sad in the cry of the wolf, something that made even the most lighthearted and careless of men pause and listen. Many persons could not bear the sound; yet to the true lover of nature it had a peculiar—if perhaps undefinable—charm. How the deep, clear, plaintive, minor strains of their voices used to grow and swell down in that lonely valley, as the shades of night drew on. Often a single old male, sitting on a commanding ridge or barren butte, would start it. Throwing back his head until the long, keen, muzzle pointed straight up to the zenith, he shuts his eyes, and from his powerful throat, through parted black lips, offset by gleaming fangs, came the wail o-o-o-o-o-o-o-o-o-o; faint at first, then rising to a resonant crescendo, and finally dying away. And presently, perhaps from the far shore of the river, came the long-drawn answer; and before it was finished others took up the refrain; here two or three, there an old female and her nearly grown family of young; and then far up and far down the valley, and out along the frowning cliffs, others and still others joined in, until the still air trembled with the burden of their voices. Oh, never, never again shall we hear the like! The days of the buffalo and wolf have forever vanished; days when it was possible for the adventurous spirit to view nature as yet unsoiled by the ruthless cupidity of civilized man; days when her children, the wild creatures of forest and plains, and the still wilder redmen, were almost the sole inhabitants of a boundless domain.

"The Scribbler," "In Frontier Days," *Forest and Stream* (January 1901).

❖❖❖

Speaking of the language of animals, the most thrilling as well as—to me—the most soul-stirring music I ever heard was the clear deep bass voice of a big gray wolf on a clear cold winter night rolling out over the ice-covered prairie. It would commence on a high note and then run down the scale to the bottom, soon to be answered by his companions from every hill and canyon for miles around. From the intonations of their voice, I understood whether it was a call to assemble or come to a carcass, or to take up their line of travel for some other locality. . . .

Lobo, the big buffalo wolf, has a deep, profound, musical howl, which can be heard for miles over the silent, frozen plains; and their music has lulled me to sleep as I lay wrapped in my blankets in the snow.

James R. Mead, *Hunting and Trading on the Great Plains, 1859-1875* (1986).

❖❖❖

It was a raw, overcast night. The carcasses of the buffaloes killed in the vicinity of the camp had drawn about it an unusual number of wolves, who kept up the most forlorn concert of whining yells, prolonged into dismal cadences and inflexions, literally converting the surrounding waste into a howling wilderness. Nothing is more melancholy than the midnight howl of a wolf on a prairie. What rendered the gloom and wildness of the night and the savage concert of the neighboring waste the more dreary to us, was the idea of the lonely and exposed situation of our young and inexperienced comrade. We trusted, however, that on the return of daylight, he woud find his way back to the camp, and then all the events of the night would be remembered only as so many savory gratifications of his passion for adventure.

Washington Irving, *A Tour on the Prairies* (1835).

❖❖❖

Editor Forest and Stream:

The long howl of the wolf has been a great marvel to your correspondent since he first heard it. The marvel is, what is the meaning of it, or what feeling it expresses? In other words, what makes the wolf howl?

When heard at any distance save very near, say a few feet or a few yards, one can detect in its sounds nothing but the profoundest spirit of melancholy. There is no other sound in nature which can compare with it in the expression of abject and hopeless misery. I have likened it to the wail of a lost spirit as it crosses the portals of the infernal regions, seeing behind it green fields from which it has forever departed, and before it a hopeless and eternal hell. It also seems to convey a deep sense of loneliness, as if the wolf had lost his last friend on earth and felt himself to be the solitary wanderer of the globe; all other creatures being dead. I have listened to this peculiar phase of the long howl till a sense of my own loneliness became most painfully oppressive.

Some say that the wolf howls so dolefully because he is hungry; others, because he is indeed very lonesome, and uses this melancholy voice to draw his friends around him. Both these, therefore, hold that it is really an unhappy feeling that inspires the long howl. But I have observed enough to convince me that it is by no means hunger that always or even generally calls forth this howl, if indeed it ever does; for I have heard the wolf howl never so piteously or with his soul so much in the work, when the region around was strewn with the bleeding carcasses of slaughtered bison, from which he had no doubt stuffed his belly. Also, I have frequently heard them howl in concert, and sometimes in packs; though it is true that the wolf when alone most frequently projects the long howl. But whether in company or alone, the sound thereof is of equal melancholy and loneliness. Some say his howl is inspired by love of his female mate, and that his sole motive is to charm her ear with a sound that is very sweet to her; in other words, that he is singing to her a melody to cheer her heart and fill her with love and admiration of himself. There may be something in this; but the marvel is that any creature should be inspired to love by such music. However, it does indeed appear that the wonderful bray of the ass is put forth with no other motive but to please his females; and it also appears that they are quite charmed therewith. So, as to what constitutes good music, ears may differ as greatly as tastes differ in appetite.

But may it not be that it is indeed a true and deep sense of melancholy and loneliness that inspires this howl? May not the wolf have a strange, unsatisfied desire, like that of the moth for the star; and that he is melancholy because the object of his desire remains distant and unfriendly? He sees it and longs for it, but dares not approach it. He waits for the gulf that separates him from his desire to diminish and fade away; but he sees years and ages pass, and the gulf is still there, profound, dangerous, impassable. What wonder that his heart grows sick as he contemplates this cruel gulf, and that he breaks forth in howls that cannot be equalled in melancholy by any other sound ever heard on earth; perhaps matched only in hell!

Verily I believe that this is all so, and that man and his friendship is the star for which this poor moth pines. And why not? The wolf is but a dog and has a dog's heart. He is the fountain from which the dog came, with all those qualities which made him the companion and friend of man. That fountain is still rich in those qualities, as we shall see later on; and they well up in it whether the fountain will or no. The dog must have man to love and to be loved by him; and if he has not he is the most lost and wretched of all beings. Who has not seen a dog lost from his master? He howls piteously, becomes wild with grief, will fawningly seek the friendship of any one who will speak to him a kind word, and he will soon lie down and die with grief if he finds not his lost master or a new one in his place. And this dog is but a wolf, with the wolf's heart.

I have often noted the peculiar manner and expression of the wolf when he and man happen to come upon one another in their travels. The wolf will not run straight from you; indeed, he will not run at all unless you force him to do so; but he will cross your path a little distance in front of you, and go circling around you in a dog trot, having his eyes all the time intently fixed upon you. Seeing them thus, I have sometimes cast my glass upon them, so as to catch the expression of their eyes and countenance; and they seemed to me as if they were saying in their hearts—"Oh, glorious man, would that you would take me to you and let me love you; but you will not!" Poor wolf! to love a star that is forever unapproachable is indeed a hard fate.

I have said that when the wolf's long howl is heard within a few feet or yards, another sound besides that of melancholy and loneliness is sometimes readily distinguishable. When a boy it befell me to pass three nights alone in a lonely cabin, in a dark mountain valley, many miles away from any human residence; for that country was then a wilderness given up to wild beasts and savage Indians. My cabin was greatly beset by wolves, and as sleep was hardly possible, I had little to do but to study this strange melody. They would often howl so near my ear that I could distinctly feel the tremulations in the atmosphere caused by their voices. Then I observed that in many of the howls there was a very deep-mouthed and wide-mouthed ferocity, as if the creature would tear something to pieces and revel in innocent blood. It was a sound as of terrible strength combined with an utterly savage and remorseless nature.

In the next chapter, should there be another, I will speak of the wolf in his social and domestic relations, and as tamed by man.

N.A.T., Abilene, Texas, Jan. 7, *Forest and Stream* (February 2, 1888).

❖❖❖

The wolf experience I like best to recall happened one day in January some years ago. In the morning it was a crisp thirty-five degrees below zero. At a cabin on the lower Toklat River in Mount McKinley National Park, my companion and I started out at daybreak, he on snowshoes, and I on skis, each of us carrying a pack containing bedroll and food, enroute to Wonder Lake along the north boundary of McKinley Park. We were making a two-hundred-mile winter trip to carry out general wildlife observations. . . . An interesting day. Toward evening it became stormy and we faced into a bitter wind blowing the first snowflakes. It became dusk, and by the time we left the river and turned in on a trail it was dark and stormy. In a few minutes we would have a fire going, a warm cabin, hot coffee, and a big meal. Now we savored the storm, for it made the cabin just ahead seem especially cozy. Then we stopped, transfixed, for out of the storm came music, the long-drawn, mournful call of a wolf. It started low, moved slowly up the scale with increased volume—at the high point a slight break in the voice, then a deepening of the tone as it became a little more throaty and gradually descended the scale and the soft voice trailed off to blend with the storm. We waited to hear again the voice of wilderness in the storm. But the performer, with artistic restraint, was silent.

Adolph Murie, *A Naturalist in Alaska* (1961).

ADDITIONAL READING

Carbyn, L.,N.,S.M. Oosenbrug and D.W. Anions. 1993. Wolves, bison and the dynamics related to the Peace-Athabasca Delta in Canada's Wood Buffalo National Park. Circumpolar Research Series No. 4. Canadian Circumpolar Institute, University of Alberta.

Harrington, F. H., and P. C. Paquet, eds. 1982. *Wolves of the World*. Park Ridge, NJ: Noyes Publ.

Klinghammer, E., ed. 1979. *The Behavior and Ecology of Wolves*. New York: Garland STPM Press.

Lawrence, R. D. 1986. *In Praise of Wolves*. New York: Henry Holt and Co.

Lopez, Barry. 1978. *Of Wolves and Men*. New York: Charles Scribner's Sons.

McIntyre, Rick, ed. 1995. *War Against the Wolf: America's Campaign to Exterminate the Wolf. Over 100 Historical Documents and Modern Articles Documenting the Evolving Attitudes Toward Wolves in America From 1630-1995*. Stillwater, MN: Voyageur Press.

Mech, L. David. 1992. *The Way of the Wolf*. Stillwater MN: Voyageur Press.

Mech, L. David. 1970. *Wolves: The Ecology and Behavior of an Endangered Species*. Garden City NY: American Museum of Natural History. 1981. Minneapolis: Univ. of Minnesota Press.

Murie, A. 1944. *Wolves of Mount McKinley*. Washington DC: U.S. Govt. Printing Office. (In print and available from Alaska Parks Association at Denali National Park, Alaska.)

Murray, John. 1993. *Out Among the Wolves: Contemporary Writings on the Wolf*. Anchorage: Alaska Northwest Books.

Rutter, R. J., and D. H. Pimlott. 1968. *The World of the Wolf*. Philadelphia: J. P. Lippincott Co.

Savage, Candace. 1989. *Wolves*. San Francisco: Sierra Club Books.

U.S. Fish and Wildlife Service. *Mexican Wolf Recovery Plan. Northern Rocky Mountain Wolf Recovery Plan. Recovery Plan for the Eastern Timber Wolf. Red Wolf Recovery Plan*. All four available from Fish and Wildlife Reference Service, 5430 Grosvenor Lane, Suite 110, Bethesda MD 20814.

Wolves in American Culture Committee, Boise, Idaho. 1986. *Wolf!* Ashland, Wisc.: NorthWord, Inc.

Young, Stanley P. 1946. *The Wolf in North American History*. Caldwell, Idaho: Caxton Printers.